TWAYNE'S
RULERS AND STATESMEN OF THE WORLD
SERIES

Hans L. Trefousse, Brooklyn College
General Editor

WINSTON CHURCHILL

(TROW 22)

Winston Churchill

By VICTOR L. ALBJERG

Purdue University

Twayne Publishers, Inc.   ::   New York

IN MEMORY

OF

MARGUERITE

Acknowledgments

The author wishes to express appreciation to the following for helpful assistance in the writing of this volume: Marguerite Albjerg, his wife, for her reading of the manuscript and for constructive suggestions; Mrs. Betsy Schuhmann for her review of the manuscript, also followed by helpful suggestions; the staffs of the following libraries who were more than cooperative in making material available: the libraries of St. Norbert College, University of Wisconsin, University of Illinois, University of Indiana, and Purdue University, as well as Indiana State Library at Indianapolis.

He also wishes to express his gratitude to the following publishing companies for permitting him to quote materials from their volumes:

Houghton Mifflin Company
Frederick A. Praeger, Inc.
Doubleday & Company
Harper and Row, Inc.
The New American Library
Wells Gardner Darton & Co. Ltd.
W. W. Norton
Pocket Books, Inc.
G. P. Putnam's Sons
Charles Scribner's Sons
World Publishing Company
And others mentioned in the volume.

Contents

Chronology

1874   Winston Leonard Spencer Churchill born at Blenheim, November 30, 1874, the elder son of Lord Randolph Churchill and Jennie, daughter of Leonard Jerome of New York.

1888-
1892   Student at Harrow.

1892-
1894   Student at Sandhurst Military Academy.

1895-
1900   Served in the army in India, Egypt, and South Africa as a second lieutenant. Became a civilian again July 7, 1900.

1900   Won election to the House of Commons from Oldham as a Conservative.

1900   Conservative member of Parliament.

1904   Shifted to the Liberal side of the House of Commons.

1906-
1908   Under-Secretary of State for Colonies.

1908-
1910   President of the Board of Trade.

1910-
1911   Secretary for Home Affairs.

1911-
1915   First Lord of the Admiralty.

1915   Began his career as an artist.

1915   Chancellor of the Duchy of Lancaster.

1916   Lieutenant Colonel on the fighting front in France.

1917-
1918   Minister of Munitions.

1918-
1921   Secretary of State for War and Air.

1922-
1924   Out of office.

1924-
1929   Chancellor of the Exchequer.

1929-
1940
Sentry against Hitlerism. Published books and articles, lectured. Reentry into the Conservative Party as First Lord of the Admiralty and member of the War Cabinet. Mobilized Britain for war. Instilled a high morale among the people.

1940 Prime Minister and Minister of Defence.

1941 Promoted acquisition of allies, Soviet Union in June, 1941, and the United States in December, 1941. Negotiated a treaty with Stalin. Supported adoption of the Atlantic Charter.

1942 Secured adoption of a plan to invade North Africa. Tobruk taken by General Rommel, and regained by the British.

1943 Participated in Casablanca Conference. Russian victory at Stalingrad. Allied victory at Tunis. Induced Roosevelt to approve invasion of Sicily, and then of Italy. Increased air bombing of Germany. Attended Conferences of Teheran and Cairo. Approved cross-Channel invasion of France. Accepted General Eisenhower as commander for cross-Channel invasion.

1944 Declining influence of Churchill in formulation of policy. Brought Britain's might to bear in invasion of France. Still hoped for a campaign in the Balkans and an advance to Vienna.

1945 Favored General Montgomery's military strategy over General Eisenhower's against Germany. Differences between Churchill and Roosevelt. Election of 1945 lost by the Conservatives.

1945-
1951
Churchill as minority leader. Churchill's nonpolitical pursuits. Fear of a Russian invasion of the West.

1951 Return to the Premiership. Acceptance of Socialist program. Acceptance of various colonial demands for independence.

1953 Failing health. Suffered a stroke.

1965 Churchill died.

CHAPTER I

The Maverick

BEFORE WINSTON CHURCHILL ENTERED SANDHURST MILITARY
Academy, his father, Lord Randolph, sent a letter to an intimate
friend in South Africa and implored him to find employment for
his son, for he saw no respectable future for Winston in England.[1] On the basis of his son's educational record, Lord Randolph was scarcely open to criticism, for Winston had given
little cause for faith in his future.[2] In contemporary educational
jargon he would have been classified as a "problem child." In
the elementary grades he had invariably maintained the lowest
academic status of all his classmates. While he was at Harrow,
from 1888 to 1892, he never got into scholastic orbit,[3] but
remained "the lowest boy on the rolls."[4] It is not surprising that
Dr. Welldon, the headmaster, informed him, "I have grave
reasons for being disappointed with you." Nor is it startling that
Winston replied, "And I, Sir, have very grave reasons for being
displeased with you."[5]

Despite such unflattering appraisals and predictions, Winston's self-confidence never flagged, for at the age of twelve
he consulted a throat specialist and implored him to correct
his speech defect. He admitted that he would enter the army
first, and then strike for the House of Commons. There, he said,
he could not be handicapped by the fixation that he must avoid
every word beginning with an *s*.[6] Before he reached the age of
twenty-one, and after he had finished with distinction his courses
at Sandhurst Military Academy[7] he gave a small dinner party
to young men of his own social class, and proposed a toast: "To
those of us under twenty-one years of age, who, in twenty years,
will control the destinies of the British Empire." Ten years later,
as Under-Secretary of State for Colonies, he had his hands on
the switchboard of power.

Churchill enjoyed a felicitous background for a political

[13]

career. Like almost everyone he was the product of his genes and environment, but in his case both of these were different from the ordinary. Sir John Churchill (1650-1722), his most illustrious ancestor, was far from commonplace in both character and ability. He had defeated the hitherto invincible armies of Louis XIV (1643-1715) and Philip V (1700-1745), in return for which his appreciative sovereign, Queen Anne, created him a duke. She also endowed him with an estate which eventually embraced 2,700 acres upon which a grateful Parliament constructed a magnificent palace of 320 rooms, and named it Blenheim after one of his brilliant and significant victories.[8]

Subsequent Dukes of Marlborough lived in grandiose style and accumulated enormous debts. To meet the insistent demands of creditors, they disposed of 450 paintings, thousands of books, and innumerable gems, the proceeds of which quieted most of the vociferous claimants. The exactions of other creditors imposed a gaunt appearance upon Blenheim. Even before Winston's birth, the Marlboroughs, when compared with the more prosperous nobility, resembled poor country cousins.[9]

While ancient European estates degenerated in wealth and significance, modern American capitalists evolved into industrial tycoons and millionaires. Simultaneously, socially ambitious American wives stalked European resorts and salons in search of titled sons-in-law while impoverished heirs coursed the matrimonial circuits in pursuit of conjugal consorts that could recoup the remnants of their family's sagging fortunes and drooping prestige. While the American Mrs. Leonard Jerome was marketing her feminine finery in the courts of Europe,[10] she and two of her daughters attended the reception given by the Commander of *H.M.S. Ariadne*, in 1873, honoring the Russian Tsarevich. There Randolph Churchill, the second son of the Seventh Duke of Marlborough, met Jennie Jerome, "masterpiece of that great artist: nature," and each succumbed to the other's allurement and fascination. Three days later they became engaged.[11]

It has been asserted that Jennie's mother, Clarissa Hall, was the granddaughter of Meribah, an Iroquois, of northern New York.[12] Gladys Caffyn in her *Fragments of the Life of Ambrose Hall*, published in 1956, regards the Indian ancestry as fiction. Ralph G. Martin, in *Jennie, The Life of Lady Randolph Churchill, The Romantic Years, (1854-1895)*, on the other hand cites three items to give credence to Jennie's Indian ancestry: (1) the lack of a genealogical record of Anna Baker, Jennie's maternal grandmother, gives the impression that it may have been deleted because of her Indian origin; (2) the Indian features of Jennie's mother and her sisters support the contention of their Indian background; (3) Leonie Leslie, grandmother of Anita Leslie of the Jerome family, spoke of her Indian ancestry.[13]

Jennie's father, Leonard Jerome, was descended from French Huguenots who had migrated to the Isle of Wight. In 1740 his ancestors had taken passage to the American Colonies. Leonard's mother's ancestors, of Scottish descent, arrived in Connecticut in the decade following 1680.

Leonard Jerome grew up in Syracuse, New York, where, as a young man, he published a newspaper. Larger challenges in New York City beckoned him, and through fortunate investments there he accumulated a fortune in excess of ten million dollars. He was keenly interested in banking, and also became part owner and one of the editors of *The New York Times*.[14] When the American Civil War broke out, he donated $3,000,000 to the federal treasury. He gave vigorous support to the suppression of the New York City riots of 1863 which took the lives of 1,600, and then he contributed $250,000 for the relief of the surviving participants. At the close of the Civil War, he gave freely to the Southern Relief Fund.

He was civic-minded and took a leading part in promoting the arts and sports. He established the first two race courses in the United States, and sponsored horse racing so energetically that he became known as the "Father of American Turf." His horse named Kentucky won many races and these triumphs augmented considerably its owner's capital assets.

He lavished funds on the Academy of Music, built a private theater, and defrayed the cost of bringing Jenny Lind and Adelina Patti to New York for a series of concerts. When he went for a Sunday afternoon drive, he whirled along in a carriage and six. Even as a boy, Winston admired his American grandfather, and this feeling endured through the years.

Fortune, however, ceased to smile on Jerome's Croesus-like capers when a huge investment in the Pacific Mail withered, and a Hoosier swindler bilked him of $600,000. The panic of 1873 deflated his investments still more. Lesser blows fell upon him, and these, combined with previous debacles, impaired his financial wizardry.

The Duke disapproved of Randolph's precipitate proposal. At first he flatly forbade the marriage, and he denounced the whole enterprise as "hasty, rash, and impulsive." He ordered his son, who was in Paris with Jennie, to return to London. Mrs. Jerome, however, beamed in fulsome gratification at the prospect of her daughter marrying into European nobility. The Seventh Duke did not respond appreciatively to this American woman's high adventure with his son's affections.

Toward the Jeromes the Duke and Duchess assumed a cool and distant posture.[15] The Jeromes soon sensed the frigid feelings accorded them and they immediately fell back upon their French-Scottish-Iroquois dignity, this eventually leading to negotiation. In the meantime, Randolph and his father arranged a deal: Randolph was to stand for a seat in the House of Commons, and, if he should be elected, the marriage might occur. The election took place on February 3, 1874, and Randolph carried the family constituency of Woodstock by a vote of 569 to 404.

Following Cupid's accomplishments, the solicitors assembled. Owing to the extravagances of his ancestors, the Duke had been left with limited resources and therefore could not be as generous as the occasion ordinarily would have required. And yet he did manage to provide a London house and an annuity of £1,100. The major burden, therefore, fell upon the American party to the contract, and Mr. Jerome settled an annuity of £3,000 upon his daughter. But even this was not enough to meet the bills of the youthful couple, and Mr. Jerome graciously liquidated the deficits, without insinuations or admonitions. With these details executed, Randolph and Jennie, on April 15, 1874, were married in the British Embassy in Paris.[16] Neither the Duke nor the Duchess was in attendance. Before the marriage they had come to Paris and had subjected Jennie to an appraisal, and she had qualified as a Marlborough-in-law.

Although Jennie had had notification of a future blessed event, she had made no preparations for Winston's arrival. She had not even assembled a layette. Several days during late November she had indulged in exhausting outdoor romping. Her doctor had cautioned her not to participate in a party at Blenheim on the 30th, an admonition which she had ignored.

On the fateful evening at the height of the festivities, she experienced violent labor pains, and dashed toward her bedroom, but got no farther than the cloakroom for the evening, and into it she plunged. Doctor Frederick Taylor of Woodstock was hurriedly summoned and he reported just in time to usher Winston into England. For that service he charged twenty-five guineas, a high fee for that time, but today no doubt looked upon as a good investment. Winston had arrived six weeks ahead of schedule, and later could not escape the sobriquet "Young-Man-in-a-Hurry."

Winston, however, was in no hurry to get an education. He did not lack intellectual interest, but the instructors, with their emphasis upon Greek and Latin, failed to arouse his interest in these courses. At St. George where he was first enrolled, he stubbornly refused to apply himself. For such a stance the instructors resorted to ferocious beatings.[17] If one application did not make him a potential Homer, his instructors administered additional birchings on the assumption that beating one end of the spinal column would activate the other. But alas, this inhumanity merely congealed his animosity toward St. George which endured to his dying day. His father transferred him to Brighton where the instruction was given by two maiden ladies. The only notoriety there was his classification as the "naughtiest boy" in the school.

Lord Randolph had very much hoped that his son would follow his footsteps into Eton, and later into Oxford, but deficiencies in the Classics excluded him from these Meccas of culture.[18] Application was, therefore, filed at Harrow, and Dr. Welldon, the headmaster, took a long chance and admitted him, and Winston became its most distinguished alumnus. Despite Winston's early aversion to Dr. Welldon, the headmaster won his undying confidence and friendship; yet even he could not awaken Winston's love of scholarship—except in English composition, history, and French, in which fields he did manifest some promise.

Winston's parents, by neglecting to maintain intimate and affectionate communication with their son, contributed materially to his frustration and maladjustments. His mother was so absorbed in social life,[19] and his father so immersed in the political game that they devoted very little time to their gifted heir. Churchill was never directly critical of his mother. As a mature man, he fully and handsomely paid tribute to her beauty and her charm and confessed that she "shone for me like an evening star. I loved her dearly—but at a distance."[20] Not until Winston, both handsome and promising, was commissioned in the army did his mother seriously interest herself in him. When he was five years of age, she wrote her mother, ". . . he is a most difficult child to manage." While he was at Harrow, she wrote him numerous letters, most of which were sharply critical of him. When he wished to spend a vacation at home she frequently denied him the opportunity, or was absent on some social engagement. Randolph Churchill, in his first volume of the biography of his father, pays his beautiful grandmother few compliments, while he cites many instances of his disapproval of her.

Randolph Churchill Sr. denied Winston the normal father-son relationship which the future Prime Minister craved.[21] Only three or four times during his life did Randolph speak intimately and confidentially with his son, and then usually broke it off abruptly just when Winston would have cherished its continuance. A good proportion of the letters which he wrote to Winston while he was at Harrow, and even some while he was at Sandhurst Military Academy, were unduly critical and condemning. Yet Churchill never ceased to admire his father and hoped some day to sit in the House of Commons with him and serve as his second in the verbal duels just as Herbert Gladstone and Austin Chamberlain had supported their fathers.

The remoteness of Randolph Churchill toward his son was accentuated by the father's political aspirations and later by his tragic collapse. Upon his entrance in the House of Commons in 1874, he embraced the doctrine of Tory Democracy propounded by Benjamin Disraeli and endorsed by his political protégés, among whom were Arthur Balfour and Sir Arthur Drummond.[22] They maintained that most of the Conservatives were political Rip Van Winkles who were unconscious of the world's advance while they had been slumbering.[23] They assumed that their survival depended upon retardation and postponement of economic development by manipulation of electoral inequalities, and the perpetuation of their myth of class superiority and other counterfeit devices.[24] Jeered at as the "stupid party," haunted by profound distrust of an ever-growing democracy, conscious that the march of progress was leaving them behind they believed that their only survival lay in "delaying and restricting the movements of the age by means of electoral inequalities, parliamentary procedure, and through the prejudice of interest and class." Randolph Churchill and his confreres believed that the pursuance of this policy would inevitably result in political suicide. They insisted that the Old Conservatives constituted the essence of a popular rhyme:

> We are the chosen few,
> All others will be damned.
> There is no place in heaven for you
> For heaven must not be crammed.

The reforms which the Tory Democrats propounded aimed at the improvement of the lot of the poor, as well as the enlargement of their rights, the realization of which would reduce the income and prerogatives of the rich. While some members of the Conservative Party, outside the Tory Democrats, endorsed the program sponsored by Randolph Churchill, they later revolted against enacting it.

Randolph Churchill had two points in his program: the reduction of appropriations for the armed services, and the application of this economy to social reform. He was in a strategic position to execute his program for in July, 1886, he had become Chancellor of the Exchequer and the leader of the House of Commons. The incumbent of that office in 1883 had insisted that he was "responsible for every shilling in the estimates."[25] This amounted to the assumption of financial dictatorship of the government and Lord Randolph confessed, "I do not disagree with that proposition."[26]

He was even more emphatic when announcing his powers as Chancellor. In 1901 William Broderick proclaimed in the House of Commons that Lord Randolph contended that the Treasury should be a dominant and despotic body, that it should dictate terms to the various departments, and that it should be "blind to the progress of science and deaf to the arguments of responsible ministers."[27] Furthermore, Lord Randolph confessed that he had only one ambition, and that was to become Prime Minister. And to achieve that objective he executed a "meteoric rise" in the House of Commons.[28] He would outdo the Liberals effecting economy and reform.[29]

In defense of this program he contended that no fleet in the world could challenge the British navy and therefore no army could cross the Channel, so why levy unnecessary taxation? The armed forces bristled with enmity against anyone who aimed to dwarf their establishments. The two departments, of the army and the navy, had presented combined requests for £31,000,000 for the ensuing year of 1887. The chiefs of the two services also asked for 30 supplementary estimates of £300,000 for the navy and £500,000 for the army. Under heavy pressure from Lord Randolph, the Chief of Staff of the Army had reluctantly accepted a reduction of his allotment, and the First Lord of the Admiralty submitted to a diminution of £700,000, not as much, however, as demanded by the Chancellor of the Exchequer.

Lord Randolph was determined to materialize his program. On two previous occasions when the opposition had blocked his requests, he had threatened resignation and he had won. Because of his expressed desire to become Prime Minister, his native capacity, and his incomparable platform performance, Lord Salisbury, the Prime Minister, could not ignore so significant a threat to his position. He believed that Lord Randolph aimed to create a cabinet crisis which would shatter the solidarity of the Party, and that he would then consolidate the fragments with himself as the Prime Minister. The Conservative Party in this crisis was not a "Hot Bed of Tranquility." Salisbury took his nephew, Arthur Balfour, into his confidence, and the two applied Tory caution and shrewdness to the situation and agreed not to challenge Lord Randolph just then, but to let him place himself in a completely indefensible position. He obliged. On the refusal of the House of Commons to pass his budget, with its reductions for the army and the navy, "in a moment of caprice," he committed political suicide by sending his resignation to Lord Salisbury who, "with profound regret," accepted it,[30] and then rejoiced in having done so.

The future with all its possibilities had beckoned Lord Randolph and had urged him to slacken his pace. Henceforth he could not escape "the role of a young man with a brilliant future behind him."[31] He spent the ensuing nine years secretly and silently cursing his fate. The hierarchy of the Party did not apply balm to his psychic wounds, but injected astringents to his despondent heart. Its members treated him with haughty courtesy as an impudent insolence. In this environment he continued to occupy his seat in the House of Commons, but he was never again considered for a place in the cabinet. The recurring and increasing virulence of his syphilitic affliction took a destructive toll and he sank ever deeper into physical and mental invalidity. By 1893 he had few really lucid moments.[32] Relief was denied him until 1896, when death in his forty-sixth year imposed its merciful easement.

Few careers in British public life have been so promising as was that of Lord Randolph Churchill. Fewer still have been so suffused with tragedy. At his death Winston was fourteen years of age. His father's profound disappointment made him increasingly aloof toward everyone, even toward his son. Furthermore, as Winston observed his father, tortured by the boycott imposed upon him by his own party, he resolved that in the event of a political divergence between himself and his party, he would not remain within its suffocating folds, but would join the Opposition.

Churchill's parents may have neglected him, but Mrs. Everest, his nurse, did not. Her first concern was his welfare, and she did her utmost to guard his health, promote his serenity, respect his confidences, and encourage him in his work. She was stooped and obese, but he ignored these externals, and remained loyal to her as long as she lived. While he was at Harrow, he insisted on her coming to spend a day with him, and he showed her every courtesy that a well-bred son might have extended to his mother. When she was ill, he wrote to her, or called upon her, and upon one such occasion he perceived the fatal nature of her condition. He remained at her bedside, holding her hand until death relieved her of her agony. Her photograph adorned his study at Chartwell. Loyalty and devotion to his friends were significant characteristics of Sir Winston Churchill, even when he was a youngster.

CHAPTER II

Warrior and Reporter

EVEN AS A SMALL BOY CHURCHILL WAS ENRAPTURED BY MILITARY problems and in his room he deployed 1,500 tin soldiers in various army formations. As soon as he developed competence in reading, he arrayed his troops as the outstanding generals had marshaled their legions for the battles of Blenheim, Oudenarde, Leipzig, or Waterloo. When guests convened in his parents' home, and occasion permitted, he rustled them into his room and exhibited his companies, battalions, and divisions, and to their amazement lectured them on the Armageddons of history.

Even Lord Randolph was impressed and in his imagination caught visions of his son reenacting the grandeur of his illustrious ancestor. In one of his rare conversations with Winston, he suggested the possibility of an army career and proposed his matriculation at Sandhurst Military Academy.[1] Winston could have clapped his hands for joy, but he stopped short of that as he recalled the ritual of the entrance examination. After intensive application, expert tutoring, and three attempts, he finally, in 1892, qualified as a cadet.

At Sandhurst Churchill found himself. Emancipated from the torments of Latin and Greek, he could apply his intellectual potential to matters which interested him. He had also attained that maturity at which the negligence and criticism of his parents no longer upset and frustrated him. This enabled him to graduate eighth from the top of his class of 150 members.

Upon graduation subalterns spent the summer months on active duty and were granted leave for the rest of the year during which many skirmished on the social front during the London season.[2] On this sector Lieutenant Churchill deployed himself briefly, but parties soon wearied him as he yearned for combat excitement. The international scene obliged. Ever since Christopher Columbus had landed in Cuba, Spain had exploited the

[22]

resources and people of that island, and had done little to compensate for its plundering. Near the end of the nineteenth century the Cubans wearied of their plight and rose in rebellion. The Spanish government sent General Martinez Campos with 80,000 troops to suppress the uprising.[3]

Churchill wrote the British Ambassador in Spain for permission to enter Cuba and this was cheerfully granted. Then he negotiated leave from his regimental officer. Following this he arranged to provide the editor of the *Daily Graphic* with stories at five pounds a piece, and thus began a distinguished journalistic career. Reggie Barnes, a Sandhurst classmate, accompanied him on the Cunard liner *Eiruria*. They left Liverpool on November 7, 1895, and en route to Cuba landed in New York and were hospitably entertained by Bourke Cochrane, a lawyer friend of his mother. On November 20 they finally set foot on the disturbed island. It took them several days, traveling by boat and train, to reach General Valdez's column which was searching for the rebels and trying to exterminate them. On November 30 they were fired upon by the unseen rebels, and one bullet missed Churchill by millimeters.[4] While he was in Cuba, he saw only three days of fighting, during which he comported himself sufficiently well to receive the Order of Military Merit.

Churchill appreciated the fact that the demand for independence enjoyed the almost universal support of the Cuban population, but despite this he had a low regard for the rebels. In his view they were ineffectively organized, poorly equipped, and badly disciplined.[5] Though he appreciated the desire of the people to throw off the Spanish yoke, his sympathies were clearly with Imperial Spain. He maintained that though the Spanish administration was bad, a Cuban government "would be worse, equally corrupt, more capricious, and far less stable."[6] On the basis of his experiences, he wrote five articles for the *Daily Graphic* in which he denounced the United States for extending recognition to the rebels in 1896, and two years later, when war broke out between the United States and Spain, his sympathies were clearly with the latter country. Since he had been reared in an imperial environment it is not surprising that he reflected the family tradition and supported Madrid against its rebellious dependency.

Upon Churchill's return from Cuba, he fell into the dinner-dance doldrums of the class to which he belonged. Many doors opened to him purely on the basis of his being a Churchill. Hostesses asked, "What is Randolph's boy like?" The most discriminating discovered that he could travel in good society on his own merits, and his calendar was soon crowded with engagements which excluded the pursuit of serious enterprises.[7] Churchill deplored the squandering of valuable time when he was driven by professional ambition. He, therefore, welcomed orders in 1896 to the 4th Hussars Regiment of 1,200 men, to which he belonged, to embark for India.

After twenty-three days afloat, their ship finally moored in Bombay harbor, and from there they proceeded to Bangalore where the mornings were largely devoted to drill, and afternoons to sleep, and evenings to polo. Churchill participated in the drills but boycotted the afternoon stagnation sessions. He took an active part in the polo games and qualified for the regimental team. While he had established an excellent academic record at Sandhurst Military Academy, he recognized that there were wide vacuities in his education. He strove to compensate for this deficiency by devoting every afternoon from one to five o'clock reading. So energetically did he pursue his self-imposed schedule, that the common saying at Bangalore was that in the afternoon only Churchill and mad dogs were about. He realized that the "man who attracts luck carries with him the magnet of preparation." Plato, Aristotle, Schopenhauer, Macaulay, Gibbon, Lecky, and Shakespeare constituted his educational diet. He was especially fond of Macaulay and Gibbon upon whose styles he modeled his own, as Lincoln had improved his by reading the Bible and Shakespeare.

Like his father, Winston could read a page at a glance and assimilate its substance. While he was a sophomore at Harrow, he manifested his magnificent memory by reciting, without hesitation or error, 1,200 lines of Macaulay's *Lays of Ancient Rome*. With a memory of such retentiveness, he accumulated prodigious quantities of information by his systematic reading.

Exciting as it was for Churchill to follow the intellectual gymnastics of distinguished scholars, he was more intrigued by the prospect of participating in the suppression of the independent tribesmen who had been harassing neighboring settlements on the North-West Frontier Province. While Churchill had been on leave in England in 1897 he had learned that General Sir Bindon Blood had been ordered to establish peace in the Frontier areas. Churchill wangled assignment to that expedition, and accompanied the force on its 2,028-mile trek to the scene of the disturbance.

Before his departure, he had arranged with the editor of the *Pioneer of Allahabad* to provide that journal with articles at the rate of £5 per column. After his departure from England, his mother had negotiated a similar contract for him with the *Daily Telegraph*.

When General Sir Bindon Blood moved into the troubled zone, Churchill rode with the advance guard, armed not only with a correspondent's pad and pencil, but also with a soldier's sword and pistol. He did not wish merely to record events but also to participate in their evolution. In an ensuing engagement he became separated from his group and he found himself exposed to a horde of hostile tribesmen with whom he was compelled to fight without any assistance. So effectively did he defend himself that he accounted for three dead tribesmen and a similar number of wounded, while simultaneously he rescued one of his comrades. For this gallantry, he was mentioned in the dispatches.

In the months following this expedition he combined and edited his letters, dispatches, and articles into his first book, *The Story of the Malakand Field Force*. It provided him with much needed revenue, for his mother had been compelled to end her annual allowance of £500 a year. He sent copies of his book to all upon whom he wished to create a favorable impression, among whom were Lord Salisbury,[8] the Prime Minister, and the Prince of Wales. They appreciated the merits of his volume and Lord Salisbury volunteered to assist him in his drive for recognition and success.[9]

Churchill already, with but little experience, possessed confidence in his capacity to assume responsibility, and he was eager for others to share his estimate of himself. In 1898, he wrote his mother from India and urged her to promote him in England. "This is a pushing age," he said, "and we must push with the best,"[10] and he did.

The commendation of his book was not unanimous. Army officers as a group abhorred it, and abominated its author. They

were especially offended by the section in which he criticized
senior officers' direction of the fighting. They bluntly questioned
a second lieutenant's competence to pass judgment upon tactics
and strategy. They deplored the brashness of this upstart in
conversing with generals on the basis of equality. They dubbed
his volume "A Subaltern's Hints to Generals."

Churchill was decidedly unhappy while he was in India. Since
he was extremely ambitious and envisioned no means there of
gratifying his aspirations he regarded himself as imprisoned.
Friends from England wrote him of political advancements of
men no older than he, men, whom he knew were less able and
less well qualified than himself to assume responsibility. But
while he was destined to remain in India, he would inform himself as thoroughly in the field of politics as he could in order
to acquit himself at his best when the opportunity for office
should occur. His second objective was to secure his release
from the army for he saw no future in frontier assignments.
While he was compelled to remain in uniform, he would proxi-
mate his military service to civilian routine: he would pursue the
career of a war correspondent, and ultimately enter politics.[11]
By 1900 he had avowed his intention to three different people
on three different continents to strike for the premiership. He
already had intimate awareness of the embarrassments of poverty.
To meet his bills he overdrew his bank account.[12] When he
took final leave of India he left behind unpaid bills, which he
later met. He needed money to escape embarrassments and to
function as a man among men. Publication of articles and books,
he believed, would emancipate him financially.

The late nineteenth century offered splendid opportunities for
impecunious war correspondents, for no sooner was one colonial
uprising suppressed than another one was simmering. As the
disturbances on the North-West Frontier were smothered, the
Mahdi leader of the Sudanese tribes gathered his forces on the
Egyptian border. Since England claimed suzerainty over Egypt,
it assumed the right and the obligation to protect it against
attack. By 1898 the British acutely felt this responsibility: since
1883 two British armies had been annihilated by the Sudanese;
the first one, of some 14,000, on November 5, 1883, was destroyed
to the last man, and a year later General Gordon at the head of

12,000 marched deeper into the interior, and all but one were killed.[13]

Britain's imperial prestige could not allow two such military catastrophes to go unpunished. The War Office chose Colonel Herbert Kitchener to lead an army into the Sudan to impose suitable retribution.

When Churchill learned of Kitchener's commission, he sensed that this operation would afford journalistic ore of high news content. It could provide spectacular adventure garnished with rich royalties. He immediately mobilized his mother and all her influential friends to secure an appointment for him under the command of Colonel Kitchener.[14] Lady Randolph in her effort to extract authorization for Winston to accompany Colonel Kitchener's army exercised the spell of her sparkling beauty and enchanting charm upon bureaucrats, high and low, including the Minister of War, but all to no avail.

In the meantime Churchill prevailed upon his superiors to grant him a furlough to England where he would plead his case. Soon after his arrival Lord Salisbury requested him to call at 10 Downing Street for a short interview. The Prime Minister listened appreciatively to Churchill's account of the situation on the North-West Frontier, commended him upon his book *The Story of the Malakand Field Force*, spoke well of his father, and finally after forty minutes dismissed him with the assurance that if ever he, Salisbury, could assist him in any way he would be glad to do so. Churchill departed flushed with confidence. The transfer seemed assured.

Churchill had, however, failed to credit Colonel Kitchener with appropriate weight in the case. This dour officer had a low regard for war correspondents in general, and a lower one for Churchill in particular. Kitchener rejected all petitions in favor of the applicant. Finally, Lady St. Helier, a friend of Winston's mother, appealed to Sir Evelyn Wood, the Adjutant General of the War Office, one of the many bureaucrats who disliked the arrogant independence of Kitchener. Sir Evelyn was preparing an independent contingent which he was dispatching to the Nile to support Colonel Kitchener's force. He assigned Churchill to it, in terms that were unique in military history: he was to be regarded as a supernumerary lieutenant of the 21st Lancers for the Sudan campaign. During his service in this organization he was to serve without pay, and in the event of his being wounded or killed no government funds of any kind would be available to defray the cost of his treatment, or his funeral in case of death.

Before the above arrangement had been made Churchill had negotiated with the *Morning Post* to submit articles on the Egyptian campaign at the rate of £15 a column. Early in August he took passage to Egypt. On September 1, 1898, he was with Colonel Kitchener's army at Omdurman.

After he had surveyed the position and the size of the Mahdi's army, he gave a report to Kitchener, who recognized him but did not give any evidence of his knowing who the young officer was. On the following day, September 2, 1898, occurred the Battle of Omdurman. Kitchener with two and one-half divisions met the Mahdi's army of 60,000 fanatics in a battle which lasted five hours. The most dramatic feature of the clash was the charge of the 21st Lancers in which Churchill participated. The charge was next to the last of its kind, the final one being executed by the Canadians in World War I. The Omdurman engagement left 10,000 Sudanese killed and between 10,000 and 16,000 wounded, while the British lost 25 killed and 136 wounded.

As soon as the battle was over, Churchill wrote an account of the conflict, to which he assigned the title *The River War*, which was acclaimed for its accuracy and style. Again he took the generals to task for their conduct. He heaped denunciations upon Colonel Kitchener for mutilating the Khalifa's body, and then tossing it into the Nile. He was even more critical of Kitchener's carrying the Khalifa's head off in an old gasoline can. Though Churchill was only a lieutenant he appreciated more fully than did Kitchener the reaction of the Mohammedan millions to this sacrilegious conduct. And he was also aware, as Kitchener should have been, that there were more followers of that faith under the Union Jack than under any other ensign. Churchill was no less critical of Kitchener's destruction by gunfire of the Mahdi's tomb, a religious shrine. He was equally condemnatory of a rumor among the troops before the battle to the effect that Kitchener had announced that he would take no prisoners, the implication being that the wounded would be shot.[15]

Military men, who regarded conduct of war beyond the competence of civilians and second lieutenants, did not take kindly to Churchill's criticisms. Therefore, even before he entered Parliament he had assembled a solid block of enemies who would not grieve over his ensuing misfortunes.[16]

Following his participation in the Battle of Omdurman Churchill returned to India to play in the polo championship finals, on the team of the 4th Hussars, which contest it won. He then returned to England and resigned from the army. After four years he was a civilian again. He had come to embrace the verdict of Disraeli, that "the army was a grand career for a barbarian in wartime but only fit for a fool in peacetime." Furthermore, his ultimate goal was not to become a field marshal, but a prime minister. To achieve this he needed entrance into the House of Commons. His interest in politics was congenital, and closely associated with that was a profound determination to vindicate his father's grievous career there, followed by his tragic death at the age of forty-six. "There remained for me," he said, "only to pursue his aims and vindicate his memory." Even in his maiden speech, he paid tribute to his father's remarkable record in the House of Commons, and ten years after Lord Randolph's death, Winston "left a biography like a wreath of a thousand leaves among the ruins."[17]

Another consideration which induced him to abandon the military camp for the political arena was the differential in income. As a subaltern his pay was 14 shillings a day. As a lecturer and war correspondent his income for a week eventually exceeded his army pay for a year. And Churchill, who already prized the good things of life, was willing to adjust his career to his appetite. Therefore, upon his return from India in 1899 he consulted a fashionable palmist, who, after communicating with her psyche, reported favorable divinations in his palm and he filed for the vacancy in the Oldham constituency in Manchester caused by the death of its member, Robert Ashcroft.

By this time he had participated in suppressing rebellions in the North-West Frontier and in the Sudan. He had publicized his experiences in the *Morning Post* and the *Daily Express.* He was the author of three books. Even though he had been absent from the British Isles most of the time for four years, his name was a commonplace in many English homes.

In his campaign speeches he stressed the virtues of Conservative principles, and the benefits of existing society. He made a brilliant plea for the Empire system, and this found great favor

with the voters generally but they did not approve of his indict-
ment of the Church of England with its ritualistic service. He
opposed the Tithes Bill, a plank of the Conservative Party's platform. He emphatically declared that if he were elected he would
not support the Bill. This was infidelity to the Party and a sacri-
lege to the Church, a double-barreled charge against his own prospect of victory, and he lost the election.

Arthur Balfour, a distant cousin and a Conservative Shogun
sent his condolence: "Never mind, it will all come out all right;
this small reverse will have no permanent ill effect upon your
political fortunes."[18]

Churchill regretted his electoral defeat without indulging in
self-pity or grief. He resolved to accumulate additional distinction and then to try again. Opportunity beckoned in South Africa
where the British Government was determined to compel the
Transvaal to extend the suffrage to Uitlanders on less exacting
terms than those embodied in their law of 1894 which denied
the franchise to all Uitlanders under forty years of age with a
residence of less than fourteen years. This law was based upon
the Afrikaner's assumption that the Uitlanders were transients
who had come to the Transvaal to extract a fortune during a
brief interval in their careers, and, having acquired their wealth,
they would return to their native lands to enjoy it. During their
short sojourn in the Transvaal, they should refrain from imposing
their dominance upon the natives. What further irked the Uitlanders were the discriminatory taxes inflicted upon them.

The British, who had been defeated by the Boers in 1881 in
the battle of Majuba Hill, had recognized the independence of
the Transvaal, though it had retained suzerain rights, which
neither side understood very clearly. Two years later (1884) the
agreement was revised and in its new form there was no reference to British overlordship, wherefore the Boers insisted that
their independence was now complete and unqualified.[19] After
the discovery of gold and diamonds in the Transvaal, the British
contested the Transvaal interpretation of its freedom while the
Boers clung to their independence and dignity with increased
tenacity and vigor. Negotiations broke down on September 8,
1899.

Open war seemed imminent.[20] Churchill regarded this as an
opportunity to redeem his political and financial stature. To take

advantage of the situation he telegraphed Oliver Borthwick, editor of the *Morning Post,* and proposed that he be dispatched to South Africa as a war correspondent. Churchill was then in a position to stipulate his terms: "Expenses, copyright of his work, and £1000 for four months shore to shore,"[21] with full payment, even if the war lasted only four days. On September 18 he wrote to his mother: "I am at their disposal."

On October 9, 1899, the Boers issued an ultimatum to the British, demanding that they withdraw all of their troops from Transvaal territory within forty-eight hours. Since the British refused to comply, hostilities began on October 12. The "best estimates" in England envisioned a three-month war at a cost of £10,000,000. It lasted three years and cost £300,000,000. It was England's greatest military effort since its encounter with Napoleon.

To report this war—and to participate in it—Churchill left Southampton on October 14 on *Dunottar Castle* and arrived in Cape Town on October 31. He wasted no time in reaching the scene of hostilities for he followed shortcuts by land and sea to reach Estcourt, about thirty-five miles from Ladysmith in Natal.

On November 15, 1899, Captain Haldane, in an armored train, consisting of three cars in front and three behind the locomotive, set out on a reconnaissance toward Ladysmith. Since Churchill assumed that such a venture might have a news lode of high content, he boarded the caravan, and off they rolled. Everything went well until suddenly everything went wrong. From a secluded spot about fifteen miles from Estcourt, the Boers opened fire on the train. Several of the cars were derailed. This was followed by a bombardment of a light field piece and then followed by a fusillade of rifle fire. Churchill, in a manner which was to become customary with him, took immediate command and issued orders and directions as if he were a veteran commander. He managed to get the cars back on the rails and the wounded into them for their protection; he also ordered the able-bodied to run on the lee side of the cars. By this means, the train began its way back to Estcourt, but Captain Haldane and seventy-five of his men were captured and imprisoned. In Churchill's attempt to facilitate the escape of Haldane's men, he found himself confronted by two sturdy and determined Boers, their rifles pointed directly at him. Escape was impossible. His choice was surrender or death. He chose the former, and was transferred to a prison camp in Pretoria. He insisted that since he was a war correspondent he was not subject to arrest. His captors, however, had observed his commanding role in directing the escape of the invaders, and they classified him according to his action rather than his deposition and accorded him the same treatment as the other prisoners. The Boers prized him and confessed, "It is not every day that we can catch a lord's son."

No sooner was he ensconced in his quarters than he planned his escape, and after a three-week sojourn there, with seventy-five pounds in his wallet and four chocolate bars in his pocket, he eluded the prison guards, slid down the prison wall, scaled the prison balustrade, and breathed the fresh air of freedom. Imitating a Boer citizen he walked down the streets of Pretoria. Then he boarded a moving freight train, and fortunately for him, it was en route to Portuguese East Africa 30 miles away. Before daybreak, like a hunted animal, he eased himself off the train and sought seclusion in a nearby thicket during the day. And hunted he was, for the Boers had circulated 3,000 posters bearing his photograph and offering a reward of £25 for him, dead or alive.

Toward evening he resumed his walking, and after several days without adequate food or water his exhaustion was easily discernible, even to a lone vulture which Churchill observed taking a deep personal interest in him. One night as he trudged along, fatigued and famished, he saw a light in the distance. His hunger and thirst were so acute that his will power yielded to their command, and he moved in the light's direction. He approached the house cautiously. It was one-thirty in the morning. He stepped up on the porch, rapped on the bedroom door, which opened to the veranda. The occupant, John Howard, the only Englishman within a radius of thirty miles and the manager of the Transvaal Collieries at Witbank, grasped his pistol and went to the door. When Howard inquired who he was and what he wanted, Churchill replied he was Dr. Bentick, that he had accidentally fallen from a passing train, and that he had lost his way. Howard refused to believe this tale and took him for a Boer spy. Churchill finally made a clean breast of it and Howard then gave him every assistance within his power. He concealed him for two days at the bottom of an abandoned coal mine in which his only companions constituted a horde of inquisitive rats. On the third night, in strictest secrecy, Howard transferred Churchill to a room in the house.

In the meantime, Howard had loaded a vast quantity of raw wool with an empty space in its center on a platform. Into this vacuum he tucked Churchill and conveyed the cargo to the nearest freight station where the shipment was transferred to a railway car.

After what seemed to Churchill an eternity, his car was coupled to a train and off it sped to Lourenço Marques. Upon his arrival there, he proceeded to the British Consulate where he indulged in a bath, a bountiful dinner, and refreshing drinks. One of his first acts after this was to dispatch a message to the Transvaal Minister of War informing him of his location.

It was later revealed that his escape and trip to Portuguese East Africa had been unnecessary, for General J. P. Joubert, on December 12, had signed an order, endorsed by Jan Smuts, for his release from prison.

To Churchill the escapade was of immense significance. Reports of his arrest appeared on the front pages of most of the British newspapers. It had made him the talk of every town. Editors exceeded all previous efforts to extoll his virtues. In a war which until then had been characterized by blunders and defeats, the British finally had a national hero.

His escape was not the end of his thrilling experiences. Churchill left Laurenço Marques on the evening of the day of his arrival there, for many of its inhabitants were fervid Boer sympathizers and he could foresee an attempt to kidnap him or perpetrate some other violence. Therefore, when the *Induna* left for Derban that night he was one of the passengers. To his amazement he found his mother and brother John there on board a hospital ship, the *Maine*, which his mother had secured and equipped with funds subscribed largely by Americans. His brother had been the first casualty to enter the *Maine* for treatment. He had been wounded in the first engagement in which he had participated.

Winston's mother urged him to abandon the fighting and to return with her to England. The lure of conflict and the thrill of reporting it took precedence over filial affection. He remained in

South Africa for another six months, reentered the army as a lieutenant in the South African Light Horse.[22] This was in violation of an army regulation which had been issued after Churchill's reports during the Omdurman campaign in which he had taken Colonel Horatio Kitchener and other army officers to task for what he considered military stupidities.[23]

In his double role as war correspondent and lieutenant he participated in the campaigns along the Tugela River, in the battles of Spion Kop and Potigieser's Ferry. He took a prominent part in the liberation of British prisoners at Ladysmith. He marched with the troops that took Pretoria and Johannesburg. He rode a bicycle through the latter city while it was still occupied by Boer forces.

After the surrender of the capitals and large cities of the two Boer states Churchill, like other responsible men, considered the Boers defeated and peace all but negotiated. This view, however, was not shared by the Boers. They resorted to guerrilla tactics and prolonged the conflict for almost two years.

Churchill not only thought that the war was over, but also that his political career was about to begin. He had good reasons for his assumptions, for all of his exploits had been well publicized and he had become something of a national hero. Henceforth he would play in the big league, and the battles would be fought in his constituencies and in the House of Commons.

CHAPTER III

Conservative Interlude

CHURCHILL'S SOJOURN AMONG THE BOERS HAD BEEN PACKED WITH excitement, drama, and danger, and during this interval he had met every situation like a hero. When he landed in England on July 20, 1900, he was overwhelmed by his reception,[1] for thousands of people lined the streets to catch a glimpse of him. He regarded this enthusiastic welcome as a favorable omen for his entrance into the House of Commons. Although he was not yet a member of that chamber, to him it was not an unfamiliar institution, for he had lived in its atmosphere ever since his childhood, his father having won his seat in the very year of Winston's birth. From his infancy the chief topic of conversation in his home had been the proceedings in Parliament, and the guests in his abode its members. In fact, the domicile of Randolph and Jenny had been the rendezvous of the most interesting people in Britain. Among its habitués were Charles Dilke, Arthur Balfour, Herbert Henry Asquith, Lord Esher, Bernard Shaw, Oscar Wilde, Lord Rosebery, Gladstone, Joseph Chamberlain, and eventually the Prince and Princess of Wales. There they congregated to exchange wit and wisdom, to relish the idiosyncracies of Randolph and to luxuriate in the beauty and boldness of Jenny. Most of the guests were charmed by her personality. Some were amazed by her sallies; others were horrified by her brazen liberties with the language, which were tolerated only because of her beauty and charm.

No one savored these soirées so keenly as did Winston who, from early adolescence, had participated in them on an easy, informal basis. Here, divorced from the agonies and anguish of Latin and Greek, and the misery of mathematics, he acquired the art and the ease of associating with the finest intellects in England. These concourses were to him pro-seminars in parliamentary procedure. Technically, he was a novice when he took his seat in the House of Commons but he had absorbed its essence since boyhood. He, therefore, entered Parliament with an advantage—his apprenticeship had begun long before his membership.

He had another factor in his favor. While his Marlborough heritage was not an undiluted blessing, yet his father in 1886 had been the outstanding Conservative of the House of Commons. Furthermore, Winston's own record was already sufficiently illustrious to presage a distinguished career.

Numerous constituencies welcomed him to serve as their candidate in the forthcoming election of 1900. He chose Oldham in which he had been defeated the previous year. During the campaign he rode through the streets in an open carriage under a banner with the inscription: "England's noblest hero." Active electioneering began on September 19 and continued until October 10 during which he made 110 speeches. His uncle, the Duke of Marlborough, provided the registration fee of £500 and met other incidental expenses. With the support of Lord Rosebery, Joseph Chamberlain, George Wyndham, Arthur Balfour, and his mother, he won one of the two seats from Oldham in which there were vacancies.

OLDHAM ELECTION OF 1900

Candidate	Party	Vote
Sir Alfred Emmott	Liberal	12,947
Winston Churchill	Conservative	12,931
Walter Runciman	Liberal	12,907
C. B. Crisp	Conservative	12,522

To commemorate Churchill's electoral triumph Joseph Chamberlain, who had been a devoted friend of Winston's father, sacrificed a bottle of 1834 port.

Churchill knew that membership in the House of Commons carried no salary and that it imposed heavy financial demands. He had three sources of income with which to meet his obligations: royalties from his books, fees from his articles, and compensation for his speeches.

His remuneration from the *Morning Post* for articles over a ten-month period plus royalties from three books had yielded him prior to his entry into the House of Commons £4,000. The proceeds from twenty-nine lectures in Britain added £3,782, 15s 5d to his account.[2] His engagements in the larger American cities yielded him £1,500. A few other sources of income enabled him to write his mother that not one person in a million at his age could have duplicated his achievement. For years Churchill's indigence had condemned him to practice what he considered asceticism. Affluence did not dispose him to austerity. Henceforth, he would live like a Marlborough, and he did.

While he was in the United States he called upon President McKinley, Vice President Roosevelt, Chauncey M. DePew, and other people of distinction. Nor did he fail to pay his respects to Bourke Cochrane, the friend of his mother, who had entertained him when, in 1895, he was en route to Cuba.[3]

William Allen White, long-time editor of the *Emporia Gazette,* maintained that survival in Ohio politics demanded the "virtues of the serpent, the shark and the dove."[4] The durability requirements in the House of Commons, Churchill discovered, were no less exacting and exhausting than in the Buckeye legislature. His prolonged career in Parliament is, therefore, a tribute to his personal and political vitality, and durability.

When Parliament opened, the novitiate took his seat on the Conservative side of the House in the chair which formerly had been occupied by his father. Nor did he overlook his mother, for on the evening of his first day in the House, he wrote her and enclosed a check for £300, and added, "I could never have earned it had you not transmitted the wit and energy which are necessary."[5]

The maiden speech of the novitiate in the House of Commons is traditionally delayed until the neophyte has observed the customary humility for a probationary as defined by the parliamentary oracles. This was generally a year or more of silence. Churchill ignored this decorum. On February 18, 1901, during the fourth sitting of the recently elected House, he won the floor and executed his hortatory debut with a carefully prepared and well delivered address.[6] Reports had circulated throughout the dining and lounging rooms that he was to speak, and the most distinguished as well as the least significant members of both sides of the House were in their seats. In the Ladies' Gallery sat his mother and his four aunts. Churchill was determined to make his performance a transcendent event in his life. He was aware that a wretched presentation would consign him to political oblivion, whereas a brilliant address would elevate him to cabinet timber. Almost the entire speech was devoted to a consideration of the Boer War. He analyzed and justified British entrance and prosecution of the conflict. He commended British officers and men, especially General Bruce Hamilton. He spoke appreciatively of the Boers, their devotion to their slogan: "Death or Independence," and confessed that if he "were a Boer," he "would be fighting with the Boers." He hoped "the Boers would not remain deaf to the voice of reason and blind to the hand of friendship."[7]

Even in his initial address he voiced the tenets of British imperialism at its zenith: Britain was justified in prosecuting the war; Transvaal was important to England economically, commercially, and strategically. Britishers away from home should feel confident of Mother England's protection. The Boer War should be fought to a victorious conclusion, and then, as soon as possible, democratic institutions should be established. Boer defeat, ill feeling, and vengeance should be liquidated. Imperialism functions at its best in an atmosphere of amicability and cooperation. While a stern parent demands obedience in his child, the progenitor's action should emanate in love. Likewise the mother country's firmness should be accompanied with affection.

He closed his speech with an encomium to his father's memory: "I cannot sit down without saying how very grateful I am for the kindness and patience with which the House has heard me and courtesies which have been extended to me, I well know, not on my own account, but because of a certain splendid memory which many honorable members still preserve."[8]

With his initial speech Churchill had scored a parliamentary triumph. He had implemented his dream. His full house confirmed his colleagues' interest in him. The delivery of the speech verified conjectures that they would hear more of him. The luminaries on both sides of the House were generous in their appraisal of his effort.

To this irrepressible political novice quiescence was insufferable. His brain was never idle nor were his ideas inert. Since nothing escaped his restless psyche, he observed that many of his fellow-men had developed a powerful army complex, that military expenditures from 1894 to 1901 had grown from £17,000,000 to £29,800,000 and that jingoists were clamoring for substantial increases.[9] Churchill viewed this as military heresy and naval sabotage. He held that this should be check-mated, and he designated himself for the assignment. He devoted six full weeks to the preparation of a verbal broadside which he fired on May 13, 1901.[10] It was one of the best speeches of his whole career.

He maintained that a large standing army was not needed for the defense of Britain. The Channel and the navy were the guardians of England's security. As long as the navy was invin-cible, an army was unnecessary for the protection of the country. And any army that England could permanently sustain would not be powerful enough to command the respect of European countries. Shortly before Bismarck was dismissed, upon being asked what he would do if a British army should invade Ger-many, he replied that he would order the police to arrest it.

Increased funds for the army inevitably would reduce allot-ments for the navy, and would in consequence, impair England's defense and diplomatic posture. To weaken the navy, which could assure victory, and to strengthen the army, which could only meet defeat, constituted a tribute to British imbecility.

In his maiden speech, he had attracted admirers but had also provoked some critics. His second exhortation won him addi-tional adherents, and again an augmentation of his critics. No one ever accused him of possessing a neutral personality. If anyone had deduced such an erroneous conclusion, Churchill's reaction to Joseph Chamberlain's advocacy of a tariff would have dispelled that misapprehension.

When England in 1845 repealed the Corn Laws, it initiated its nineteenth-century free-trade program. By 1859 almost all of its tariff legislation had been abandoned, and thereafter Lib-erals and Conservatives alike regarded free trade with almost the same conviction as they did the Thirty-nine Articles. By 1890 some had begun to question, if not the sanctity, at least the sanity of laissez-faire as applied to commerce. Abundant raw materials, modern and efficient machinery, and the appli-cation of science to industry enabled Germany, Japan, and the United States to undersell the British in the world market.

England itself was becoming the dumping ground for its rivals. When Japanese cotton fabrics, in 1890, appeared on the textile counters of Manchester, Big Ben hesitated to strike the hours of the day, and some Britishers felt like exhuming the corpse of Adam Smith and mutilating it. The industrial and commercial interests, however, limited themselves to insist that imports from Germany be stamped "Made in Germany," in order to discourage patriotic customers from buying the denounced articles. But like Adam in the Garden, they found it of excellent quality, and repeatedly returned to it. "Made in Germany" became a trademark of excellence and customers rushed to the Teutonic counters.

The days of British industrial and commercial supremacy had vanished. In the interval of their glory, British commercial men had been high-handed, and high-priced, and had left their customers with the opinion: "Take it or leave it." By 1890 the hustling German, American, and Japanese salesmen, with better goods, frequently at lower prices, had driven the British out of many of their former preserves. Unemployment began to plague England.

Joseph Chamberlain, the former Birmingham businessman, perceived the malady and prescribed a remedy: a tariff, with preferential rates for the colonies and dominions. This, in his opinion, would rescue business, and tie the colonies and dominions closer to Mother England, a painless treatment, accompanied by the ring of guineas into cash registers.

Churchill viewed this as political and economic apostasy.[11] Free trade, he maintained, had lifted England from agrarian poverty into industrial abundance and national affluence. With an ardor for open trading equal to Chamberlain's vehemence for tariff, Churchill denounced the program of the Birmingham sage. He insisted that it was free trade that was the Conservative Party's traditional policy, and that his opponents were extolling political and economic heterodoxy.[12]

In his encounters with Chamberlain and his proselytes, the latter peppered Churchill with facts and fiction, and when these did not silence or subdue him, they resorted to expletives of "Hear! hear!" "Oh!" and "No! no!" The Speaker of the House reminded the hecklers that "Orders of the House as they existed 250 years ago, make it the duty of every member to maintain silence whilst a member addresses the House."[13] With exquisite courtesy, Churchill remained within the House decorum and imposed upon his opponents savage rejoinders.[14] The discord between himself and the vast majority of the party became harsh and acrid.

Churchill also took issue with the Conservative Party's acquiescence in the exploitation of the native population, the Hindu migrants, and the Chinese coolies in South Africa of whom there were more than 80,000 at one time. All of these worked for pitifully low wages. To earn a return passage of £17 10s from Transvaal to China, a coolie would have to work for two and one-half years. They resided within compounds, and were forbidden to roam at will. They were subjected to severe flogging for real and assumed misdeeds.[15] Safety devices to protect those who worked in the mines were piddling, and mine disasters occurred too frequently. When South Rose Deep Mine was flooded, fifty-four miners were drowned.[16] Among the Chinese coolies "unnatural crimes,"—homosexuality—prevailed.[17] Many of the mines were owned by wealthy absentee Britishers who were indifferent to the hardships, brutalities, and abnormalities of the coolies. Their only concern was for luscious returns on their investments, most of which were fabulous. Since the mine owners preferred to sacrifice their morals to their dividends, they serenely maintained their diabolic system without any interference from the Conservative regime in London. Churchill with all his vigor and eloquence was unable to redress the situation. Conservatives did not enjoy being exposed by their enemies; they abhorred being betrayed by one of their own.

The controversy between Churchill and his party hung fire over a period of years, smouldering and sputtering by turns, and, as usual, he placed himslf in the vortex of the storm. He publicly commended other Conservatives for supporting him in his differences with his party. He even paid tribute to a Liberal who had castigated Chamberlain and his tariff policy. He did not ingratiate himself with the Conservative hierarchy by his thanking God for the existence of the Liberal Party.

The rupture occurred on May 16, 1904. As Churchill was addressing the House of Commons, Arthur Balfour, the Prime Minister, left the Chamber, and was soon followed by the members of the cabinet, and most of the members of the Conserva-

tive Party, some 250 in all.[18] And as they departed, some of
them halted at the door and jeered. It was a discourtesy almost
without parallel in English history. Six days later, Churchill
formally severed relations with the Conservative Party. On May
31, after the Whitsuntide recess, as he entered the House of
Commons, he crossed the floor and selected a seat beside Lloyd
George.[19]

The conflict between Churchill and the Conservative Party
did not cease with his withdrawal from it. His defection merely
intensified its virulence and expanded its scope. The weaklings
of the party, too cowardly to enter into individual conflict,
congealed into a solid phalanx of animosity and became as
ferocious and cruel as only cowards can be, when fortified by
consciousness of their numerical superiority and supported by
their organization. Even members of the Marlborough family
repudiated him for what they considered infidelity to his own
kinsmen and their traditions.

What was more important to Churchill was the reaction of
his Oldham constituents to his break with his party. Already
on January 8, 1904, the General Executive of the Oldham Conservative Party Organization had passed a resolution which
declared that because of his action he had forfeited the confidence of Conservative voters of his constituency, and that in the
next election they could not support him.[20] Churchill was not
greatly shocked by their action. In his incipient liberalism,
"Conservativism was too sterile for his adventurous mind."

CHAPTER IV

The Essence of the Man

GENERAL SIR GEORGE TEMPLER, ONE-TIME HIGH COMMISSIONER of Malaya, after reflecting upon Churchill asked in amazement, "What is there about this man which no one else has?"[1] A wide gulf, indeed, differentiated him from the common run of humanity.

In the first place, Churchill was extremely ambitious, and he was willing to pay the price to satisfy his ardent hunger for success. In his one and only novel, *Savrola,* the main character, who was none other than Winston by another name, pondered, "Would you rise in the world, then you must work while others amuse themselves. Are you desirous of a reputation for courage? You must risk your life. Would you be strong morally and physically? You must resist temptation."[2] Churchill was his own most faithful disciple. Few people have been so willing to expend their energy in productive employment, and fewer still have worked so efficiently. Generally, he did not rise in the morning until the middle of the forenoon, but by that time he had toiled for hours, and with the exception of an afternoon nap, in which he faithfully indulged, he maintained his energetic pace until past midnight. In his early years in the House of Commons, then an agreeable bachelor, he was in considerable demand at country-house parties. Generally he accepted such invitations, but with the reservation that he might work in the forenoons while the other guests dozed away the morning hours. Like Sinclair Lewis he "wanted to be somebody." He not only wanted renown, but he insisted upon achieving it at a crescendo pace, for his Marlborough antecedents had been short-lived, and he assumed that he would help to perpetuate the family longevity record. Because of this fixation he strove to reach his ultimate goal before he would be forty. Yet Churchill by his very nature would in all likelihood have maintained a hectic pace even if all of his ancestors had been Methuselahs. During his boyhood he spoke with assurance of his future membership in the House of Commons, even in the cabinet. When he was first Lord of the Admiralty, 1911-1915, Sir Edward Grey observed, "Winston will very soon be incapable, from sheer activity of the mind, of being anything in the cabinet except Prime Minister."[3] To attain his objective he rebelled against conforming to the conventional tempo. He would capture distinction on the run.[4] His craving for eminence led him to agree with the statement credited to Milton that "It is better to rule in Hell than to serve in Heav'n."[5]

To realize his self-imposed fate demanded exacting qualifications and, fortunately for Churchill, he possessed them, and he was willing to exploit them to the maximum.

Physically, his appearance differed little from that of other men, but his bones, tissues, and brain cells possessed an unusual vitality, and though he subjected them to exhausting demands, they survived the shocks and strains.

To fortify his physique to meet these requirements, he stoked it with hearty meals. He consumed bountiful breakfasts embodying a variety of meats, followed by sumptuous lunches accompanied by champagne and followed by brandy. Late in the afternoon he enjoyed his whiskey and soda, while his dinners comprised volume and variety. Before coming to the United States for a lecture tour in 1930-1931—during the prohibition era—he required his entrepreneur to provide him with a bottle of champagne after each engagement.[6] In a friendly conversation with Lord Cherwell, Churchill inquired if the equivalent of his consumption of champagne at the rate of a pint a day were poured into railway coaches, how many it would fill. Lord Cherwell made some calculation, and replied, "Only part of one." To which Churchill replied, "So little time and so much to do."[7] Until his doctors restricted his smoking, he consumed sixteen cigars a day. During World War II, meat rationing was imposed upon everyone within the realm. Even the Royal Family faithfully observed the edict, but not Churchill. With everyone's knowledge, and approval, he enjoyed his customary daily dimensions of roast beef. He justified this indulgence on the thesis that "the carnivores would win the war." According to a good friend, the Earl of Birkenhead, "Mr. Churchill's tastes are very simple. He is easily satisfied with the best of everything."

While he was First Lord of the Admiralty his love of the good life was facilitated by his free and full use of the *Enchantress,* a 3,000-ton yacht. On it he gave weekend parties "with magnificent dinners," with such celebrities among the guests as John Morley, Herbert Asquith, Arthur Balfour, and many others of distinction. On such occasions nothing was spared to make the events memorable, and few, if any, enjoyed them as much as did the host.

His luxurious living was not confined to England. While he was traveling in East Africa, in 1907, he had a special train at the service of himself and his entourage and it was equipped with the best of food and liquid refreshments. Nothing was spared to give him the comfort of home and the excitement of being abroad.

In 1904, in a letter to his mother, he went into raptures about the enjoyment he derived from being the guest of Ernest Cassel in Switzerland. He described the four-story house, "complete with baths, a French cook, ... and every luxury that could be expected in England." It was situated on a 7,000-foot mountain elevation from which he could survey the surrounding landscape. On many occasions he visited his aunt, Lady Londonderry, in one of her numerous establishments in various parts of Europe, and while he was there no effort was spared to make life a pleasant dream. Other friends extended gracious hospitality, and if he had wished merely to luxuriate in their bounty and munificence he could have floated through life on a cloud of enchantment. This bountiful indulgence in good living and pleasant environment generated in him enormous energy and vitality. Not without good reason he was called "a steam engine in breeches."

Churchill's intellectual vigor was quite as superior as his physical constitution. Not without justifiable grounds did Stanley Baldwin maintain that he had a "one hundred-horsepower brain."[8] Absence of intelligence tests during his educational career precluded a statistical rating of his mental equipment, but all those who had any dealings with him confirm Baldwin's appreciation of his faculties, and he had reasons for knowing its dynamism. When Anthony Eden was asked what he considered Churchill's greatest characteristic, he replied, "his ability to probe," i.e., his capacity to get at the core of a problem expeditiously. During World War II, subordinates entered his office with problems which they believed insoluble. Churchill, after "probing" them, often found solutions.

He made a conscious effort to keep his intellect in good working order. Unlike many college graduates who cease to improve their minds the moment they step off the commencement platform, he intensified his intellectual development almost immediately after he had received his commission in the army. No sooner had he reached his first military assignment, in India, than he began to compensate for his educational deficiencies by wide reading. Even while he was imprisoned in South Africa he frequented the jail's library and read. On one of his trips to France he returned with 276 volumes.

Books were Churchill's constant companions, and with a phenomenal memory he absorbed their contents.[9] He could recall events of the past with almost unbelievable accuracy. On one of his trips to the United States, while traveling through Frederick, Maryland, it stirred his memory and prompted him to wonder audibly what the reason might be. Harry Hopkins then recounted the Barbara Fritchie incident, and began reciting Whittier's poem,

> Shoot if you must, this old gray head,
> But spare your country's flag, she said.

but then he bogged down and no one else could recall any more of the poem—except Churchill—who recited the remainder without a slip, although he had not thought of it for sixteen years. While his Harrow sojourn was decidedly lacking in luster he "could quote whole scenes from Shakespeare's plays."

With such a phenomenal retentivity it is not surprising that he committed almost all of his major speeches to memory, and delivered them with poetic cadence and rhythm, and, withal, they possessed the ring of spontaneity.

One reason for his mental efficiency was his immense power of concentration. While considering some problem his whole being was given to the point at issue, and all distractions were deflected.

With all his nutritious food and efficient metabolism, it is not surprising that he had an avid zest for living. To him every project was an adventure, a dramatic enterprise in which he was determined to play the stellar role. Whatever venture engaged his interest he pursued with all the excitement he displayed when he rode to the hounds, or played polo. In each endeavor he bore himself like "Job's horse which paweth the earth before a race." To him every day was an exciting drama, and every evening was not so much the close of the day as the prelude to the ensuing morning. At seventy-two, he maintained that life should be a grand and glorious episode, an ideal which he made reality.

In 1900, in Ladysmith, while a group of officers was engaged in conversation, Winston Churchill, with a surplus of audacity, elbowed his way to Sir George White, the commanding general, and engaged him in a noisy conversation which attracted all within hearing range. Finally, one of the officers questioned who the ostentatious and noisy fellow was, and he was told that the intruder was the son of Randolph Churchill. The informant admitted that he did not like the stranger, but added that some day he would become prime minister.[10]

Aggressiveness and pugnacity were outstanding characteristics of Churchill. "He was never a man to languish unnoticed." In this regard he closely resembled President Theodore Roosevelt, who was determined "to be the bride at every wedding, and the corpse at every funeral."[11] No sooner had Churchill secured a cabinet post in 1906 than he bombarded all his colleagues on the improvement of the administration of their departments. At cabinet meetings he frequently provided his colleagues with dossiers of projects which he urged them to execute. He insisted upon "having an oar in every boat and a finger in every pie." This did not particularly endear him to his ministerial associates. It is not surprising that the *Daily Chronicle* dubbed him "Pushful the Younger."

During the early days of World War I the British had a horror of the possibility of a German occupation of Antwerp, directly across the channel. Churchill was in full agreement with this apprehension and he volunteered to command a British force to prevent Belgian surrender of the city. He rushed to Antwerp, and gave orders to everyone including King Albert. When his troops did arrive he acted "as though he were Napoleon and all within range of his voice were the Old Guard."[12]

Before the opening of World War II, Neville Chamberlain opposed Churchill's entry into the cabinet. He contended, "If I take him into the cabinet he will dominate it. He won't give others a chance even of talking."[13] And no sooner was he incorporated, on September 1, 1939, than he did just that. He outlined to most of the other cabinet members the action that they ought to adopt and how each one could contribute to the successful prosecution of the war.

Intelligence without emotional power is about as useless as a gasoline engine minus spark plugs. Fortunately for Churchill he possessed the ingredients of both intelligence and emotion and in the proper blend. He made no effort to conceal his spirit. His emotional power ignited his intellectual convictions and mobilized them into action. His tears, "the noble language of his eyes," were not revelations of weakness, but disclosures of supercharged feeling which could explode into a chain reaction of blows appropriate to the situation.

When Sir Edward Grey, in August, 1914, announced that England was at war, Churchill joined Lloyd George in a gush of tears, and within minutes the fleet was running down German ships. As Churchill bade farewell to General Sir Henry Wilson, Commander of the British Expeditionary Force, he wept so that he could not finish a sentence in the leave-taking.[14] When during World War II, his grandson was baptized, his lips quivered and he mumbled something about the inhospitable world into which he had come. In 1947 at Blenheim, one of his superior speeches aroused the audience to sustained and enthusiastic cheering, after which all joined in singing "Land of Hope and Glory," and Churchill was overcome with pride and joy. When he visited British cities which had been bombed and devastated, he registered his grief with sobs. This was not only "the agony of reluctant tears," but the release of compressed emotion. It was this prodigious feeling which, given expression in oratory, mesmerized the British to hang on after the fall of France, and then to finish the job.

Though he was the poorest student in his class at Harrow, he made no apologies for his depressed academic index. Quite the contrary. After he had been involved in an altercation with Nugent Hicks, another student, who concluded the incident by giving Churchill a thrashing, Winston growled defiantly, "I shall be a greater man than you."[15] Even when his scholastic performances were at their worst, he was still conscious of his unexploited potentialities. In almost any situation, he regarded himself better qualified to manage it than anyone else. Anthony Eden, an ardent admirer of Churchill, admitted that he was at times arrogantly confident. While he was fighting and reporting during the Boer War, he regaled his comrades with his experiences in India and Egypt. The more amusing he made his escapades, the more dubious his listeners became of the authenticity of his tales.

When he was on his first speaking tour in the United States in 1901, he was more self-assured than usual. When he met the American Winston Churchill, the novelist, he told his namesake, "I mean to be Prime Minister of England." He urged the American to strike for the presidency. He hoped that they might become chiefs simultaneously.[16] It is not surprising that he should have been called the most "self-assured individual, not to say egotistical, that has happened in recent history." Throughout World War II, he never lost hope for ultimate victory. Less than two weeks after he came into the premiership, he observed, "I have been Prime Minister ten days of unmitigated disaster ... but one thing is sure, we shall win."[17] Suffused as he was with confidence in Britain's cause and her ability to redeem it, he imparted his mood to millions of people in Britain and beyond its shores. And all of this was essential if Hitler was to be humbled.

Allied with his confidence was his courage. If there was a chance of positive results, he dared to try the hazardous. Immediately before he entered Sandhurst Military Academy, while he was playing with his brother Jack and other youngsters who were trying to catch him, he recognized that he was cornered, for the bridge upon which he stood was guarded at both ends. To elude his prospective captors he jumped from the bridge to an adjacent tree hoping to grasp a branch. This he failed to do and he fell thirty feet to the ground. Three days later he regained consciousness, a year later he left his bed, but he retained the disposition to dare, which he never outgrew. Proof of this he demonstrated on one of his trips to Africa when, without any weapon, he strolled right into lion and rhinocerous territory in order to observe the gaily colored butterflies. "He longed to see

what danger was like." Often his courage bordered upon recklessness.

This he confirmed during the first year of World War I. Before
the opening of 1915 he had conceived the plan of opening the
Dardanelles to trade with Russia, without reckoning with its
defenders, General Liman von Sanders and Mustapha Kemal
Pasha. These risks imposed catastrophic results upon Churchill.

Madcap strategy of this kind led Roosevelt to declare that
Churchill "had a hundred ideas a day, and four of them were
good...."[18] The Prime Minister did not altogether appreciate
this appraisal as his reaction revealed: "It is impertinent of
Roosevelt to say this. It comes from a man who hasn't any
ideas at all."[19]

During World War II Field Marshall Alanbrooke, the Chief
of the Imperial General Staff, lamented that one of his greatest
torments was to confute Churchill's multiplicity of military
proposals.

Churchill was one of England's pioneers in aviation, and that
demanded courage. Repeated wrecks did not dispel his fervor.
Reports of his mishaps became proverbial. Once while flying
across the English Channel his plane caught fire. On another
occasion while attempting a takeoff his plane somersaulted. On
another flight the steering mechanism failed as he was trying
to land and he crashed on Croydon Airfield. When a young man
who had been invited to join him on a flight, reported late for
the takeoff, Churchill disapprovingly inquired the reason for
his tardiness. The passenger replied, "I was drawing up my will."

He indulged in even more dangerous flying. Just before
France surrendered in 1940, he flew to Tours for an interview
with the French Cabinet in an effort to induce it to remain
in the war. Just before his departure, he strapped a revolver to
his waist and announced to his astounded spectators, "If I fall
in with the Germans, I shall have the satisfaction of shooting at
least one." His attempt to retain France in the war proved futile,
for Marshall Pétain had already superseded Paul Reynaud as
Prime Minister. Upon his return to London he announced to
his cabinet colleagues France's decision to leave the war. "Then
we shall be alone," he said. "For myself, I find that rather
inspiring."

Fear was an alien instinct to Winston Churchill, whether it

involved facing the king of beasts in Africa or the Chief Commissar in Moscow. He was equally courageous in proposing political, diplomatic, and military programs, and in assuming responsibility for their execution. He was in Washington on June 21, 1942, when Rommel captured Tobruk and drove the British pell-mell back into Egypt. This created a serious threat to the whole British position in the Middle East.[20] When news of the catastrophe reached Churchill, he did not seek solace in hysteria, although he did admit that he was the most embarrassed Englishman in America since Cornwallis surrendered Yorktown. After a moment's reflection he merely remarked: "What do we do?" He knew that the situation had to be met, and he ignored irrelevancies. What fortified him in such embarrassing situations was, to a large extent, his calm courage. He never panicked.

Churchill enjoyed work. To him it was not drudgery, but purposeful creativity.[21] If he was not preparing a speech, organizing a report, planning a campaign, painting a mural, writing a book, building a wall, digging a ditch, he was off in the *Enchantress* inspecting dockyards or observing naval maneuvers. Each enterprise, whatever it was, constituted an entrancing experience which, in its performance, held him spellbound. "No statesman in British history, not even Gladstone or Wellington, had such an enormous range of careers as Churchill,"[22] nor so much enthusiasm for what he was doing.

Many people can impose a sharp reproof; only few can confer a delicate compliment. In speaking to a group, Churchill once remarked, "You are the kind of people I should like to find in heaven."

Churchill did not subscribe to the conventional interpretation of religion. It is, therefore, not surprising that he had an aversion to dogma, ritual, liturgy, and ceremony. This attitude may have been induced by a redundancy of it at Harrow, where students were subjected to three services every Sunday, and morning and evening worship throughout the week. "All this was very good," he contended. "I accumulated in these years so fine a surplus in the Bank of Observance, that I have been drawing on it confidently ever since."[23] The emphasis upon faith and formalism backfired within him. Immediately after he had participated in communion following his confirmation he vowed to his cousin, "Once, and never again."[24]

He did not accept the creation of the universe as revealed in Genesis. In *Savrola* he hypothesized that "when the human race was emerging from the darkness of its origin, and half animal, half human creatures trod the earth, there was no idea of justice, honesty or virtue, only the motive power which we call the 'will to live.' "[25] He believed that this was still a vital force. He contemplated death with composure.[26] He envisaged it merely as black velvet—eternal sleep.[27] In a letter to his mother, on August 24, 1898, from the Sudan, written immediately before the Battle of Omdurman, he confessed, ". . . I do not accept the Christian or any other form of religious belief."[28]

Even if he did not embrace the traditional conception of religion, he endorsed it for the masses.[29] For himself, he appreciated its ethical code, although when Hitler inaugurated his blitz upon London, he did not turn the other cheek. But he did believe that Christianity offered a better set of principles by which men could associate agreeably with one another than any other creed. His own career, one of the most remarkable in history, was notably free from anything sordid, either in his personal or public conduct.

He was also a master of denunciation when he thought the occasion demanded it, and it was always on tap. A mere aspersion against his policy or character triggered it, and then the torrent of verbal fulmination deluged his critics. Any commendation of Socialism ignited the detonation, and then the chief priests of Marxism were administered a decisive dressing-down. He kept this within limitations, for he did not want to rupture the coalition of which he was the head. Despite his occasional abuse of Attlee,[30] the latter was frank in acknowledging the greatness of his chief. Attlee insisted that Churchill was a great leader "because he was able to solve the problem that democratic countries in total war find crucial and could be fatal, among them the relations between civilian and military leaders. Lloyd George had an instinct that told him when the generals were doing anything wrong, but he did not have the military knowledge to tell the generals what was right. Churchill did."[31]

Although Churchill had been reared in a democratic environment, he nevertheless possessed many of the attributes of an autocrat. His lucid and superior intellect, combined with an ambitious and aggressive nature, propelled him into the leadership of Britain in its direst crisis. Like his father he "liked to be boss." With this disposition, and placed in the vortex of a critical situation, he could not escape being dictatorial. Lord Moran, his personal physician, maintained that he was a "pasha," and that he cowed his colleagues.[32] When one of his ministers failed to comply with one of Churchill's wishes, he was severely disciplined.[33] He exploited all the power that inhered in the two offices which he held: the Premiership and the Ministry of Defense. The exigency of England's danger magnified the justification for his dominance.

Harry Hopkins, who was intimately acquainted with Churchill, confessed: "I learned that the provisions of the British Constitution and powers of the War Cabinet are just what Winston Churchill wants them to be at any given moment." His dictatorship, however, rested upon the sufferance of the majority of the House of Commons. Several times during the war he was subjected to votes of confidence, but in each case he was sustained by an overwhelming majority. During the war he was indispensable.

In repartee he was superb, sometimes devastating, a proficiency of high utility in a parliamentary body. He and Aneurin Bevan, the Welsh politician, had mutual appreciation of each other's verbal weaponry. As a group of men in the House of Commons was conversing in a lounge, someone observed the absence of Bevan. Another one informed them that Bevan was sick, to which Churchill remarked, "Well, I hope it is nothing trivial." On another occasion George Bernard Shaw sent Churchill two tickets to one of his plays which had just opened in a London theater. Shaw informed him that the tickets were good for either one of two nights, and that one ticket was for himself, and the other one for "a friend of yours, if you have one." In replying Churchill thanked him for the tickets. He regretted that he could not go the first night, but that he would go the second night—"if there is one."

One of his most outstanding characteristics was his magnanimity. In sponsoring his programs he could not avoid disappointing, or even offending, some people. And those who were aggrieved repaid him in kind in multiple measure by sinking the shafts of attack deep into his vitals. But once the fray was over, Churchill erased it from his memory. Admiral Fisher, in 1915, double-crossed him in the Dardanelles campaign in consequence of which Churchill had to surrender the post of First Lord of the Admiralty. The blow to him was devastating and tragic. Churchill bore no grudge against the old sea dog. The following year he recommended Fisher for the post which he had vacated.

Horatio Kitchener emphatically and repeatedly had denied Churchill assignment as a war correspondent to his Army of the Nile. Churchill did not let this impair their mutual relations; even when he was First Lord of the Admiralty and Kitchener was Minister of War, the two associated agreeably though without enthusiasm in the prosecution of the war.

Churchill, with all his virtues, also had his faults, one of which was a chronic unpunctuality. He was almost always late for an appointment. He was often tardy for his cabinet meetings, or his sessions with the Imperial General Staff, and he manifested no remorse or embarrassment over his failure to be on time. Because of a prolonged conversation with someone he was even late in meeting President Roosevelt at a railway station to which the President had come to meet him and Clemmie. She reported on time, and left Churchill in conversation with an acquaintance. Roosevelt wearied from waiting and drove Clemmie to the White House and returned to the station to pick up Churchill.[34] The Prime Minister had merely been faithful to his customary conduct.

Some enlightened Englishmen during the war served patriotically without salary, and Churchill was one of these. As Prime Minister his stipend was $14,000 a year, but he did not accept it. His patriotism did not evaporate with the loss of the Premiership in July, 1955, for when he became leader of the opposition he was entitled to $7,000 a year, and again he declined it.[35] To him service was more important than salary.

CHAPTER V

The Liberal Interlude

Since the Conservative Party of Oldham had resolved not to support Churchill in the election of 1905, he scouted for another constituency and selected North Manchester, a liberal district, warmly sympathetic toward his political convictions. These views included the championing of free trade in opposition to Joseph Chamberlain's crusade for a tariff. Churchill maintained that England had grown prosperous because of the free flow of commodities, and to abandon a policy which had created wealth would constitute economic heresy. He pledged his loyalty to England's traditional commercial policy. Already he was an effective campaigner, for he was young, vigorous, handsome, and colorful, and he exploited all of his attributes. The publication of his *Lord Randolph Churchill* had generated favorable publicity, and it soon yielded substantial royalties.

His opponent was William Joynson-Hicks, a divine, who, with ecclesiastical vehemence, denounced free trade, alcohol, and Churchill. He was an effective speaker, and possessed considerable ability, and sixteen years later he entered the cabinet as a colleague of Churchill. Because of Joynson-Hicks's endorsement of a tariff, Churchill's mother, who had joined the campaign, warned the voters that by electing him they would impose dear food; she offered them "dear Winston" and the electors preferred him to Joynson-Hicks by a majority of 1,241 votes.

The result of the election was not merely a victory for "dear Winston" but also for the Liberal Party, since it secured a majority of 377 seats while the Conservatives were cut down to 132, and many of their bellwethers were not returned to the fold, among them Arthur Balfour, the erstwhile Prime Minister, Joseph and Austin Chamberlain, and others of great ability and distinguished careers. Henry Campbell-Bannerman, who became

[55]

Prime Minister, organized a cabinet of political celebrities, among whom were Herbert Henry Asquith, David Lloyd George, John Morley, Sir Edward Grey, and also Winston Churchill who would be a political asset to the party as Under-Secretary of State for Colonies. While the Conservatives did not appreciate him, the Liberals did, and to the Tories that made his defection all the more odious.

Thus began an administrative career which closed fifty years later and during which he held more cabinet posts than any other Englishman. "No other ruler in history, from Pericles to Stalin, had had a longer or more variegated experience in the craft of governing men."

ADMINISTRATIVE POSTS HELD BY CHURCHILL

Under-Secretary of State for Colonies . . . 1906-1908
President of the Board of Trade 1908-1910
Secretary of State for Home Affairs 1910-1911
First Lord of the Admiralty 1911-1915
Chancellor of the Duchy of Lancaster . . . 1915-1916
Minister of Munitions 1917-1918
Secretary of State for War and Air 1918-1921
Secretary of State for Colonies 1921-1922
Chancellor of the Exchequer 1925-1929
First Lord of the Admiralty 1939-1940
Prime Minister and Minister of Defense . . 1940-1945
Prime Minister 1951-1955

Despite allegations to the contrary, Churchill was an able administrator. He loved power, and he gloried in its exercise. He was unhappy unless he could be the leader of any group of which he was a member. To the exasperation of his cabinet colleagues, he tried to be first among equals. Within his own department, however, its members welcomed dynamic leadership and they got it. When he initiated a project, he knew precisely what he wanted, and how to convey directions to his subordinates. Furthermore, he was able to infuse his own enthusiasm for the enterprise into the minds and hearts of those who were to execute it. He made them feel that it was their project as well as his own. They knew that he was able to defend his policies in the House of Commons, that their completed assignment would not wind up in the alley of blunders and be left there.

What was more, he was willing to assume responsibility for his blunders, and when his programs evolved into successes, he assigned generous credit to those who had contributed to their triumphs. When the Germans, in 1940, expelled the British from Norway, Churchill shouldered the blame for their ejection. When the Germans in 1941 drove the British out of Greece, he again shielded his subordinates at his own expense, the kind of conduct that inspired loyalty and devotion. Long before his World War II popularity, a small group of ardent followers supported him when his future appeared bleak. Among them were Edward Marsh, Professor Frederick Lindeman, Anthony Eden, and Duff Cooper, merely to mention a few.

When Churchill became Under-Secretary of State for Colonies he was thirty-two years of age. In that role he became custodian of the British Empire, the largest in the world. In 1900 it embraced 13,000,000 square miles, populated by 370,000,000 people.[1] This was the largest piece of real estate in the world having a common allegiance. Its administration and supervision proved to be a full-time occupation. In regions so diverse, with populations so varied, its management demanded judgment and tact, qualities which Churchill's enemies did not attribute to him.

The main administrative work technically should have been Lord Elgin's, the Secretary of State for Colonies, but two factors prevented this: Lord Elgin sat in the House of Lords, remote from the acrid inquiries customary in the House of Commons; and being rather ineffective, he interposed no objection against his subordinate's assumption of the primary duties of his office, provided the junior officer accorded him all the dignities of his seniority, and Churchill cheerfully and handsomely met this requirement. He was willing to sacrifice the husk for the kernel.

In the period from 1906 to 1908, while Churchill was Under-Secretary of State for Colonies, England had a multiplicity of problems within the Empire, but none challenged the attention of the government so acutely as did the form of government that should be accorded to the subjugated Transvaal and Orange Free State. Liberals and Conservatives, with few exceptions, agreed that the Boer states should be extended self-government.[2] Preliminary to this, Churchill urged the withdrawal of all military forces from the Transvaal and Orange Free State and appropriation of funds from the British treasury for the resettlement of the people who had been driven from their homes. Since the war was over, he wished to effect a reconciliation, and in this Britain should take the initiative.[3]

A committee was dispatched to South Africa to study the problem of self-government. It returned with a report strongly endorsing Boer autonomy. Churchill ushered this through the House of Commons, which approved the measure with a large majority.[4] In 1906 the Transvaal was accorded responsible home rule. On June 20, 1907, the Orange Free State inaugurated self-government.[5] The Transvaal chose General Botha as its President, and Churchill extended his blessings upon him despite the fact that he had just learned that it was Botha who had captured him in South Africa in 1900.

Another problem, according to Churchill, called for consideration: the condition of the Chinese coolies who had been imported into the Transvaal as contract laborers to work in the mines. In 1904 the wages of a majority of them amounted to £1 10s a month while a very few received £3 10s a month. There was no disposition among the imperial-minded Britishers to meddle with the profitable practices of their acquisitive compatriots thousands of miles away in South Africa. Churchill, himself an imperialist, but with a more sensitive conscience, abhorred the system, and favored a more humane establishment under the Union Jack even though far removed from Downing Street. The treatment of the coolies was, however, a problem between the mine owners and the Transvaal government, beyond the jurisdiction of London's control, and he was compelled to acquiesce in an imperial practice which he regarded as abominable.

With the death of Henry Campbell-Bannerman in 1908, Herbert Henry Asquith entered 10 Downing Street and remained there until 1916. He elevated David Lloyd George from the Presidency of the Board of Trade to the Exchequer, and Churchill to the Board of Trade, which office he held until 1910. This became the radical phase of the descendant of a long line of Tories.

Campbell-Bannerman's election slogan in 1906 had been "Peace, Retrenchment, and Reform," all of which his ministers strove to transform into statutes. Churchill was fully conscious of the disruptive effect of war upon England with its far-flung commercial and imperial interests. He, therefore, was an advocate of peace unless the country's vital interests were jeopardized. His intimate and congenial association with John Morley, Augustine Burrell, Sir Edward Grey, and Herbert Asquith, all strong advocates of peace, strengthened him in his conviction.

Furthermore, Britain before World War I was no longer clamoring for additional colonial territory. Its worldwide markets, though vulnerable to German, Japanese, and American penetration, helped to absorb the country's production. What Britain needed was peace, and Churchill strove to neutralize animosities. Only after he entered the Admiralty in 1911, did he appreciate the dangers, and prepare to face them.

Because of the unjust and unsound economic conditions of vast numbers of the British population, Churchill became a zestful reformer. He recognized poverty as a potential threat to the stability of the country. In 1900 three per cent of the people were wealthy, nine per cent were well-to-do, and eighty-eight per cent were poor, and despite moderate increases in wages, their purchasing power was declining. In 1906 agricultural laborers were getting 18s 3d a week, and metal and shipbuilding engineering workers, the highest paid laborers, were receiving 28s 1d a week.[6] The average weekly income of all industrial laborers was 26s 7d. A family's subsistence on income so low exacted a shocking human toll, for fifty per cent of those who attempted to enter the armed services in 1900 were rejected for physical disability.[7] During the closing years of the nineteenth century, thirty per cent of English children died before they reached their fifth birthday.[8] Among the depressed classes, infant mortality was still higher. In London, in 1900, one-fourth of the adults died in charitable institutions. In 1904, 30,000 children had been abandoned by their parents.[9]

In contrast to this indigence and squalor, many of the wealthy few indulged in uncurbed luxury and irresponsible sybaritism. Five thousand four hundred and eight of the largest landed proprietors owned more land than all the rest of the landowners combined.[10]

DISTRIBUTION OF THE LAND IN 1909

Size of the holding in acres	Number of owners	Acreage
Less than 1	825,272	629,852
1-10	121,983	478,680
10-50	72,640	1,750,000
50-100	25,839	1,791,606
100-500	32,317	6,317,346
500-1000	4,799	3,317,678
1000 and more	5,408	18,695,528

The Duke of Sutherland, the greatest landowner, possessed an estate of 1,250,000 acres. Among others of the nobility whose individual estates were measured in the hundreds of thousands of acres were the Dukes of Northumberland, Richmond, Devonshire, Portland, and Westminster, all of whom enjoyed prodigious incomes. They lived in houses with hundreds of rooms, tended by an army of servants.[11] The chief occupation of the owners and their families consisted of going to house parties, where they rode, hunted, ate, and drank. During the entertainment season, from twenty to fifty guests assembled with their valets, maids, horses, and dogs at the home of the host to revel in ease and luxury. Occasionally, the parties lasted a week, and so extravagant was the entertainment that some of the nobles were driven to the brink of bankruptcy.[12]

It was almost inevitable that these jolly millionaires should assume that the country and its government had been ordained to gratify their lusts, and that anyone who threatened their establishment was an enemy of society, especially if he had defected from its own ranks. Churchill could scarcely have expected anything but venomous hostility from this class of society.

Edward, Prince of Wales, shortly before he was crowned, realized the contrast between the glittering world of wealth and privilege and the squalor, filth, and vermin of the peasants and the urban proletariat, and he reported this discrepancy to the House of Lords of which he was then a member.

The upper orders, however, refused to be disturbed by the Prince's revelations. They rationalized that the poor had always been an element in the population, and were, therefore, a permanent fixture of society. It was useless and senseless to invoke governmental action for their relief. The aristocrats, to calm their consciences, quoted Adam Smith's belief in the merits of noninterference by the government in economic affairs. At Christmas, they dispensed charity, not so much to relieve the distress of the poor as to convince themselves of their virtue, morality, benevolence, and patriotism, and that existing society met the needs of all.[13]

In the past, peasant and proletarian had found pleasure in romantic contemplation of the splendors of the rich. By 1906, the poor no longer gloried in the magnificence of the titled prodigals. They somehow sensed their own potential dignity, and found heralds who were willing to champion their cause.

These spokesmen were David Lloyd George and Winston Churchill. The former's sympathy for the poor and the oppressed sprang from his boyhood rearing in Wales, while Churchill's was acquired through study and observation. John Morley had informed the latter of Seebohm Roundtree's volume, *Poverty: A Study of Town Life*, and after Churchill had read it he confessed, on January 9, 1902, that it ". . . has fairly made my hair stand on end."[14] And when he and Edward Marsh strolled through the streets of a factory town, Churchill commented that life for the poor appeared to him like an "everyday hell." He resolved that something should be done for the people.[15] This became all the more urgent as he reflected upon the fact that the index of the cost of living from 1896 to 1901 had risen from 91.7 to 102.4, and simultaneously employers pressed by foreign competition were striving to solve their problem by reducing the wages of their employes. Here was latent social and political dynamite.

As a result of his reflections upon these statistics Churchill wrote the Prime Minister a moving letter in which he called for action to ameliorate the conditions of the poor. He pointed out that Germany with a harsher climate and less financial resources had created a more humane condition for its proletariat than that which existed in England. This had been achieved by a comprehensive social security system which held hunger and hardship at bay. In the House of Commons, on the public platform, and in private gatherings he was a powerful second to Lloyd George in fighting for a social security system which embraced workmen's compensation, unemployment insurance,[16] the Mines Act, and the eight-hour day, as well as health insurance. Most of the unhappy human exigencies were covered by the social code enacted between 1906 and 1912.

In his reforming zeal Churchill was motivated not alone by sympathy for the poor but also by his determination to strengthen England by having its power based upon a healthy and productive economy. Well-nourished workers would be more productive employes than famished laborers. Physically fit soldiers and sailors would be better defenders of Britain than enfeebled starvelings.[17]

New revenue would be needed for implementation of this code, and Lloyd George, the Chancellor of the Exchequer, devised a system of taxation which fell more heavily upon the aristocrats than ever before. It seemed especially burdensome to them for in the past they had generally shifted the affliction to others.

The Lords aimed to kill the bill, not by defeating it in the Upper House, but by mobilizing the public against it, then calling an election which they hoped would give the Conservatives a majority in the House of Commons, which would then defeat the measure. Mr. Asquith, the Prime Minister, accepted their challenge. Parliament was dismissed. A vociferous campaign was staged against the bill, and in the election of January, 1910, neither party won a clear majority. A second election was therefore arranged for December, 1910. Its major issue was whether the House of Lords should have the power to defeat money bills. In this election, again, neither the Liberals nor the Conservatives secured a safe working majority. The Conservatives in the House of Commons, however, allowed Lloyd George's budget to pass; and the Lords did likewise, for the Prime Minister warned them that if they defeated the measure he would ask the King to create enough peers of liberal persuasion to enact the measure. Lloyd George and Churchill and the rest of the members of the Liberal Party could now proceed to enact England's New Deal, and this they did.

Lloyd George was the chief architect in effecting this change and Churchill was an enthusiastic abettor. For his part in gaining the Lords' approval of the legislation, Lloyd George was hated, while Chuchill, as his coadjutor, was despised. Since it was more difficult for his former colleagues to refute his logic than to heap scorn upon him, they drenched him with their contempt. They confirmed that their animosity toward him still festered and that the longer it brewed the more noxious it became.

Churchill repaid his antagonists in kind by denouncing them as a "party of vested interests, banded together in a formidable federation: corruption at home, aggression abroad to cover it up. . . . Sentiment by the bucketful, patriotism by the imperial pint; the open hand at the exchequer, dear food for the millions, cheap labor for the millionaire."[18] This coruscating denunciation, far from silencing his foes, merely impassioned their enmity. Despite all of his immense ability and ingratiating charm, when he turned it on he was the most hated man in the kingdom, a solitary sentinel in no man's land.

In encounters between Churchill and his foes, Lloyd George did not remain a silent auditor but administered his own brand of astringents on the raw wounds of the nobility. When the Lords attacked his naval budget, Lloyd George insisted that "A fully equipped Duke costs as much to keep as two dreadnoughts, and Dukes are as great a terror, and they last longer. He has one man to fix his collar in the morning, a couple of men to carry a boiled egg to him at his breakfast, a fourth man to open the door for him in and out of his carriage and a sixth and seventh man to drive him."[19]

Churchill's transfer to the Home Office in 1910 did not diminish the animosity toward him. There he was, the Chief of Police of the Realm, and as such he was expected to maintain peace and order during an era of increasing violence and lawlessness. This he strove to do, and with a dramatic flourish. When a couple of desperadoes, after having killed several people, took refuge in a house and fired at the gendarmes, Churchill, after appeals from the police for troops, despatched himself in top hat, striped trousers, cutaway coat and spats, not as an observer, but as the embodiment of law, justice, and power, and exposed himself to the flying bullets. After the police had fired a barrage of their own against the house, the convicts' firing ceased and a mortuary silence ensued. The gendarmes then entered the house and found both of the culprits dead. When Churchill returned to his office his secretary entreated him against taking unnecessary risks to which he replied that the incident had been "such fun."

The more conventional and sophisticated members of officialdom regarded Churchill's conduct as a degradation, not only to him, but also to all in the political hierarchy. Balfour outdid himself in scorn and ridicule.

Since, as Home Secretary, Churchill had placed himself in the vortex of an explosive environment, he found additional "fun" in store for himself, for England, in the period before World War I, experienced an epidemic of strikes which grew in numbers and intensity.

Year	Number of people in Britain out on strike
1909	170,000
1911	830,000
1912	1,250,000

Churchill was hostile to strikes. Intrinsically, as a high government official, he was authoritarian. He opposed any section of the population's attempt to impose its policy upon another one, or to defy the government. Secondly, he perceived a potential conflict brewing between Britain and Germany. To be prepared for such an eventuality, Britain should have a naval force superior to that of any competitor. To maintain that goal Britain could not allow strikes to impede production.

The strikes occurred mainly in dockyards, the railways, industry, coal mines and allied industries. Churchill did not react gently to these developments. To suppress them he ordered troops and the metropolitan police to the scenes of disturbances to compel resumption of operations. So precipitately did he invoke military intervention in strikes that Ramsay MacDonald, leader of the Labour Party registered emphatic disapproval of settling strikes with bayonets and bullets. Since Churchill had a lower regard for MacDonald than he did for the labor union leaders, this effort to stay Churchill's strong-arm pacification ended in failure. Keir Hardie, another Scot and Labour Party member, also strove unsuccessfully to restrain Churchill. Finally, Lloyd George, Churchill's big brother politically, cautioned the

Home Secretary that his policy would alienate Labour support, and when this was repeated by Asquith, the Prime Minister, Churchill reduced the militancy of his campaign against Labour and strikes. But by that time he had estranged Labour almost beyond repair. Not until England faced Germany alone, twenty-eight years later, did Labour tender him its support. In the meantime, Churchill could expect only jeers and taunts from the Conservative Party, and the last Liberal administration came to an end in 1915. Churchill's political posture was precarious.

His despotism, however, embraced redeeming elements of benevolence, for as Home Secretary he secured the enactment of the Mines Act. His object was to promote safety for the miners, and this legislation was urgently needed, for during the first six months of 1909, mine disasters each month had taken the lives of one hundred twenty-two men.[20]

Police and prisons also came under his control, and in this post he effected real improvement. He had suffered imprisonment in South Africa, although for only three weeks, and there he had experienced the loneliness and indignity of incarceration. Furthermore, infliction of punishment was abhorrent to him. He aimed to surround inmates with a wholesome environment, and to that end he introduced lectures and convocations into the prisons.[21] He also inaugurated employment that would appeal to the convicts' creative instincts. He separated adolescent prisoners from seasoned convicts who would otherwise indoctrinate the youngsters in the finesse of skillful and sophisticated criminality. He also issued orders that pubescents who had committed no crimes should be released from prisons. He extended his reforms even farther by releasing 4,000 convicts from prisons on the supposition that, in appreciation of this humane act, they would conform to legal and social conduct. Four years later three out of four had been returned to prison on long sentences.[22]

No death sentence could be executed without the Home Secretary's signature. With his reverence for human life, he found it exceedingly abhorrent to terminate a mortal career. On the other hand it was repugnant to him to contravene the judgment of a jury which had listened to all the facts involved in a case, and had rendered a mature decision. Whenever he reviewed a case ending in a death sentence, he was always deeply disconcerted for days following his decision.

Even before his entry into the House of Commons, Churchill had been unable to ignore the distractions of romance, for he was sensitive to feminine beauty and sparkle. Furthermore, he was also a man of action who usually executed his ideas the moment they were conceived. His pursuit of a young woman, therefore, was that of a conscientious suitor rather than a counterfeit litigant.

On October 26, 1896, he wrote his mother from India that he had met an exceptionally beautiful girl, a Miss Plowden,[23] whose father was Sir John Chiechle-Plowden, in the Indian service. Churchill associated with her in India, South Africa, Toronto, and England. Each admired, even loved the other, and both hoped that their camaraderie would crystallize into marriage, but obstructive elements prevented this. She had her doubts regarding his capacity to exalt her above everything and everyone in the world. He lacked money, even though he was a Marlborough—or because of it. His mother enhanced this embarrassment by imposing enormous financial obligations upon him without even informing him of her monetary maneuvering. On one occasion she made him accountable for the annual interest obligation of £700 on a £17,000 loan which she had negotiated without consulting him. His own fixed income at the time was his subaltern's salary which scarcely defrayed the cost of his polo ponies' oats.[24]

Professionally and politically he was tormented by the realization that he had scarcely passed the first rung of the ladder. His consciousness of failures prevented him from acting decisively. His emotional fervor slumped into an intellectual appreciation. Controversies, though dignified, weakened the ardor. This opened the opportunity for Victor, 2nd Earl of Lytton, who was fortified with rank and wealth, and in 1902, he walked off with the prize. In 1965, when Churchill died, she was still living.

Very soon after his return from India, with a book to his credit, and adventure to his name, he met Muriel Wilson, an English beauty with considerable wealth, and proposed to her, but she declined to become Mrs. Churchill. Thereafter he resolved not to approach women with money when he was moved by romantic motives.

His third prospect was Ethel Barrymore, but she too declined his proposal on the ground that their two divergent careers could not be fused into a happy union.

In the election campaign of 1908, when he was thirty-three, he met Clementine Hozier, ten years younger than himself, at the home of a friend in London. After a relatively short acquaintance they became engaged,[25] and this triggered London Society into a carnival of gossip. The old dowagers and the young hopefuls were amazed that he had not selected an heiress, and who was Clementine Hozier, anyway? She was the child of a broken home, and she was compelled to give lessons in French to supplement the living expenses of herself and her mother. Duchesses' eyebrows elevated at quizzical angles. Clementine, however, had no cause for issuing apologies for herself for she was one of England's outstanding beauties, and she had sterling character. Harry Hopkins maintained that she was "the most charming and entertaining of all the people that he had met on these weekends. . . ."

The wedding was a notable social event. Invitations were issued to eight hundred people, most of whom appeared on September 12, 1908, at St. Margaret's Church, in London, to witness the ceremony. Significant as was the event in his life, Churchill, while waiting with Lloyd George in the vestry to make his entry, engaged the Little Welsh Attorney in a lively political discussion.

After the wedding Lord Rosebery, the last of the Victorian Liberal Prime Ministers, avowed that "The marriage won't last six months." His estimate was off by fifty-six years, for in the last months of his life Churchill announced, "We lived happily ever afterwards." The durability and congeniality of that nuptial contract must, however, be credited to Clemmie's patience, tolerance, and devotion. He did not abuse her, but his moodiness and tension did not augment his allurement. Clemmie adjusted herself to all his varying dispositions. They became the parents of five children, one son and four daughters: Diana, 1909; Randolph Jr., 1911, who passed away in 1968; Sarah, 1914; Marigold, who died in 1921; and Mary, 1922.

Churchill confessed that his political duties encroached upon his parental obligations. There was, however, no estrangement between him and his children; and on many occasions, even diplomatic conferences, he enjoyed associating with them, and they reciprocated his affection.

Even though he fell in love with and married a suffragette, he had no enthusiasm for her cause. During his early years in the House of Commons he not only opposed but ridiculed the Women's Suffrage movement. He contended that governing was a peculiarly masculine function, and on that account women who wished to exercise that prerogative were encroaching on men's vested interest. The legitimate sphere of women's activity, he insisted should be nonpolitical.

Emmeline Pankhurst, "The Madonna of the Militants," in her crusade to enfranchise women, embodied all the fanaticism of martyrs. She exhorted thousands of young people, both men and women, to dedicate themselves to the enfranchisement of her sex. Despite her eloquence, and the justice of her cause, as revealed by its subsequent adoption all over Europe and in many other areas, the great majority remained inert and dormant to her appeal, while members of Parliament g.nerally remained passive and quiescent. Though eight bills had been introduced in the House of Commons before 1913, none of them was given serious consideration.

Women, chiefly of the upper-middle class finally resorted to violent demonstrations in their effort to secure the franchise; in consequence of this they were imprisoned. In their defiance they resorted to fasting. When forced feeding was imposed upon them, Churchill, as Home Secretary, refused to countermand the compulsory nourishing. During World War I, however, British women performed so magnificently that in 1918 women over thirty were given the vote. To this enactment Churchill raised no objections, nor in 1928 when they were accorded the franchise on terms of equality with men.

In neither term of his premiership did he select a woman for a cabinet position, although precedents for that had been established by both Ramsay MacDonald and Clement Attlee.

After about a year as Home Secretary, before his enemies could wreak vengeance upon him, he shifted from the Home Office to the Admiralty as its First Lord. Several reasons contributed to this transfer, the first and most important of which was the challenge of the German navy. Until 1911 the British fleet was the unquestioned master of the seas. If the assertion that Germany was an army with a country had any validity, it was equally true that Britain was a navy with an empire. Several factors account for the German threat. England had lost its supremacy in the production of steel. In 1850 it produced more steel than all the rest of the world combined. Even in 1871 it had forged 50 per cent more than did Germany, but by 1914 the tables were turned. Then Germany produced 85 per cent more pig iron than did England, and 143 per cent more steel.[26] Because of these factors Germany's *Weltpolitik* enhanced Churchill's concern.

In 1905, Britain laid the keel of the first of its dreadnoughts. It had three characteristics which made it superior to all other warships: heavier armor, greater offensive power, and higher speed. Momentarily the British rested secure in their naval supremacy, and then suddenly realized that the dreadnoughts made obsolete all or nearly all of their battleships. If Germany should build dreadnoughts, as of course it would, a naval race would then be instituted, starting from an even base. Since Germany had a greater population and more steel than Britain, the latter was at a serious handicap.

When the British became aware of their self-imposed embarrassment, their mood approached panic-stage for, referring to battleships, they chorused

> We want eight
> And we won't wait.

By 1913, the German navy's threat to the British was serious, and month by month it became increasingly acute.

COMPARABLE STRENGTH OF THE
BRITISH AND GERMAN NAVIES IN 1914[27]

	Dreadnoughts	Predreadnoughts	Battle Cruisers	Light Cruisers	Destroyers	Submarines
British	20	8	4	12	42	54
German	13	16	3	15	88	28

In this ominous situation, Premier Asquith and his colleagues agreed that whatever personal objections they might have to

Churchill, he, more than anyone else, possessed the qualities that the circumstances demanded. No one could dispute his great administrative ability. The urgency of the posture necessitated the presence of the First Lord of the Admiralty in the House of Commons to expound on the need and objectives of the Navy, and few, if any, in that body were as articulate as he.

Churchill, at thirty-seven years of age, rejoiced in his appointment. It challenged his ability and he gloried in the exercise of power. His vibrant and dynamic personality infused verve and enthusiasm in the performance of duties all the way from the humblest apprentice seaman to those of the exalted First Sea Lord. All who did not emulate his earnestness were replaced by disciples of Theodore Roosevelt's gospel of the "strenuous life." One of the first casualties was Sir Arthur Wilson, the First Sea Lord, who was replaced by Prince Louis of Battenberg. Others who were more interested in the dignity than the duty of their offices soon joined the aggregation of naval discards. Churchill replaced these with young men with reputations yet to make, and eager to do so. He chose Admiral Sir John Jellicoe to command the home fleet, and made David Beatty his secretary. From the best of the most promising officers, he created a Naval War Staff to bring the fleet into battle readiness. He made each officer feel that he was a prospective Lord Nelson. The whole navy soon vibrated with zest and efficiency. Also, he improved the battleships by increasing the thickness of their hulls; he enlarged their guns from 13.5 to 15-inch bores; he substituted oil for coal as fuel. He was instrumental in acquiring oil fields in Persia for meeting the needs of the fleet in Far Eastern waters.

Despite his inclination to sea sickness, he made the *Enchantress,* the Admiralty yacht, his part-time office. For three years he used it in visiting bases, dockyards, and shipyards in all parts of the empire. He maintained high-ranking officers on duty at naval headquarters twenty-four hours a day to issue the appropriate orders in any eventuality. He prepared a chart of the seas frequented by German vessels and upon it pinned each ship's location day by day. Each morning he asked one of his subordinates, "What would happen if Germany began war today?" He wanted others to sense the responsibility which weighed upon him.

Without adequate appropriations, Churchill would have been

unable to strengthen the fleet as demanded by British public opinion. In 1913, he asked for £50,000,000, a sum which seemed an extravagance to Lloyd George who was able to whittle it down by £5,000,000.

Parliamentary appropriations were designed chiefly for the construction of ships, but this did not deter Churchill from diverting £70,000 for the building of eighteen "landships" (tanks). Skeptics, of whom there were many, referred to these vehicles as "Winston's folly."

Churchill's initative was not stymied by ridicule and criticism. He proceeded to develop the first naval air force in history. In 1925, he projected his vision to the development of an atomic bomb. He envisioned a device "no bigger than an orange ... which could blast a township at a stroke."[28]

While trying to maintain a safe naval lead over Germany, he strove to negotiate an agreement of naval limitation with Von Tirpitz. But in this he failed, for the Germans refused to make themselves vulnerable to commercial blockade in case of war. To them, this was of the utmost importance, considering their position in the center of Europe, and their necessity of import-ing raw materials and of maintaining an outlet for their exports.[29] In 1913 Von Tirpitz emphatically rejected the prospect of a naval holiday with the British. Since the Germans refused to negotiate on such a basis, the naval race between the two countries became increasingly tense.[30] Churchill's insistence that for Eng-land the navy was a necessity, and that for Germany it was a luxury did not meliorate the relations between the two countries, especially after the publication in 1890 of Admiral Mahan's *The Influence of Sea Power on History,* in which he maintained that that nation or that group of nations which controls the seas is always victorious in a war.

The European crises which succeeded one another from 1906 until 1914 convinced Churchill that a military confrontation between the European powers was almost inevitable, and acting upon that conviction he prepared the navy for instant action on the outbreak of hostilities. Years later when Lord Grey of Fal-lodon wrote *Twenty-five Years,* he declared that the country was under deep obligation to Churchill for the exceptionally good state of preparation of the fleet at the opening of the World War.[31] Few, if any, took issue with that verdict.

CHAPTER VI

World War I

WHEN CHURCHILL WAS A NOVITIATE IN THE HOUSE OF COMMONS, Sir William Harcourt confided to him, "Believe me, nothing of importance ever happens." Fourteen years later the quiescence abruptly changed, for on June 28, 1914, Gavrilo Princip assassinated Archduke Francis Ferdinand and thereby drove international repose from the earth. The two sides, England, France, and Russia versus Germany and Austria, precipitately squared off and instituted an exchange of blows. William II proceeded to implement the Schlieffen Plan for the seizure of Paris. Churchill, ahead of authorization, had mobilized the fleet, and the war got off to a roaring start.

Even before the inception of the war, Churchill had drafted the naval strategy in the event of a conflict. It was to:

1. Blockade Germany.
2. Convoy British shipments of troops and matériel to the fighting front.
3. Maintain open trade routes for the British on all the oceans.
4. Induce the German fleet to come out and fight—and then to defeat it.

So well was the fourfold naval campaign executed that by Christmas of 1914 the German navy had been sunk or driven from the oceans, and shipments of men and matériel to the Continent had been executed with remarkable safety and expedition. Churchill, however, received little commendation. When a British fleet scored a victory, the Tory press heaped praise upon the commanding admiral, and when a German squadron sank a British flotilla, Tory newspapers simmered with ominous forebodings against Churchill. When a German squadron, on December 14, 1914, bombarded Hartlepool, Scarborough, and Whitby on the east coast of England and killed or wounded 500 civilians, the public generally agreed that Churchill should not have permitted such an "outrage." Tory patriarchs never relaxed their determination to destroy him. They were willing to pay a high price for his political scalp. A naval disaster in their view, would not have been an undiluted misfortune. His enemies waited watchfully, and not in vain, for the time to strike.

Before this happened Churchill came into possession of the German Naval Code book. When the German ship *Magdeburg* was wrecked in the Baltic Sea, in September, 1914, the communications officer drowned, and a few days later his body surfaced with the code book still held firmly in his embrace. The Russians recovered the body, and the code book, and forwarded the latter to their naval attaché in London who turned it over to Churchill. This enabled him to ascertain in advance the movements of the German fleet, and from that information he could draw strategic conclusions.

Churchill did not confine his activity to naval affairs but participated in land warfare as well. The Germans in executing the Schlieffen Plan reached the outskirts of Paris on September 6, and from then until the 13th, in a futile effort to take the city the Battle of the Marne ensued. Following that unsuccessful effort the Germans made a rush for the Channel ports, among them Antwerp. That city in German hands would constitute a threat to British shipping in the Channel. On the other hand, Antwerp under British occupation would serve as a menace to the German right wing. With very little coaxing General Kitchener, British Minister of War, prevailed upon Churchill to assume command of the expeditionary force to prevent German occupation of the city. With a mixed force of about 9,000 men, of which only a marine brigade of 3,000 was fully trained, Churchill arrived in Antwerp on October 4. Upon landing he took complete charge. He fired a barrage of orders as if he were "Hannibal taking his army across the Alps." He directed King Albert as if he were a Belgian intendant, and the members of his cabinet as if they were local sheriffs. His purpose was to encourage the Belgians and to harry the Germans in their rear, and to induce them into thinking that his troops were but the vanguard of a vast horde that was soon to follow. So enthusiastic was he about his enterprise that he offered to resign as First Lord of the Admiralty and to accept the commission as Brigadier-General that Kitchener had offered him. Asquith, the Prime

Minister, refused to honor his request on the ground that to make a former lieutenant senior to two major generals, several brigadier-generals, and a number of colonels would not have been conducive to harmony. Furthermore, his services were needed at the Admiralty.

From the 4th to the 9th of October the Germans attacked Antwerp with heavy artillery, whereupon they took the city. Churchill's forces, a hastily organized, ill-prepared detachment, were unable to meet the German onslaught. The attempted defense had cost the lives of 20,000 Belgians and 1,500 British, while two battalions had wandered off into Holland and were interned for the duration of the war. When the Germans entered the city, they imposed a levy of £20,000,000.

The assessment which Churchill's enemies imposed upon him were equally extravagant. While they deplored the loss of the hundreds of men who were killed, captured, and interned, they rejoiced in the charges of incapacity which they could level against him. Churchill's prestige suffered a blow. He had initiated the project, not in anticipation of expulsion but rather in the expectation of a triumphal achievement, of holding the city against the Germans. This he had failed to do, and his enemies would invoke it against him later.

The rampaging German commerce raiders—the *Emden, Goeben, Breslau, Königsberg, Gneisenau,* and *Scharnhorst*—were still at liberty and sinking Allied commercial vessels with impunity. The Conservatives maintained that Churchill should have put a stop to that. Did not Britannia rule the waves, or did she? Almost simultaneously a German submarine sank three British cruisers—the *Aboukir, Cressy,* and *Hawke*—with the loss of 1,600 lives. This provided Churchill's enemies with additional ammunition for their assault upon him.

He attempted to neutralize the opposition by his appointment of Sir John Fisher to the vacancy left by the resignation of Prince Louis of Battenberg, who had been First Sea Lord. The addition of Sir John to the Admiralty was regarded by many as toying with combustibles, and later, Churchill did not dispute this allegation. Nor did Fisher's presence in the Admiralty prevent a German squadron commanded by Graf Maximilian von Spee from sinking on November 4, 1914, three cruisers and an armed merchantman in the Battle of Coronel, off the coast of

Chile. For this, the Conservative press figuratively suspended Churchill from the yardarm, and then gave Vice-Admiral Sturdee the credit for destroying at Falkland Islands the German Fleet which had sunk Cradock's squadron at Coronel. For Churchill, the Antwerp incident was a "rabbit punch" in comparison to the solar plexus that was in store for him in the Dardanelles Campaign.

A number of reasons prompted Churchill to prosecute the Dardanelles expedition. Of first importance was the necessity to keep Russia in the war. In March, 1914, the Russian press had informed its readers, in all likelihood at the behest of General Sukhomlinov, the Minister of War, that "Russia is ready!"[1] Its artillery, the release continued, was superior to the German or the French, and the army had the necessary shells.[2] If Sukhomlinov's braggadocio had been as lethal as chlorine, the Germans would have been struck dead at Tannenberg. Sukhomlinov's pronunciamento was a skewed revelation of his country's unreadiness for combat. "By November 1914, the Russians had practically run out of ammunition."[3] Some guns were silent for lack of ammunition; others were limited to three or four shells a day.[4] The war had scarcely gained full momentum before one Russian general lamented, "Today our artillery and infantry are mute, and the army is drowning in its own blood."[5] So acute was the shortage of rifles that "30 per cent of the Russian soldiers at the front had no weapons. They were expected to stand by until their comrades had been killed, then pick up their rifles and fire."[6]

In this dire extremity Churchill believed that Russia might abandon the war. He maintained that the most assured way of preserving an Eastern Front was to dispatch supplies to the Russian army, and that the speediest route was through the Dardanelles through which before 1914 80 per cent of Russia's seaborne commerce had passed. The reopening of this route would enable the West to provide Russia with vast stores of foodstuffs, and war matériel. A second reason for opening the Straits was the establishment of a third front against the Germans. This effort would reduce their effectiveness on the other two. The third front would comprise, in the main, the Balkan states.

Furthermore, a successful penetration of the Balkans would

eliminate Turkey as an ally of Germany; it would also make possible the creation of a Balkan League for military action against Austria-Hungary. According to Lloyd George, the Balkan states could mobilize 800,000 troops.[7]

These forces supplemented by French and British troops would have constituted a formidable army. Churchill believed that a combined Balkan attack against Austria-Hungary would have animated Balkan nationalism within the Dual Monarchy. Such a development might well have disintegrated the Old Empire. Prince Aleksander Mikhailovich Gorchakov, Russian Foreign Minister 1856-1882, had characterized Austria-Hungary in 1883 as "a cadaver already in a state of putrefaction."

Since the beginning of the war, the armies on the Western Front had demonstrated the impossibility of a "break-through," or of a successful flanking attack. But Churchill was confident that this deadlock could be broken in the Balkans, and that this would spell the defeat of the Central powers.

In his *Gallipoli*, Alan Moorehead contends that the Dardanelles Campaign was "the most imaginative conception of the war, and its potentialities were almost beyond reckoning."[8] C. R. M. F. Cruttwell maintained that it "was unquestionably the most fruitful and feasible of all those which flitted through the brains of the War Office Council Sub-Committee."[9] Among the many who did not embrace this view before the campaign opened were David Lloyd George, and Reginald McKenna, whom Churchill had superseded.

The strategic plan for the attack on the Dardanelles was drafted by Admiral Carden, accepted by Churchill, and adopted by the Cabinet and the War Council. Sir John Fisher, however, lacked enthusiasm for it because he had a plan of his own which involved an attack on the Baltic coast of Germany.

The final decision to strike at the Dardanelles was made on January 28, 1915. Sir Edward Grey contended that the attacking force should be strictly naval.[10] It was under no circumstances to involve the use of troops. The naval strength assigned to penetrate the Straits comprised ten British and four French pre-dreadnaught battleships besides the battleship *Queen Elizabeth* and the battle cruiser *Inflexible*, supplemented by a large number of cruisers and torpedo craft. With this force, Churchill, in his own words, hoped to push through "in the nature of an

organized rush." At the time it seemed like a plausible supposition, for the guns of the battleships from February 19 to
March 7 silenced the Turkish batteries, while landing parties
demolished the fortresses. By that time the large Turkish guns
had a reserve of only twenty shells. The Turks had lost confidence in their capability of resisting, and General Liman von
Sanders had ordered his special train to be prepared to take
him and his staff back to Berlin. The Turks were already discussing surrender terms with Henry Morgenthau, the United
States Ambassador to Constantinople.

On March 18, the situation was reversed when three Allied
battleships, after having run into a minefield, were sunk and
three others were seriously damaged.[11] Admiral De Robeck,
commander of the joint fleets, broke off the action. On the supposition that the naval attack would be resumed, Churchill
remained hopeful, but on April 14 De Robeck telegraphed
Churchill that he would not renew the attack until he could
secure the support of the army. This message drove Churchill
to exasperation. He was desperately determined to resume the
attack and in this he was supported by Asquith and Balfour. Sir
Henry Jackson, who, after Churchill's resignation from the Admiralty, became First Sea Lord opposed further attacks until
naval action could be supported by land forces. On April 28,
1915, 29,000 troops, chiefly Australians and New Zealanders,
landed on the Gallipoli peninsula. From the very beginning of
the invasion, Allied troop losses were abnormally high, and few
in England were hopeful of a victorious issue. Sir John Fisher
supplied the Tory press with synthetic incrimination against
Churchill. Anti-Churchill Conservatives read these with glee.
Liberal members of Parliament viewed Churchill as the author of
the difficulties that afflicted their party,[12] and petitioned their
chiefs of staff to bar him from membership in the ministry under
consideration. They recalled his firm suppression of labor strikes
and his role in the Ulster Plot in 1913, in which the Protestants
of Ulster demonstrated against the pending bill for the union
of Northern and Southern Ireland under Home Rule for the
island under the suzerainty of Britain. Churchill exercised a
significant role in the disturbances, and reaped the ill will of
many of the liberal-minded people. It was widely believed at
this time that Churchill was conniving to establish a Department

of Public Safety "which would have allowed him to exercise an overriding control over all wartime operations. . . . Still others hinted that he coveted nothing less than the premiership."[13] With all this simmering, Churchill was vulnerable to the intriguing against him. Daily the opposition against him grew. On May 15, 1915, Sir John Fisher resigned as First Sea Lord, and this precipitated the crisis which led to Churchill's expulsion. Bonar Law, the leader of the Conservatives, expressed lack of confidence in the administration of the war, and demanded a fused ministry of Liberals and Conservatives. Asquith yielded to this ultimatum, because he was eager to "prolong his lease on Downing Street."[14] He also yielded to Law's second demand that Churchill should be dropped from the cabinet. King George V endorsed this requirement, for writing to the Queen on May 19, he expressed satisfaction that "the Prime Minister is going to have a national government. Only by that means can we get rid of Churchill at the Admiralty. He is intriguing also with [General] French against [General] K; He is the real danger."[15]

This development fell upon Churchill like a bolt from the blue, for he was unaware of the volume and intensity of the animosity against him. Administrative responsibilities had monopolized his time and prevented his attendance in the House of Commons where he would otherwise have sensed the antipathy of the Conservatives toward him.

Churchill fully realized the significance of the blow to his career. In the greatest of all dramas, he had wished very much to be in the cast and to play a leading role. He, with ability, energy, and zest found himself dropped and discredited. Others in the war would make names for themselves while he would be classified as a blunderer. They would return with citations, medals, and trophies heralding their heroic adventures. They would exploit their luminous careers to his disadvantage. In sadness Churchill announced more to himself than to any possible listener, "I am finished."

To soothe his wounded pride Asquith appointed him Chancellor of the Duchy of Lancaster, a prodigious sinecure. This did not assuage his mortification. The ablest and the most enterprising man of British public life could not so easily be blinded to his humiliating dismissal.

The Dardanelles campaign continued until December, 1915, seven months after Churchill's ouster. It was ". . . one of the most striking examples of willing the end without willing the means."[16] It imposed a toll of 250,000 casualties of whom 150,000 died. It was a huge bill for a frightful failure since the Straits continued under German control. The Russians overthrew the Tsar, succumbed to a Communist coup, and in March, 1918, signed the Treaty of Brest Litovsk. The opening of the Straits might have prevented these developments. A parliamentary investigation exonerated Churchill from the charges of incompetence and mismanagement of the Dardanelles campaign. The injury to his reputation, however, remained until the opening of World War II.

While Churchill was exhilarated by many incidents in his life, few, if any, depressed him so much as his dismissal from the Admiralty. His appointment as Chancellor of the Duchy of Lancaster, and Kitchener's assurance that the "fleet was ready" were sources of gratification, but they constituted merely surface sedatives to his psychic wound, and gave but temporary relief to a trauma that was deep and lacerating.

Churchill believed that the most efficacious way to neutralize pain was to smother it in pleasure. To practice that therapy he purchased a painter's equipment, and proceeded to the park to confiscate its beauty and carry it away on a canvas. As he was fumbling his brushes, Lady Lavery appeared and initiated him into the art "not bound by the laws of the syllogism." Other painters cheerfully donated their time and talent to the evolution of a statesman into an artist. Churchill viewed the canvas as a battlefield and his brushes as swords as he deployed them as his artistic sense commanded.[17]

During his career with paint and brushes he completed more than 500 paintings.[18] During World War II he painted only one, of the Atlas Mountains in North Africa, while he was recuperating from pneumonia.

Recognition for his artistic achievement was generous. In 1948 he was made an Honorary Royal Academician, a distinction extended only to few. He was also accorded membership in the Society of British Artists. Some of his paintings were shown in the Royal Academy's Exhibition, and in 1958 forty of them were on view in the Metropolitan Museum of New York.[19] Thirty-five paintings were shown in the Smithsonian Institution in Washington.

Despite these honors, Churchill never acquired the competence of a professional painter because he had not subjected himself to the exacting discipline which excellence demands.[20] At best he developed into an able amateur,[21] chiefly in the field of landscape painting. "His pictures lack the ultimate magic of the artist who has spent his life searching for the hidden beauties that nature only reveals to her full-time admirers."[22]

It is not surprising that Churchill was not the twentieth-century Rembrandt or Da Vinci, but it is amazing that, engaged in a great variety of activities, he could paint as well as he did. His painting is another evidence of his extraordinary versatility.

The demands upon an amateur artist did not exhaust the compressed energy of this human dynamo. In the great conflict that was raging, the role of a mere observer was anathema. Since he had known General Sir John French, the Chief of the General Staff, since their Boer War days in South Africa, Churchill appealed to him for a military assignment in France. Sir John, remembering former times, offered him a commission as a brigadier general after a month's experience in the trenches. When Asquith learned of this he was aghast, and exclaimed, "For God's sake, don't give him a brigade—don't give him more than a battalion!"[23] Churchill, in consequence, was demoted to the rank of major and when, in November, 1915, he reported to the colonel of the Grenadier Guards for his assignment, the commanding colonel gave him an insolent reception: "We were not consulted in the matter of your coming to join us." This was hardly an auspicious welcome, and Churchill felt the full force of the impertinence. During the month with the Grenadier unit there was only slight relaxation in the haughty mood of the officer staff. Upon his transfer to the Scots Fusiliers, the officers' conduct gave proof of a continuity of frigidity toward him; but with a difference, however; he was advanced to the rank of lieutenant colonel.

With the enlisted men he fared well for he made it very clear that he was their advocate. He organized committees to scour the countryside for extra food, especially of a better quality than that served in their barracks, the cost of which was defrayed from his personal funds, or from those of the mess hall. He assured the men that upon the end of the war if they should need assistance in securing employment, he would be glad to be of service to them. What was most appreciated was his establishment of delousing stations where the men could rid themselves of vermin.

He did not ignore the officers. Somehow and somewhere he had come into possession of an old bath tub the use of which he made a ritual. He invited his fellow officers to avail themselves of its comfort and cleansing potentialities.

Even while he was at the front Churchill received distinguished guests from France and England. Among the more illustrious were F. E. Smith, Lord Chancellor of England, and Georges Clemenceau, soon to become the Prime Minister of France. The latter was on an inspection tour of the front line and upon his arrival Churchill and Clemenceau vied with each other in display of courage, or recklessness, by disporting themselves auspiciously above ground along the front trench in full view of the Germans. When one of their shells landed in close proximity of the "Tiger," he gleefully exclaimed, "This is delicious!"

Churchill survived this hazardous bravado and devoted himself to the writing of *Variants of the Offensive* in which he condemned the stupid slaughterhouse tactics pursued on the Western Front which consisted of frontal attacks across no man's land against all the death-dealing devices of the enemy. Instead, he urged the construction of a vast number of tanks and airplanes with which to outflank the Germans. Rather lethargically the General Staff embraced this view, which Churchill had proposed before the opening of the war. General Ludendorff's memoirs authenticated this contention for there the German general maintained that the enemies' tanks constituted the most vital factor in bringing Germany to defeat.[24] In urging the use of the new weapons, Churchill was not ahead of his time; the military diehards were behind schedule.

In December, 1916, Lloyd George superseded Asquith in the premiership, and in July, 1917, some of the violent antagonism toward Churchill had subsided. Lloyd George had high appreciation of Churchill's administrative ability, and was eager for his admission into the cabinet long before he asked him to join. The Prime Minister feared that Churchill's reentry into the cabinet would induce the Conservatives to withdraw from the coalition. Nevertheless, in July he was appointed Minister of Munitions.

Churchill justified his superior's confidence in him by improving the organization of the department. He reduced the number of major units within it from fifty to ten, and made all the men within each unit directly responsible to its head. The heads of the ten units constituted a council responsible to Churchill. This simplified the operation within the ministry, and greatly improved the efficiency of the whole system. Within a short period production increased 20 per cent. This resulted in part from the increase in the number of munitions plants, a development initiated by his predecessor and advanced during Churchill's administration of the department. England was, therefore, prepared to render assistance in equipping the U. S. Army after the American declaration of war in April, 1917. France provided even greater quantities of war matériel for the American Expeditionary force.

Upon the entry of the United States in the war, it had only fifty-five serviceable planes, all antiquated models, and sixty-five pilots who were qualified to fly them.[25]

Toward the close of the war, Lloyd George assigned the Ministry of War and Air to Churchill; his new duties consisted primarily in demobilizing the troops without antagonizing any units of the armed forces more than absolutely necessary. This required delicacy in administration, for each unit, with martial insistence, demanded precedence over all others in the schedule of disbandment. Churchill's predecessor had inaugurated a plan for the demobilization of units according to the urgency of the national need for their services. The uniformed men who had lived in the trenches for years, in facing this situation were motivated more by personal than national considerations. They insisted that those units which had been in the service the longest should be the first to be mustered out, and, if necessary, they were ready to reenforce their arguments with their weapons. Churchill realized the explosiveness of the situation, and yielded in a large measure to the wishes of these troops, and, thereby, avoided what might have become a critical affair.

Another development with which Churchill played a significant role was the Allied intervention in Russia after 1917.

The original purpose of the Allies was to maintain an Eastern fighting front against Germany after the fall of the Tsarist government, and to prevent Allied war matériel shipped to Vladivostok and Archangel from falling into German hands. All of the major Western powers, including the United States, dispatched troops to achieve the realization of these objectives. Since the intervention continued for almost two years after Germany's defeat in 1918, other motives came to the fore, and Churchill became the spearhead of these designs.

With the advent of the Bolsheviks to power, he strove to rally the West "to strangle Bolshevism at its birth," for he regarded the Leninists as mortal foes of "civilized freedom," and as "murderers and ministers of hell." He admitted that the Bolsheviks had come to power because of the moral bankruptcy of the Romanov regime. "With victory in its grasp it [Russia] fell upon the earth and was devoured alive, like Herod of old, by worms." In 1919 he denounced the "foul baboonery of Bolshevism," and the "bestial appetites of Leninism," whose leaders were "soap box Messiahs." Lloyd George had good grounds for declaring that Churchill, more than anyone else, was responsible for the Allied intervention in Russia. While he was Minister of War he dispatched almost 100,000 tons of arms, ammunition, and clothing to Admiral Kolchak, who enjoyed Allied recognition, and to General Denikin, also operating against the Bolsheviks; he sent 250,000 rifles, 200 guns, 30 tanks, and vast quantities of ammunition, as well as several hundred officers and noncommissioned men to instruct the White Russians in the use of the matériel. A similar consignment of ordnance and instructors was sent to General Yudenich who was attempting to take Petrograd. British troops were stationed at Murmansk, Vladivostok, and the Caucasus region. Churchill deplored the pauperism, starvation, and misery that prevailed under the Bolshevik regime, but overlooked his own contribution to that pitiful situation by his prosecution of the intervention which included the maintenance of a blockade of Russia until 1920. Nor did the Allies, largely because of Churchill's influence, permit League of Nations relief to reach the Russians. Allied intervention against the Bolsheviks contributed materially to the death of two million people afflicted with scarlet fever, typhoid fever, malaria, cholera, diphtheria, and smallpox.

Many Britishers, especially within the Labour Party, finally questioned the justification of their country's intervention. British dockworkers refused to load the ships bound for the Allied forces in Russia. Soldiers who had fought in Germany rebelled against their being dispatched to Russia, and those who were there demanded their return to England. Newton D. Baker, the American Secretary of War during this period, declared that the intervention was "nonsense from the beginning."

CHAPTER VII

Return to the Conservative Fold

IN THE ELECTION THAT FOLLOWED THE FALL OF THE LLOYD GEORGE coalition in 1922, Churchill lost his seat in the House of Commons and found himself excluded from Parliament for the first time since 1900. A number of factors account for this political reverse. Since 1905 he had been closely associated with Lloyd George, and during the heyday of the Little Welsh Attorney, Churchill had shared some of the political glory. Following the general disenchantment with Lloyd George, Churchill could not escape his idol's subsidence. With the defeat of the coalition which had governed England since 1915, loyalties lapsed and dormant passions rallied. All the former antipathies toward Churchill were revived. His former enemies on the right and his opponents on the left reinvigorated their old animosities and aimed their venomous denunciations against him.

Another factor that militated against him was the postwar mood of Britain. During the war the public had toiled, sacrificed, and suffered in order to achieve victory. With a triumphant peace achieved it had hoped for an era of security and sufficiency, but instead of this the years had been marked by shortages and disturbances.

At a time when the national mind was one of frustration and dissatisfaction, Churchill, in 1923, ran for a seat in the House of Commons from the constituency of West Leicester as a supporter of the temporarily resurrected Asquith-Lloyd George coalition. In this contest Churchill was defeated by 13,000 to 9,000 votes. This was a blow, but he did not lose heart.

In February, 1924, when a vacancy occurred in the Abbey Division of Westminster owing to the death of an M.P., Churchill filed for the seat. He was considerably handicapped in the campaign, for the Conservative Organization had committed the party to the support of Captain O. W. Nicholson. Emotionally he could not affiliate with the Socialists, and the Liberals, what was left of them, had a very uncertain future as a party. Churchill, therefore, welcomed whatever support he could secure from the Conservatives, many of whose members were favorably disposed toward him. Among these were Lord Arthur Balfour, Lord Birkenhead, Austin Chamberlain, and Stanley Baldwin. These and others who favored Churchill could not publicly declare themselves in support of him, but they could insinuate it, and this they did, and it almost insured him victory, for the election brought him within 39 votes of winning.

With this encouragement he tried again, this time in the Epping Division, in September, 1924, where he scored a decisive victory, polling 6,000 more votes than the total ballots of all the other candidates. He refused to admit that he had reentered the Conservative Party, but he maintained that the conflicting issues of the past had been extinguished by time and events. Consequently, there was no difference between himself and the current Conservative Party. The two, he said, had coalesced.

Churchill not only returned to the House of Commons but also reentered the cabinet, because Stanley Baldwin, Premier from 1924 to 1929, confessed that he was more afraid of Churchill out of, than in, the governing body. Baldwin offered him the "Chancellorship." Wonderingly, Churchill asked, "Chancellorship of Lancaster?" Baldwin replied, "No, the Chancellorship of the Exchequer," and Churchill literally wept for joy.[1]

After the resignation in 1886 of Randolph Churchill from the Exchequer, one of the officials, in traditional routine, called at his home for the robe that he had worn while he held the office. The caller was met by Winston's mother, who refused to surrender it, for she was determined to retain it for her son to wear, when, some day, he should hold the office. This was delayed thirty-eight years, until 1924, when he donned the identical garment that his father had worn when he headed the Treasury.

His administration of the Exchequer was the least successful of all his ministries. National finance was one of the fields in which he not only lacked interest, but also competence, in consequence of which his political enemies denounced him as the "worst Chancellor of the Exchequer" Britain had ever had. In retrospect, he confessed, "I am inclined to believe with them."[2] Stanley Baldwin, within a year after his appointment of Churchill to the Exchequer, indirectly admitted his error in naming him to that post. Baldwin in a comment to a friend remarked: "I thought we should have taken another line," but he had yielded to Churchill's persuasion.[3]

Churchill's first blunder was to restore the pound to gold at the prewar parity of exchange. This was nineteenth-century finance in twentieth-century economics after an unparalleled war, and was well received by the Midas-minded moguls of the party because it would redound to their advantage. England had borrowed 74 per cent of the cost of financing World War I. During the first two years of the war, patriotism and faith in ultimate victory had stimulated the sale of bonds at low rates of interest. The shrewd financiers, however had held off for a better bargain, and, as the war dragged on year by year with declining prospects of victory, the government, to secure funds, finally elevated the interest rate to 5½ per cent with the price of the bonds considerably below par. By this time the pound had dropped to $3.18. To the smart investors this had the golden glow, and they bought. With the restoration of the pound to gold their $3.18 purchases could be redeemed at $4.87 at a net profit of 52 per cent. This was class legislation in favor of the rich, for almost all of the poor investors had disposed of their bonds by 1925.[4]

The bonus to the opulent in itself would not have been disastrous had it not resulted in a serious retardation of economic life. The elevation of the exchange rate of the pound and the simultaneous depreciation of the currencies of other countries in Europe induced foreign customers to boycott British counters, with the result that British exports in 1927 stood at 78.6 per cent of the 1913 level.

In defense of this restoration of the pound to gold, Churchill maintained that every expert and every conference on economics and finance had urged the return to the gold standard. Likewise, he said that members of Parliament and high governmental officers had endorsed his proposal to return to gold.

In his enumeration of authorities on the currency issue, Churchill made no reference to John Maynard Keynes, who took emphatic exception to Churchill's financial measure, and embodied his criticism of the Chancellor of the Exchequer in *The Economic Consequences of Winston Churchill.*

The economic situation was at its worst in the coal fields. Wages there stood at $12.12 a week when the miners had employment. "In the Welsh valleys and Northumberland children walked barefooted and in rags through the snow. . . ." Undernourishment and emaciation pushed the death rate up. The miners were almost the lowest paid of the depressed classes in Britain, and so they had been for centuries, because the upper classes, the governing caste, had indoctrinated themselves into believing that "the poor have always been with us, and therefore there can be no possible improvement. It must be so." On the other hand, it was estimated "that one per cent of the population owned 55 per cent of the nation's private property."[5]

Other factors beside the loss of markets through the restoration of gold contributed to the depressed conditions in England, such as the exhaustion of the coal mines, antiquated mining equipment, and the German delivery of 40,000,000 tons of coal annually to Britain's former customers.

The coal operators resolved to meet the situation by invoking the age-old formula of reduction in pay and lengthening the day for the workers. The 50,000 miners refused to submit. In 1926 they organized a strike, and in sympathy 1,500,000 other labor union members joined them. This, however, did not make the strike "general" for there were still 4,500,000 members of organized labor who held aloof from the contest, as well as 10,000,000 unorganized laborers who refused to participate. But if the "general strike" had persisted it would have paralyzed the economic life of the nation.

The strike could have been averted by reasonable concessions to labor, whose demands were not unjustifiable. They had not asked for higher pay or for less hours of work. They struck because employers reduced their pay and lengthened their day. This was the employer's substitution for modernization of his industry. In the impasse between the operators and the miners, the Archbishops of Canterbury and York tendered their services to break the deadlock. They proposed that the government should renew its offer of assistance to the coal industry for a short definite period; that the mine owners should withdraw their recently announced wage scales.[6]

The Home Secretary, who attended the clerical conclave, agreed with the conclusions made. Churchill approved the publication of the church recommendation, but his endorsement lacked his customary zest.

Though his problem came within the jurisdiction of the Home Secretary, Churchill, Chancellor of the Exchequer, with gusto, took charge. He reigned as editorial tsar of the British press.[7] He organized England into districts, placed an intendant over each one, shut down all newspapers, drafted editors and journalists to publish *The British Gazette* that disseminated his view of the strike, which maintained that it was Communist inspired. He imposed all the pressures of the state against the strikers, in consequence of which the general strike, which had begun on May 3, was terminated on May 12. The coal miners, however, continued to strike until November, when their funds were exhausted. Churchill had campaigned against the labor unions much as if they had been an alien element determined to demoralize the country's economy and society. He did not see the coal miners as hungry, ill-clad, insecure Englishmen.

A report by a parliamentary commission that the government purchase the coal mines for £100,000,000 met vigorous opposition from Churchill.[8] To him it smacked of socialism. Furthermore, he disapproved of so vast an expenditure. Twenty years later Parliament enacted such a proposal into law.

In his contest with labor he won largely because the trade union membership was not of one mind in prosecuting the strike. It had been instigated in the interest of only one group, the miners. There was no demand for an improvement of the trade union membership generally, the consequence being that miners lacked sympathetic support. Also, the leaders of the trade unions, who lived under conditions similar to those enjoyed by the middle class, were not deeply sensitive to the views of the people whose destinies they controlled.

Furthermore, by invoking the general strike labor had instituted major changes in the British constitution, without desiring a revolution. It had substituted the doctrine of direct action for the voice of the nation as manifested in the balloting booth. The question at issue resolved itself into whether Britain should be governed by King and Parliament or by shops and trade unions, by organized capital or by organized labor. At the time the voice of England declared in favor of organized capital.

Labor submitted but it remained sour and sullen toward

Churchill. His implacable action to defeat the strikers, in an area outside his own jurisdiction reminded labor of his harsh solution of labor problems in 1911, and confirmed its aversion to him and his social policies.

The cost of the strike was high. The miners lost £60,000,000 in wages, and the country as a whole incurred a debt of £800,000,000. This was a financial shock to a country afflicted with heavy unemployment and a stagnant economy.

The Conservative Party, with Churchill in agreement, was determined to prevent a recurrence of such a disturbance. To that end, in 1927, it was instrumental in passing the Trades Dispute and Trade Union Act which made general strikes illegal, prohibited intimidation of strikebreakers, and denied government employees membership in trade unions.

The governing classes by this act attempted to immunize themselves against disturbances from the proletariat. They had been less concerned with the welfare of the toiling masses, who, on the other hand, could not forget Churchill's energetic action in the general strike and how previously he had suppressed labor unrest. The simmering of their antagonism to Churchill continued until the opening of World War II.

Upon reflection, Churchill and his Conservative hierarchy considered their flagellation of labor injudicious, and somewhat hypocritically attempted to assuage the feeling of the masses by enacting a pension law for widows, the aged, and orphans which assured them allowances from a fund established by contributions from the state, employers, and workers.

In order to ingratiate themselves further, the Conservatives, with Churchill's approval, in 1928 enacted the Fifth Reform Act, which extended the ballot to most males previously denied the suffrage, and to women between the ages of twenty-one and thirty, who, by the Reform Bill of 1918, had been denied the suffrage. This granted the vote to 7,000,000 women who previously had not possessed the franchise. This legislation established a feminine electoral majority. In the election of 1929, 15,000,000 women voters cast their ballots while only 13,500,000 men exercised the franchise.[9]

Though Churchill finally endorsed the franchise for women and their election to the House of Commons, he still did not favor their membership in the Cabinet. These electoral sops did not obliterate labor's memory of his Philistine efficiency in suppressing their strikes.

In his capacity as Chancellor of the Exchequer, Churchill negotiated the terms for the partial repayment of the British loans contracted in the United States during World War I. While Americans admired Churchill and the British for their financial integrity, the British taxpayers were less favorably impressed by his financial probity.

In the election of 1929 the Labour Party was returned to power and Churchill was consigned to the back bench. From there he viewed Ramsay MacDonald as the philosopher of failure who preached a gospel of envy, and the Conservatives led by Stanley Baldwin, glorifying repose and resignation. Churchill insisted that the combination of these two, with their followers, "had decided to be undecided, resolved to be irresolute, all-powerful for impotence." They were, however, in the driver's seat and could ignore him, and this they tried to do.

CHAPTER VIII

Ostracized and Redeemed

FROM 1929 TO 1939 CHURCHILL DID NOT LANGUISH IN IDLENESS but wrote a great number of articles that appeared not only in British journals but also in American and Continental magazines. He also published ten books, among them the monumental six-volume biography of the Duke of Marlborough, which he wrote in part as a refutation of Thomas Babington Macaulay's treatment of his distinguished ancestor. Although Churchill had designed it as a rebuttal, it did not take a splenetic approach but constituted a study based upon scholarship at its very best. He consulted libraries in Continental capitals as well as enormous numbers of documents which had been stored in Blenheim Palace and had never before been used. The result was a masterpiece of such merit that even his enemies could not restrain their appreciation.

This publication, added to earlier ones, elevated his reputation as an author and enhanced his income. During the period from 1929 to 1939 the receipts from his pen grew to more than $100,000 a year.[1] During that decade only George Bernard Shaw enjoyed greater revenue from writing.

But all of this income did not suffice to meet the demands of his way of life, and when it needed replenishing he arranged a lecture tour of forty engagements in the United States at $2,500 per lecture. Almost immediately upon his arrival in New York, on December 13, 1931, in crossing a street according to London traffic rules, he collided with a taxicab and was dispatched to a hospital for several weeks. While thus immured, he wrote an article on the subject of his accident for which he received $2,500. He capitalized even on his misfortune.

Churchill, though a member of the Conservative Government from 1924 to 1929, enjoyed neither the confidence nor the benevolence of his party colleagues. The Conservative Central Organization likewise viewed him with skepticism. This lack of intimacy with his party associates constituted a permanent feature of his political career. He rarely fitted himself comfortably into close relationship with any association. If a group's policy or personnel did not accord with his views, he made few sacrifices to harmonize his principles with its program. If he could not induce others to embrace his views, he, in no way, weakened his attachments to his own convictions, but remained faithful to them and pursued his course. But even with this limitation he always had a small group of devoted followers who remained loyal to him.

In the decade prior to World War II Churchill found himself at odds not only with the Conservative Party, but also with British public opinion. A considerable element of his party and larger components of the Liberal and Labour Parties no longer shared Churchill's fervor for imperialism, especially as it applied to India. He still regarded the subcontinent of India as the "brightest pearl in the British crown," and he aimed to keep it well polished. Many Britishers, on the other hand, had weakened their ardor for the "white man's burden." In his enthusiasm for imperialism Churchill resembled an arbitrary father in his relations with his wayward children.

Another of his divergencies with many Britishers was his attitude toward the Treaty of Versailles. Germans generally regarded it as a *Diktat*, and, by 1930, a large section of influential Englishmen had come to believe that it was punitive. Churchill did not embrace this view. Considering the preliminaries to World War I, and its prosecution, he insisted that it imposed no serious injustices.[2] Speaking in the House of Commons on April 13, 1932, he maintained,

When we think of what would have happened to us, to France and to Belgium if the Germans had won; when we think of the terms which they imposed upon Rumania, and the terms of Brest Litovsk; when we remember that up to the end of the war the German authorities refused to consider that Belgium could ever be liberated, but said that she would be kept in thrall for military purposes forever, I do not think that we need break our hearts in deploring the treatment Germany is receiving now.

In the same discourse he contended that

Germany got off easily after the Great War. . . . The facts repudiate the idea that a Carthaginian peace was in fact imposed upon Germany. She underwent no serious territorial loss, except Alsace-Lorraine, which she herself had seized only fifty years before.[3]

Whatever unfairness the Treaty embodied, he insisted, could have been corrected. Before Hitler reached the Chancellery, Churchill proposed redress for those grievances which he considered real.[4] By such an approach, he maintained, vexations could have been liquidated, not by threats, but by reliance upon reason and justice.

Through wide reading of German history, Churchill was conscious of the continuity of the Reich's foreign policy. Even though Bismarck is generally credited with having satisfied his foreign-policy objectives when the German states were unified, his interests in larger objectives were already then developing. In 1861, when he wrote his sister, he said, "Hit the Poles till they despair of their lives. I have no sympathy for their existence, but if we have to survive, our only course is to exterminate them."[5] The yearning of industrialists and bankers clearly indicates the temper and direction of German foreign policy, even if not expressed as blatantly as did Hitler's entries in *Mein Kampf*.[6]

In March, 1918, the idea of a German-dominated Europe was incorporated in the Treaty of Brest Litovsk. This document deprived Russia of Estonia, Latvia, Lithuania, the Ukraine, Bessarabia, Baku, Batum, and also of its Polish provinces, and acknowledged the independence of Finland. This constituted a loss to Russia of 1.3 million square miles and 62 million people.[7]

Richard Kuhlmann, the German foreign secretary at the time, was not so indiscreet as to voice Germany's demand for *Lebensraum* but his policy was nothing less than that. If there was any doubt about Germany's intention to expand eastward it was dispelled by the Treaty of Bucharest which Germany imposed upon Rumania as it made its exit from World War I. When a member of the Rumanian delegation protested against its Draconian features, a German staff officer protested: "A *harsh treaty*, you said, you call it a *harsh peace*? Just wait till you see what we are preparing for France and England."[8] Hitler in comparing the Treaty of Versailles with that of Brest Litovsk considered the latter document one of "infinite humanity" as contrasted with the former, despite the fact that the Brest Litovsk document deprived Russia of its richest provinces and 50 per cent of its productive capacity. Churchill, better informed and more realistic than the appeasement-minded ministers, realized that if Hitler should win a war against the democracies his "infinite humanity" would be even more demanding than that of William II in 1918.[9]

While Churchill was absorbed in the biography of his ancestor, he did not overlook the character of his contemporaries, one in particular: Adolf Hitler. Churchill never met the Fuehrer, although in 1932, while both were in Munich, Ernst Hanfstaengel, an ebullient Hitler protégé, had all but clinched an introduction. However, when Hitler learned that Churchill lacked enthusiasm for him as well as his tenets, he claimed another engagement.[10]

Even before this incident Churchill recognized Hitler as a "maniac of ferocious genius," with a charismatic dominance over individuals and the ability to captivate audiences. The high and the low alike succumbed to his malevolent tirades. Churchill perceived the shrewdness of this unvarnished fanatic. He identified him as the incarnation of the sullen and vengeful disposition of the Germans following their defeat in 1918. Churchill believed that this "Messiah of the discontented" would, while Germany was still impotent, limit his damnation of its conquerors, but that once it had recovered its military might, he would attempt to crucify its vanquishers.[11]

Hitler's schedule of aggrandizement was spelled out in *Mein Kampf*, which Churchill had read before Hitler became Chancellor; Neville Chamberlain, however, had neglected this volume until after the Munich Conference. Churchill was an omnivorous reader, and a constant stream of intelligence from individuals living abroad, even in Germany, enriched his fund of information.[12]

Even before the military situation became acute, different solutions to German grievances had been proposed by British statesmen and commentators. Early in 1932 Churchill had pointed to the potential threat of Germany and had proposed a consolidation of powers with which to resist German threats.

Ramsay MacDonald and George Lansbury, leaders of the Labour Party, and Stanley Baldwin had been inoculating the British people against the assumption of danger. In this atmosphere of denial of threat, Churchill viewed proposals of disarmament as inappropriate as profanity at a prayer meeting. And for MacDonald's brand of negotiation he had a low appreciation. "The Boneless Wonder," as Churchill called him, proposed disarmament first followed by negotiations with Germany regarding redress of grievances. Churchill, on the other hand, insisted upon negotiations first, then disarmament. MacDonald's formula, he maintained, was as if someone said, "I will go tiger hunting with you, my friend, on condition that you will leave your rifle at home."[13]

To Churchill the most abominable feature of MacDonald's plan was the provision which called for an increase of the German army to 200,000 men, and a reduction of the French from 500,000 to 200,000. He regarded this last stipulation as more "boneless" than the first. He insisted that French acceptance would constitute defeat before the battle, since Germany's population and its industrial power were almost twice those of France.[14] MacDonald's proposal, he maintained, also constituted betrayal of an ally, and recognition of Germany's dominance of Europe, as well as the submission of the democracies to the dictatorships. France would have none of it, in consequence of which MacDonald's proposals were interred before their birth.

In the face of the Hitlerian threat, Churchill was disturbed by the status of England's defenses. Baldwin's pessimism regarding Britain's capacity to defend itself compounded Churchill's concern; early in 1933 Baldwin had declared that there was no defense against air attack from the Continent. This roused Churchill to assert on March 14, 1933, in one of his great speeches in the House of Commons:

Our island is surrounded by the sea. It always has been, and, although the House does not realize it, the sea was in early times a great disadvantage because an invader could come across the sea and no one knew where he would land; very often he did not know himself. On the continent the lines of advance are fixed by the mountain passes, the roads and the fertile plains and rivers. We were under great disadvantage a thousand years ago in being surrounded by the sea and we suffered terribly by it. But we did not give up, we did not evacuate the island and say that we must live on the mainland. Not at all. We conquered the sea; we became mistress of the sea, and the very element which had given the invader access to the heart of the country, to our hearths and homes, became its greatest protection, became indeed the bridge which united us to the most distant parts of our empire throughout the world. Now here is the air. The sea, perhaps, is no longer complete security for our island development; it must be the air too.

Why should we fear the air? We have as good technical knowledge as any country. There is no reason to suppose that we cannot make machines as good as any country. We have, though it may be considered conceited to say so, a particular vein or talent in air piloting which is in advance of that possessed by other countries.[15]

Simultaneously he announced that the British air armada ranked "only fifth in the gamut." On November 28, 1933, he declared that the German air force was rapidly approaching the size of the British; in response Baldwin assured the House that British air power was not to be second to any on the Continent, but this pledge proved as spurious as a counterfeit guinea. On December 18, 1934, Churchill again warned that "by December 31, 1935, the German Luftwaffe will be as strong as our own. By the end of 1936 it will be 50 per cent stronger and in 1937 nearly double."[16] At the end of 1934 Germany, he said, already had between 200 and 300 machines of long range, with great speed, of from 220 to 330 miles per hour.[17] Some of these were employed in carrying mail and were so constructed that they could easily be converted into bombers, their bomb racks being stored in shelters and ready to be installed with great dispatch. And this was confirmed by developments during the following year.[18] In consequence, Parliament appropriated funds for the creation of forty-one additional squadrons, a total of 802 planes. Churchill's great delight rapidly changed into deep desolation when he learned that this program covered the expansion, not for one year, as he had supposed, but for five. This information drove him into increasing efforts to accelerate production of planes and enlistment of pilots. Reflecting upon the sluggish British plane production, he declared on November 28, 1934: "A disaster of the first magnitude has fallen upon us." "A ten day period of intensive bombing of London," he declared, "would kill from 30,000 to 40,000 people." The use of firebombs, he learned, would incinerate large sections of the city. From three million to four million people would have to be evacuated.[19] But even this lurid prediction failed to stir Parliament into action.

Before the opening of World War II Churchill had confidence in Britain's navy to protect the United Kingdom and its farflung interests. He maintained that as far "as Europe was concerned, we are relatively stronger than we were then [in 1914] and the measures which we are taking now will make us relatively stronger."[20] He maintained that Britain was the only country in Europe which could "draw out an effective battle line...." Owing to its expenditures of from £50,000,000 to £60,000,000 a year "Britain was in a position of considerable strength as far as Europe was concerned."

In 1937 he believed that ships were secure from air attacks. "Dropping a bomb down the funnel of a battleship which, from a height of 15,000 feet would look smaller than a housefly on the face of a clock, is a thing, the ease of which has been much overrated by some of the modern strategic thinkers.... The battleship is not obsolete. The contrary is the case.... The navy will be able to afford us a substantial guarantee ... that we shall be permitted to continue our peaceful and free island life."[21] The sinking, on December 10, 1941, in the Bay of Bengal of the *Prince of Wales* and the *Repulse* by Japanese planes refuted his thesis. And when hostilities broke out in 1939 he was compelled to admit that his navy was not so omnipotent as he had claimed, for he plaintively appealed to President Roosevelt for fifty destroyers.

The small size of the British army caused him grave concern. Before 1938 it comprised only two divisions, just enough to suppress possible domestic disturbances. He maintained that the army lacked "almost every weapon which is required for the latest form of war."[22] He asked, "Where are the anti-tank guns, short distance wireless sets, field anti-aircraft guns?" He wanted an army commensurate with England's prestige in the world, mechanized to the highest degree. British tanks, he said, were antiquated, "surpassed by those of Germany, Italy, Russia and the United States."[23] Germany's army, on the other hand, comprised, by May 31, 1935, twenty-one divisions, and was increasing at the rate of one division a month.[24]

Churchill strove to enlarge the regular army and to equip it with modern weapons. Against stern opposition he also urged the arming of the Home Guard with the most modern equipment and to merge it with the Regular Army. Appeasers and the hierarchy of the Regular Army defeated this.

A great number of Churchill's proposals from 1929 to 1939 were rejected because of his personality, but another significant reason was the fact that a large proportion of the British people still believed that peace could be maintained. World War I had taken the lives of more than 700,000 Britishers and wounded three times as many.[25] It had cost more than forty billion dollars. The United States and Japan had encroached upon British commercial preserves. The British generally had no enthusiasm for a repeat performance and so they surrendered to their wishes rather than submitted to their wisdom, and beguiled themselves into believing that somehow they could escape another war.

Furthermore, the appeasers suffered from a guilt complex. They conveniently assumed that the Treaty of Versailles had been too harsh, and that it had been based upon vengeance. They insisted that it was time to redress grievances of the past, and to restore Germany to its rightful position of dignity in the family of nations.

They extended the sophistry to the realm of genealogy. They rationalized that the British and the Germans had common ancestry, the Anglo-Saxon, rather remote they admitted, and that therefore brotherly love, rather than fraternal enmity, should prevail in their relations, quite ignoring the prevalence and viciousness of family feuds. While the genealogical basis of appeasement was less important than others, it revealed the desperate effort of its proponents to justify their bias.

For hundreds of years the British had been a commercial people, ever alert to the possibility of expanding their markets. They recalled that before 1914 Germany had been one of England's best customers, and exporters were eager to recover their commercial relationships and were willing to sacrifice a moral point to achieve an economic advantage. The past, after all, belonged to the past, and the balance of payments established from German purchases served the same purpose as those from other countries. Commerce, they insisted, should be independent of international morality, as long as the customer paid his bills. Exporters, therefore, urged the resumption of Anglo-German trade for it would accelerate production, decrease unemployment, reduce the dole, and lower taxes. England might yet become the "precious stone set in the silver sea."

For almost five hundred years previous to 1918 Britain had pursued the balance of power policy toward the Continent, aligning itself with the weaker major power and supporting it against the stronger. In so doing England made the weaker the stronger, and prevented the establishment of a powerful Continental country from pursuing a hostile policy toward Britain. Before 1914 England had supported France, the weaker one, against Germany. After 1919 British ministries assumed that France had become the most powerful of the European countries, and that Germany was weaker than France. England, therefore, generally supported Germany against France. Georges Clemenceau was not only keenly disappointed but grievously provoked, and bluntly accused Lloyd George: "Ever since the war you have been against us," to which the Little Welsh Attorney replied, "Has that not been our traditional policy?" After World War I Britain, materially influenced by appeasers, reverted with some antipathy toward the French and benevolence toward the Germans.

Another factor which generated appeasement was the fear among the upper classes of any social or political tumult that might disturb the system which assured them their wealth and privilege. The well-to-do feared that their involvement in another holocaust might be followed by some form of Communism. They preferred Hitler to the heirs of Marx. In any event, they would utilize Hitler as a buffer to slay the Communist dragon. To shift his direction of aggression from the West to the East, appeasers, by indirection, assured him that Britain's sphere of influence did not embrace the small countries bordering Russia's western frontier. Hitler's conquest of some small "distant country about which we know so little," should not rile the British lion. Such a sacrifice would be more economical and less disturbing than another war, except to the victim.

Many of the appeasers were tinged, if not suffused, with anti-Semitism. Even Gilbert Murray confessed that the Jews were ". . . in some peculiar and exceptional way a pernicious element."[26] Lord Lothian, during the first five years of Hitler's rule, found much about him that he considered commendable.[27] Lord Londonderry, a relative of Winston Churchill, was reported to have commended Hitler upon his remilitarization of the Rhineland. Distinguished scholars like Arnold Toynbee and John Wheeler-Bennett continued to admire Hitler until it was only too obvious that he was a threat to anyone within his reach.

Outstanding journalists also acclaimed Hitler, among them Geoffrey Dawson of *The Times*, J. L. Garvin of *The Observer*, an Astor publication; Vernon Bartlett overlooked the Fuehrer's crudities and savagery, and lauded him for his regeneration of the Reich.[28]

While Churchill voiced a fleeting admiration for Hitler's energy and vitality in his efforts to lift Germany by its bootstraps, he did not join this chorus of approbation. In the House of Commons, on April 13, 1933, he declared, "As surely as Germany acquires full military equality with her neighbors while her own grievances are still unredressed, and while she is in the temper which we have unhappily seen, so surely should we see ourselves within a measurable distance of general European war." Hitler, even before he came to power, and no less afterward, was the soloist in the German chorus of vengeance and aggression.[29]

Among others who defended and supported Hitler was T. Philip Conwell-Evans, an intimate friend of Joachim von Ribbentrop, who, in 1936 became German ambassador to London. Conwell-Evans served as intermediary and arranged appointments for Englishmen with Hitler. Among Hitler enthusiasts was Lord Mount Temple. He regretted the formation of the Franco-Russian alliance and proposed an Anglo-German rapprochement as a counterweight. All of these believed in the sincerity of Hitler's peaceful protestations, and urged the withdrawal of England from European troublesome questions, a step which would have left Europe to Hitler's mercy or terror.

Until the immediate approach of World War II, the appeasers constituted a significant group in English public life. Without their influence Neville Chamberlain could not have enjoyed the popular support which was his until immediately prior to World War II. These appeasers had a profound dislike of Churchill and strove to liquidate him politically.

Among the appeasers in the House of Commons in the nineteen-thirties was Arnold Wilson, who in 1934, insisted that Hitler was "absolutely honest and sincere."[30] Even a year later, following his visit to Germany, he believed that the Reich would be one of the last of the great powers to attack Great Britain. Sir Thomas Moore maintained that Hitler's policy was "based upon peace and justice."[31] Appeasers were not the dominant group but they made appeasement from 1933 to 1939 the dominant issue.

The favorite haunt of the appeasers was Cliveden, the home of Lord and Lady Astor. The people congregating there, the so-called "Cliveden Set," justified the development within Germany as the reasonable evolution of a well-ordered society. Whatever excesses were committed, they rationalized as the inescapable development of a country striving to survive an acute depression while surrounded by hostile neighbors. Appeasers overlooked the brutalities and vulgarities of the Nazi elite. Political responsibility, they reckoned, would make their character and their conduct more palatable. The appeasers aimed to transform the Nazis by the exercise of patience and tolerance.

It would be erroneous to interpret all appeasement as wicked, immoral, and unjust. Nations, like humans, cannot escape living in association with one another, and this process can be eased and facilitated by an adjustment of differences. A concession here and a dispensation there in line with justice and tolerance can liquidate differences between individuals and nations, but when a nation or an individual imposes unjustifiable demands and threatens violence against noncompliance, a dangerous situation arises. Before Hitler came to power numerous concessions had already been extended to the Weimar Republic, among them allied military evacuation of the Rhineland ahead of schedule, construction of a German navy in excess of treaty stipulations, and reduction of reparations payments. And liberal concessions continued after Hitler.

It would be difficult to sustain the contention that Hitler was mentally normal. Churchill maintained that repetitive concessions to his demands would not insure sanity or safety. He agreed with Publilius: "One man's wickedness easily becomes all men's curse."

Churchill had a few supporters in the House of Commons, twenty or thirty, and among them were Anthony Eden, Duff Cooper, Brendan Bracken, Page Croft, Harold Nicolson, Roger Keyes, and Leopold Amery. Eden in 1935 had hoped to tranquilize not only Hitler but also Mussolini by assigning them territory in Africa. Their conduct and policies disillusioned him.[32] The compact majority of 360 Tories regarded Churchill and his band as a disgrace to the House of Commons and a misfortune for England.[33]

With such a solid phalanx against him Churchill's future appeared dismal, but his devotion to England took precedence over his concern for himself. With all the fervor and none of the fanaticism of William Lloyd Garrison, he felt as the abolitionist had proclaimed, "I will be as harsh as truth, and as uncompromising as justice. On this subject I do not wish to think, or speak, or write in moderation.... I am in earnest. I will not equivocate. I will not retreat a single inch."[34] Churchill's agitation in favor of rearmament and his efforts to thwart Hitler did not instill in the House of Commons an environment in which "joy ruled the day and love the night." But an increasing number in the House admired him for his constancy and his courage.

As time advanced and the government did not prosecute a massive rearmament program, he implored the House of Commons to abandon a certain helplessness and hopelessness, "which had characterized the production of equipment." "For the first time," he said, "we are not fully equipped to repel or retaliate an invasion.... That, to an island, is astonishing.... We are the incredulous, indifferent children of centuries of security behind the shield of the Royal Navy, nor yet able to wake up to the woefully transformed condition of the modern world.... We are entering upon a period of danger and difficulty.... Is there no grip, no driving force, no mental energy, no power of decision or design?"[35] He was afraid that the British would be caught "fat, opulent, free spoken and defenseless." He reminded members of the House that the delivery of planes, guns, and tanks could not be improvised at will. "The first year you have to sow; and in the second you have to harrow; the third year is the harvest."[36]

True as this was, and emphatically as it was proclaimed, the great majority of the House refused to accept his thesis. They imagined that they had established safety for England by denouncing Churchill as a warmonger.[37] Some maintain that British policy in the thirties was formulated not only in response to appeasement, but to other considerations, especially economic.

This is undeniably true, and that was England's misfortune. Too many were willing to take a long chance on prosperity, even at the risk of security.

Another factor which, according to Churchill, made hasty rearmament urgent was the increased speed in transportation. A whole army, he said, could be conveyed one hundred miles into enemy-occupied country overnight. Hitler, on March 9, 1935, aroused Churchill's apprehension by proclaiming publicly the official Constitution of the German Air Force, and a week later he decreed universal military conscription for an army of 500,000 men.[38] Churchill maintained that the "German action was an open and formal affront to the Treaties of Peace upon which the League of Nations was founded."[39] France's response to this breach was the extension, within a week, of the military service from one to two years.

Beyond this action the French and British leaders limited themselves to some vigorous finger-shaking. They refrained from sending a joint army into the Ruhr or the Rhineland, an action which would have been sanctioned by the Treaty of Versailles. On the contrary, the British government accepted an invitation from Hitler for Sir John Simon, the British Foreign Secretary, and Anthony Eden, Lord Privy Seal, to come to Berlin for a discussion with the Fuehrer. They arrived in Berlin on March 24, 1935. While there they learned that Germany had attained air parity with the British.[40] This was another violation of the Treaty of Versailles. On April 11, representatives of France, England, and Italy met at Stresa and condemned Germany's rearmament. On April 15-17 the Council of the League of Nations adopted a resolution to the effect that "treaties should not be broken by unilateral action."

At the moment Hitler had no desire to challenge Britain's naval supremacy, and on that score he wanted to put the British people at ease. To that end, he proposed to limit Germany's navy to thirty-five per cent of the British tonnage. In June, 1935, this proposition was incorporated into the London Naval Agreement.

Churchill was acutely disappointed with the British acquiescence in Hitler's violations, and when his country approved the enlargement of Hitler's navy beyond the provisions of the Treaty of Versailles, without even consulting the French or the Italians,

Churchill's exasperation was almost boundless. Just because Hitler had withdrawn from the League of Nations did not release him from observing the provisions of the Treaty of Versailles and other international commitments. According to Churchill, Hitler had clearly violated a treaty, and he was liable for prosecution.

What infuriated Churchill still more was the information that Simon at the Conference at Stresa had offered Mussolini territorial concessions in Africa if he would call off his threatened war in Ethiopia. A year later the British cabinet considered returning one or more former German colonies in order to satiate Hitler's *Lebensraum* hunger.[41] This induced Churchill to propose joint action by France, Russia, and Britain to compel compliance with the Treaty of Versailles.

The appeasers criticized Churchill for stirring up a "panic feeling," to which he replied, "It is better to have a panic feeling before and then to be calm when things happen than to be extremely calm beforehand and then to be in a panic when things happen."[42]

A year later, in 1936, things did happen: Hitler sent 35,000 troops under the command of General Jodl into the Rhineland in violation of the Treaty of Versailles and the Treaty of Locarno. If ever there was a breach of treaties, this was it. Hitler was fully conscious of this fact and of the enormous risk which he was taking, for he had instructed Jodl to evacuate the Rhineland if the French made any demonstration of resistance. He also ordered his secret agents in London and Paris to wire him half-hourly reports of the reaction in those capitals.

The French, contemplating resistance, craved assurance from England that they could rely on her if they should attempt to expel the intruder.[43] Stanley Baldwin, the new Premier, however, bluntly told the French that even if there was only one chance in a hundred of war, he could not pledge British support. The vast majority of the British people was more responsive to Baldwin's rejoinder: "There must be no war, there must be no large rearmament," than it was to treaty obligations. Churchill regarded this policy as stupidity reinforced by cowardice. Lord Lothian insisted that "the Germans, after all, are only going into their own backyard garden,"[44] and Lord Halifax expressed an almost identical reaction. Dawson of *The Times* commented:

"What has it got to do with us? It's none of our business." This was the atmosphere in which Churchill had to function. It is not surprising that at the Rhodes Dinner in 1936 he confessed, "Of course, I know that I have no future as a politician."[45]

Though France and its allies, Poland and Czechoslovakia, could have mobilized an army of ninety divisions, and had one hundred more in reserve, they took no measure to expel the Germans from the area it had occupied. At the Nuremburg Trials high-ranking German officers maintained that the least show of French resistance would have compelled the Germans to retire. This was a fateful incident,[46] for if the French had stirred, the German generals, who already had a plot gestating to overthrow Hitler, might have acted. The army chiefs confessed that French resistance would have compelled them to evacuate the Rhineland "like a dog with his tail between his legs." Subsequently Hitler admitted, "I have never been so scared as in the days of the Rhineland undertaking. . . . I would not have had one brigade at my disposal to challenge even a mere threat of war from France. Am I glad, my God, am I glad that everything turned out right."[47]

While appeasers in England considered Hitler's remilitarization no concern of theirs, Churchill viewed it as a matter of essential importance to the British. In the debate which opened in the House of Commons, on March 26, 1936, he averred:

We cannot look back with much pleasure on our foreign policy in the last five years. They certainly have been disastrous years. . . . We have seen the most depressing and alarming change in our outlook of humanity which has ever taken place in so short a period. Five years ago all felt safe; five years ago all were looking forward to a peace, to a period in which mankind would rejoice in the treasures which science can spread to all classes if the conditions of peace and justice prevail. Five years ago to talk of war would have been regarded, not only as folly and a crime, but almost as a sign of lunacy.[48]

For years Churchill had pleaded for a stronger Britain. After the Rhineland crisis he voiced the same appeal for France, and urged the buttressing of the smaller states of Central and Eastern Europe which might be or become allies of France. As early as 1938 he envisioned the United States as a potential ally of the forces opposing Nazism.

National strength was imperative in negotiating with Hitler, who frequently said one thing and meant the opposite. In a speech to the Reichstag, on May 21, 1936, Hitler announced that "Germany neither intends nor wishes to interfere in the internal affairs of Austria, to annex Austria, or to conclude an Anschluss." Ten weeks later, on July 11, 1936, he reaffirmed his vow of disinterestedness in the internal affairs of Austria. This was the kind of assurance that warranted apprehension, for almost simultaneously he ordered his Chief of the General Staff to prepare plans for the conquest of Austria. On February 12, 1938, he summoned Kurt von Schuschnigg, Austrian Chancellor, to Berchtesgaden, deluged him with insults and threats, and concluded his tirade by demanding the appointment of Artur von Seyss-Inquart, leader of the Austrian Nazis, into the cabinet as Minister of Security, the release of Austrian Nazi prisoners from jails, and the inclusion of Austrian Nazi Party members in the Fatherland Front Party.[49] This in effect would "Nazify" the Austrian government and bring Austria into the German Reich. Schuschnigg was astounded, astonished, and overwhelmed. He appealed to Mussolini, his erstwhile guardian and defender, but French and British blunders and Hitler's cunning left Schuschnigg helpless and defenseless. On March 11 German troops entered Austria, and Schuschnigg resigned. Austria was annexed to Germany and Seyss-Inquart took over the administration under orders from Berlin.

Churchill appreciated fully the significance of the Austrian coup. He realized the advantages which had accrued to Germany. Austria, he maintained, was the strategic gate to the Balkans.[50] Being in control of it, Hitler could dominate the land and water transportation to southeastern Europe. The countries in that region depended upon Viennese banks for credit, upon Austrian and Czech factories for industrial goods, and upon Austria as an outlet for their exports. All of this had now fallen to Germany, which needed everything that this part of the Continent produced. Strategically, too, this region was of great value to the Reich for it could dominate each of the small countries by preventing them from uniting against Berlin. Diplomatically, Czechoslovakia was isolated. If Germany assimilated that country, Poland would be in peril. The expansion of *Lebensraum* had made a propitious beginning.

Churchill with solemnity again warned the House of Commons of the significance to England of these developments. On March 14, he declared:

The gravity of the events of March 11 cannot be exaggerated. Europe is confronted with a program of aggression, nicely calculated and timed, unfolding stage by stage, and there is only one choice open, not only to us, but to other countries who are unfortunately concerned, either to submit, like Austria, or to take effective measures while time remains to ward off danger, and if it cannot be warded off, to cope with it. Resistance will be hard . . . but if we were to go on waiting upon events for a considerable period of time, how much should we throw away of resources which are now available for our security and for the maintenance of peace? How many friends would be alienated, how many potential allies should we see go, one by one, down the grisly gulf, how many times will bluff succeed until behind the bluff ever gathering forces will have accumulated reality? Where will we be two years hence for instance when the German army will be much bigger than the French army, and when all the small nations will have fled from Geneva to pay homage to the ever waxing power of the Nazi system, and to make the best terms that they can for themselves.[52]

Churchill endorsed Russia's proposal of a joint action with France within the League of Nations. Neville Chamberlain, the Prime Minister, vetoed this for he was very suspicious of the Russians, and still hoped to propitiate the Germans by concessions. Chamberlain's distrust of Churchill was only slightly less than his aversion to Stalin.

For some time Churchill had been urging the creation of a triple alliance comprising Russia, France, and Britain. He realized that Hitler took full advantage of an opponent's weakness, and that mere equality of strength was no deterrent. Churchill, therefore, hoped to assemble a preponderance of power in order to discourage Hitler from indulging in military gambling. Since Chamberlain and his appeasement-minded colleagues did not appreciate Churchill's logic, this proposal was consigned to the dustbin of neglected opportunities.

It was not only Churchill who disapproved of Chamberlain's supineness toward the dictators, but also Anthony Eden, his Secretary for Foreign Affairs. Until 1936 he had tolerated the expansionism of Hitler and Mussolini. But when the Fuehrer sent his army into the Rhineland and began constructing the massive West Wall along the French border some of the appeasement scales began to fall from Eden's eyes. What induced him to shift from obeisance to opposition vis-à-vis his Prime Minister, was Chamberlain's acquiescence in Mussolini's conquest of Ethiopia and the latter's assignment of 100,000 troops to intervene in behalf of Franco in the Civil War in Spain. What added insult to injury was Chamberlain's negotiation with Italy without taking Eden into his confidence. What further irritated him was Chamberlain's endorsement of Dino Grandi's proposal that the British send a delegation to Rome with a view to acquiesce in Italian aggression in Africa. Emphatically, but courteously, Eden registered his dissent, whereupon Chamberlain told him, "Go take an aspirin." Rather than accept his chief's policy and medication he resigned, on February 20, 1938. This was comfort to Churchill. A significant figure in the government had come to his side. Others would follow.

Another problem was already on the Fuehrer's desk, and on his mind: Czechoslovakia. On the day of Austria's incorporation Goering consoled the Czechs: "Germany has no evil intentions against Czechoslovakia." On the day following the incorporation Hitler remarked, "This will be very embarrassing for the Czechs." He was not languid in creating those conditions within the Sudeten area which would keep the region in constant turmoil and facilitate a pretext for intervention.

The Sudeten area, on the western and northern rim of Czechoslovakia had never constituted a part of Germany. While its population was mainly German, it had long been a part of Austria. By March, 1938, Austria had become a part of Germany, and this reenforced Hitler's plea for self-determination in the region. Since President Wilson, with canonical conviction, had espoused self-determination as one of the main bases of the peace, Hitler claimed a justifiable reason for insisting upon its observance twenty years later. For its implementation he prosecuted so violent a propaganda campaign in the Sudeten area that the major European countries feared the possibility of his dispatching an army to take physical possession of the region.

Churchill, fully conscious of the delicate and explosive situation, steadfastly opposed any measure taken by Hitler to violate Czechoslovakia's independence or territorial integrity. He realized that Hitler aimed at the incorporation of all European areas populated by Germans in order to create that Great *Vaterland*. He was also aware that the Fuehrer craved territory in Southeast Europe in order to control its economic resources as well as to create potential *Lebensraum* for the growing population of Germany. Churchill was also mindful of the fact that Hitler fully realized that the strategic location of Czechoslovakia made it a potential air and military base from which France, Russia, and Britain could operate against Germany. This option Hitler was determined to deny them.[53] Thus for the sake of Czechoslovakia's survival and England's security Churchill strove to block Hitler's acquisition of Sudetenland.

He found it almost as difficult to obstruct Chamberlain's policy of noninterference with Hitler's aggression as to impede the Fuehrer. The essence of the Prime Minister's policy in 1938 was to avoid war at all cost. To realize that ideal, he would pressure the Czechs to accept Hitler's demands "without sacrificing anything essential to their own state."[54] Churchill was in complete sympathy with this objective but he realized that the Czechs could not comply without enlisting wizardry of a high order. Thereupon Chamberlain dispatched Walter Runciman to Prague,[55] where he remained for six weeks and associated almost exclusively with German princes and Czechs with Nazi sympathies.[56] Neville Henderson, British Ambassador to Berlin, was also hostile to the Czechs. In a letter to Lord Halifax he characterized them as "a pigheaded race" and maintained that Beneš was "the most pigheaded of the lot."[57] Even Sir Robert Vansittart, Chief Diplomatic Adviser to the British Government at that time, refused to heed Churchill's warnings. Appeasers mesmerized themselves into a trance of security by denouncing Churchill as a warmonger. Even in the House of Commons many found it burdensome to listen to him.

Nor could Churchill find much comfort from many French leaders, among them Georges Bonnet, the Foreign Minister, who had assured the German Ambassador to Paris that this country and England would try to induce Czechoslovakia into seeing the situation from the German viewpoint. Since many of the well-to-do French citizens shared Bonnet's views, Churchill put little credence in the pledges of Edouard Daladier and Léon Blum, successive French Premiers, who had assured the Czechs that France would honor its pledge of 1935 to protect Czechoslovakia against attack. Churchill pleaded with Lord Halifax, who in February, 1938, had succeeded Anthony Eden as Foreign Secretary, to draft a joint note with France and Russia in which they should express to Germany their amicable intentions, but also inform it of their apprehension over its aggressive militarization, their eagerness for a peaceful solution of the Sudeten question, and that Germany's efforts to solve the issue by military action would arouse their serious concern.[58] Since this would involve a more adventurous policy than Lord Halifax dared to prosecute, he vetoed it and Churchill encountered another rebuff.

One country, however, was prepared to take positive action to prevent further expansion of Germany at the expense of its neighbors, and that was the Soviet Union. On September 19, 1938, the Czech government inquired of the Soviet government if it was prepared to meet its obligations under its treaty with Czechoslovakia by which it had committed itself to come to the assistance of the Prague government if and when France should come to its defense. In response the Moscow administration had replied unequivocally in the affirmative.[59]

Churchill at the time maintained that it was profoundly regrettable that neither the French nor the British government had given serious consideration to this Russian pledge. Here, he maintained, was an opportunity to confront Germany with major force on two fronts, and the mere threat of this would have diminished the Nazi martial ardor. Churchill admitted that neither Hungary nor Rumania would have welcomed Russian troop movements across their countries, but he contended that international diplomacy could overcome this situation.[60]

If one expedient failed, Churchill always had another in reserve; and in the Sudeten crisis he now urged Lord Halifax to ask President Roosevelt to join Britain, France, and Russia in their protest to Hitler against his plans.

To impress the Fuehrer with their earnestness Churchill proposed that the nations which opposed him should mobilize their fleets and place them in strategic locations vis-à-vis German ships and harbors. He aimed to impose as much diplomatic pressure against Hitler as peacetime conditions would permit.

As the Fuehrer became increasingly intent upon the applica-

tion of self-determination to the German people in the Sudetenland, the French eagerly wanted to learn the extent of assistance
the British would render in the event of German military action
against the Czechs. Upon Bonnet's inquiry, Lord Halifax replied, "Two motorized divisions and 150 planes." Churchill was
not only disappointed but also embarrassed that this was the
best that once mighty Britannia could do in so serious a crisis.

Hitler's threats energized Chamberlain into unusual activity.
Though he had never flown, he boarded a plane for Munich,
and on September 15-16 at Berchtesgaden he and Hitler sketched
out the general principles for the solution of the Sudeten issue.
Upon his return he expressed his impression of Hitler thus: "In
spite of the hardness and ruthlessness I thought I saw in the
face, I got the impression that here was a man who could be
relied upon when he had given his word...."[61] A week later
Hitler corrected this assumption, for when the two met, on
September 23, at Godesberg the Fuehrer presented Chamberlain "with a totally unexpected situation." Hitler had discarded
the Berchtesgaden terms and presented a new set of demands,
which Chamberlain refused to endorse. The meeting adjourned
with the situation unresolved. Chamberlain flew back to London,
and Hitler to Berlin, following which violent disturbances were
generated in the Sudeten area, and tension mounted in European
chancelleries. Hitler threatened to occupy the territory which he
wanted, but before that happened Czechoslovakia mobilized its
field army of 800,000 men and the French army manned the
Maginot Line. Chamberlain, Mussolini, and President Roosevelt, to a lesser degree, then prevailed upon Hitler to meet the
representatives from France, England, and Italy at Munich to
resolve the Sudeten problem. Russia, though it was the largest
of all the European countries and the problem under consideration concerned a Slav country, was not invited to send a
representative; nor was Czechoslovakia, although it was to be on
the diplomatic vivisection table. At a two-day meeting Daladier
representing France, Chamberlain Britain, Hitler Germany, and
Mussolini Italy assigned the Sudeten area, embracing 10,800
square miles and including Czechoslovakia's line of defense and
the Skoda works to Germany. Most Europeans found relief in the
avoidance of war, but a good many, like Léon Blum of France,

condemned themselves for their cowardice and moral bankruptcy.

Upon his return to London Chamberlain was accorded a heroic welcome, "There is no other example of worldwide popularity comparable to that which Chamberlain was accorded."[62] A staff of secretaries toiled for seven months responding to letters and telegrams from kings, presidents, and ordinary citizens.[63]

While the British at this time were not specifically bound by treaty to support Czechoslovakia, their customary fidelity to the maintenance of the balance of power on the Continent was breached. This precept had been scrupulously preserved for centuries, but in 1938 England defaulted on this cherished principle in order to escape war. And England lavished honors upon its Prime Minister for abandoning it. This was appeasement at its zenith.

It has been contended that Chamberlain could not have done otherwise than he did, for England's military leaders would not have tolerated war. If that is true, the Prime Minister must bear a large responsibility for their convictions, for in his official capacity he had by his speeches and actions helped to instill a spirit of defeatism rather than arouse a mood of courage and confidence.

If, without conviction, he had endorsed military action in cooperation with France and Russia, contrary to the sentiment in the House of Commons, he could have exercised his prerogative and resigned. But he preferred to practice appeasement, and in so doing he assured Hitler a free hand on the Continent, for the time being.

Churchill was not among those who congratulated Chamberlain, nor did he vote approval of his work at Munich. In a frantic attempt to impress the public with his own acute anxiety he implored the British to reflect upon all the instances they had yielded to Hitler's coups until England was now confronted with a military giant who threatened all Europe. He insisted that the Czech crisis was "the most grievous consequence which we have yet experienced of what we have done, and of what we have not done, and of what we have left undone in the last five years of futile good intentions, five years of search for the line of least resistance, five years of uninterrupted retreat of

British power, five years of neglect of our defences. These are the features I stand here to declare and which mark an improvident stewardship for which Great Britain and France have dearly to pay."[64] In the same speech he declared, "All is over. Silent, mournful, abandoned, broken Czechoslovakia recedes into darkness. She has suffered in every respect by her association with the western democracies and with the League of Nations of which she has always been an obedient servant."[65]

But even this failed to awaken the government against the ominous threats. Chamberlain, until February, 1939, still adhered to his policy that "war changes nothing, cures nothing, ends nothing."

Churchill, on the other hand, maintained that Britain had had a choice in the Sudeten affair, either submission or war. He insisted that if it had warned Hitler that an unprovoked aggression against Czechoslovakia would bring Britain to its aid, such an announcement would have saved the situation. After Hitler's occupation of the Sudetenland, with its valuable military resources, England could no longer rescue it.

Churchill insisted that France and England found themselves in this sorry situation because Chamberlain had been "viewing the problem through the wrong end of the Birmingham drain pipe."

After his acquisition of the Sudetenland, Hitler announced that this was his last demand for territory in Europe. While some of the credulous appeasers embraced this declaration as a bona fide pledge, Churchill regarded it as another bogus statement. He expected additional Hitlerian assurances of friendship, supplementary intonations of his integrity, further avowals of his reasonableness, and continued aggression.

In preparation for the next Nazi onslaught, Churchill continued his efforts to achieve solidarity among France, Russia, and Britain. Since he still viewed France as the dominant power in Europe, he continued to urge closer relations between it and the smaller countries of the Continent. He hoped for a Continental bloc, which, with the support of England, could checkmate further incursions.

Churchill did not have long to wait for the next aggression. On March 14, 1939, Emil Hacha, President of Czechoslovakia, arrived in Berlin for "discussions" of the relationship between

Germany and Czechoslovakia. Since a chronic cardiac condition prohibited his flying, Hacha's arrival was delayed until forty minutes past ten in the evening. He was kept waiting until one o'clock in the morning and was then ushered into Hitler's presence. The Fuehrer then demanded Hacha's written approval of his country's incorporation into the Third Reich, in a manner so insulting and abusive, followed by a barrage of indignities and accusations by Goering and Ribbentrop, that Hacha finally collapsed into unconsciousness. Goering had provided for just such an eventuality; a doctor in an adjoining room was summoned and after a few injections Hacha recovered sufficient sensibility to inscribe his signature on a previously prepared document by which he "... confidently placed the fate of the Czech people and the country in the hands of the Fuehrer and the German Reich." Almost simultaneously Hitler effected the establishment of Slovakia as an autonomous state under Father Tiso.

On March 15, the day following the incorporation of Czechoslovakia, Chamberlain announced in the House of Commons Hitler's latest aggression. He then stated that the guarantee which he himself had made to Czechoslovakia assuring it of independence and territorial integrity was no longer binding. "It is natural," he said, "that I should bitterly regret what has occurred, but do not let us on that account be deflected from our course. Let us remember that the desire of all people of the world still remains concentrated on the hope of peace."

His own spurious logic, emphasized by Hitler's occupation of Memel on March 23, offended even Chamberlain, for two days later, like Saul en route to Damascus, the Prime Minister en route to Birmingham reversed his previous policy. In his home city he denounced Hitler and his chicanery, as strongly as if the speech had been written by Churchill. By this time the appeasement scales had finally peeled from Chamberlain's eyes and he could see Hitler in his true colors. He realized that the Fuehrer was not aiming at the revision of a few provisions of the Treaty of Versailles, but at the domination of Europe, and after that a more pivotal influence in world affairs. Churchill warmly commended him upon his address. On March 31, two weeks after the Birmingham speech, Chamberlain initiated measures to throttle Hitler's ambitions: He assured Poland of British assistance in the event that it should be attacked by Germany. This was the death knell of appeasement in the House of Commons, for the Prime Minister's followers conformed to his revised diplomatic liturgy.

The Soviet Union on April 16, 1939, proposed to England a pact which should comprise France, Russia, and Britain, and also Poland if it could be induced to enter.[66] This coalition should also assume the obligation of protecting the small countries to the east of Germany against Nazi aggression.

Churchill welcomed the Russian proposal for negotiations which might lead to an alliance, and he insisted that England should not delay in accepting it. The situation, he contended, called for precipitate action. With Russia as an ally of the West, Hitler, if he instigated a war, would be vulnerable on two fronts, a military situation which had proved calamitous for the Kaiser. In order to augment its strength Churchill urged the inclusion of Estonia, Latvia, and Lithuania in the alliance.

Chamberlain demurred and delayed his reply until May 8. This postponement elevated still higher Stalin's lofty suspicion of the West. Even five days prior to his reception of Chamberlain's reply, on May 3, he had instituted feelers for some kind of an arrangement with Hitler.

The nature of Chamberlain's reply, when it did arrive, did not alleviate Stalin's deep distrust of the West, for it stipulated that Russia was obligated to assist France and England if they were involved in a war in consequence of their treaty obligations toward Rumania and Poland. Conversely, if the Soviet Union should enter a conflict under terms of its treaty with England and France they were not obligated to reciprocate their services.[67]

Stalin may not have been wise, but he was cautious, and ever had Russia's security in mind. The part played by England and France in the Czechoslovak crisis in 1938 and 1939 had made him lose faith in their integrity. He, therefore, fell back on his Georgian wariness. War, he believed, was inevitable, and Germany could inflict greater injury upon the Soviet Union than could England and France. To him Russia's survival was more important than the Western Powers' emotional reaction to him.

Churchill was keenly disappointed with the slowness of the negotiations. He had reasons for his uneasiness, for on May 3 Stalin replaced Maxim Litvinov, Commissar for Foreign Affairs, with Vyacheslav Molotov. The former had pursued a pro-Western policy, and the latter was pro-German in his views. Like Churchill, Stalin appreciated the urgency of the hour. In the meantime, Chamberlain and his coterie were haggling with the Russians over details of the proposed alliance.

Since May 3, plenipotentiaries of Germany and Russia had been negotiating, and finally, on August 23, they signed their Non-Aggression Pact in which each country pledged itself to neutrality if the other should become involved in war with a third party. Simultaneously, they staked out spheres of future conquest in Eastern Europe.

This compact did not receive a hospitable reception from Chamberlain. In a letter to his sister he relieved himself of his feelings toward the Soviet leaders. He frankly admitted that he had no confidence in any commitment to which they might pledge themselves. He doubted their capacity to wage a military campaign successfully. Furthermore, the hostility of Russia's neighbors toward the Soviet Union would contribute materially to its military weakness.[68]

Chamberlain did not let his aversion to Russia deflect him from his abhorrence of Hitler. Proof of this he revealed in his introduction of compulsory military service for six months for all men upon reaching twenty years of age, just long enough, the Germans maintained, to acquire the skill necessary to carry an umbrella. This was the first time in English history that con-scription had been imposed during peacetime. Churchill had been promoting such a measure for several years.

A deluge of denunciations from France, England, and the United States descended upon Stalin for combining with Hitler. Churchill refused to join this chorus. He maintained that if Stalin's "policy was cold-blooded, it was also realistic in a high degree."[69] Denunciation would merely increase the difficulty of inducing Russia to shift to England's side later.

Hitler did not envisage such an eventuality, nor did any of the appeasers in England. The Fuehrer again based his policy upon customary British protests, followed by the usual remon-strances, and finally succeeded by acquiescence. He presented Poland with what amounted to an ultimatum, which, among other demands, insisted upon a right-of-way for a road and a railway across the Corridor. Poland, with faith in British and

French assurance of assistance, rejected Hitler's demands and prepared for war.

As a last effort to restrain Hitler from plunging all Europe into war, Chamberlain dispatched a letter to him in which he solemnly and emphatically warned him that in the event of war on the Continent England would not remain neutral. To reinforce his warning Chamberlain, on August 25, announced a formal Anglo-Polish alliance which repeated the British pledge of assistance to Poland in the event of its being attacked. These two announcements jolted Hitler sufficiently to postpone his attack on Poland from August 25 to September 1. During the interval he hoped that England would give him some assurance that it would not intervene.

Simultaneously with the German invasion of Poland, on September 1, Chamberlain ordered the mobilization of the British armed forces. For some weeks a movement for Churchill's inclusion in the cabinet, sponsored by the press, the public, members of Parliament, and the cabinet, had been growing in volume and intensity to the point that Chamberlain could no longer ignore it. On September 1, he summoned Churchill and asked him to head the Admiralty as well as to serve in the War Cabinet. Churchill accepted without any demonstration other than an eagerness to prepare England for the perilous days that lay ahead.

CHAPTER IX

Potentate of Downing Street

UPON CHURCHILL'S RETURN TO THE CABINET HE WASTED NO TIME on ceremony, and was soon issuing suggestions and dispatches to his cabinet colleagues on matters within their own departments, and orders within his own. His first victim, or beneficiary, was the Prime Minister. Only a few hours after assuming his new duties, he wrote to Chamberlain and reminded him that the cabinet comprised too many old men. He indicated that the total age of the six members of the War Cabinet was 386 years, or an average of sixty-four. Churchill proposed to lower this age by the inclusion of younger men, and suggested Archibald Sinclair, who was forty-nine, and Anthony Eden, who was forty-two. Chamberlain cheerfully accepted this suggestion and made both men members of the cabinet. This reduced the average age to sixty. Churchill also recommended that the cabinet be composed of representatives from all the parties. Chamberlain accepted this suggestion also, but the Liberal and Labour parties declined the invitation.

On September 1, Lord Halifax, the British Foreign Minister, dispatched a note to Von Ribbentrop, the German Foreign Minister, which demanded the withdrawal of German troops from Poland within forty-eight hours. Hitler's noncompliance led to the British declaration of war on September 3. When the Fuehrer was apprised of Britain's action, he focused his gaze upon Von Ribbentrop and queried, "What now?"—an insinuation that his foreign secretary had given him the wrong cue. Goering, who was present, remarked, "If we lose this war, God have mercy on us."

Upon the expiration of the ultimatum on September 3 Churchill said, "In our hearts this Sunday morning there is peace. Our hands may be active, but our hearts are at rest. We must not under-rate the gravity of the task that lies before us, nor the temerity to which we shall not be found unequal. We must expect many disappointments, and many unpleasant surprises, but we may be sure that the task we have freely accepted is not beyond the compass and strength of the British Empire and the French Republic."[1]

Churchill's remarks appealed to the noblest and bravest sentiments in the British people, from the most exalted duke to the humblest millhand. It instilled in every Briton a willingness to sacrifice himself, if necessary, in order to save his country.

Churchill's position as First Lord of the Admiralty imposed difficult and heavy responsibilities. In 1939 Britain's navy was not as well balanced nor as powerful as it had been in 1914. And the Germans possessed new marine weapons. At the opening of World War I Britain had 400 destroyers and by 1918 the Allies had a total of 900.[2] In 1939 England had only 190 destroyers. Between the wars the destructive power of the submarine had multiplied. In 1938 Chamberlain negotiated a treaty with the Irish by which England relinquished the right to use Irish ports for war purposes. Furthermore, in 1940, the Germans were to overrun Denmark, Norway, Holland, Belgium, and Luxembourg. Britain was, therefore, more vulnerable than previously, and had fewer offensive weapons with which to combat German submarines.

There were, however, antisubmarine weapons. Among these was sonar detection which projected a sound wave into the ocean, and upon striking a solid substance, i.e., a submarine, the sound was returned. This was of immense importance to the British; without it mercantile losses would have been much greater. Churchill had these instruments installed in as many vessels as time permitted. He equipped trawlers with guns, and he armed merchant vessels. As in World War I, the British hunted German cruisers and battleships, but not until 1943 were the surface ships driven from the seas. During the intervening months they imposed immense shipping losses and aroused anguished concern.

At the opening of the war the Germans dropped magnetic mines in channels of congested navigation. These devices exploded merely upon proximity of a vessel. When the tide subsided several of these mines became visible and Churchill assigned naval engineers to ascertain their mechanism, after which he

ordered copper wires stretched around British ships to neutralize their magnetic attraction of the mines.

During the first four months of the war German submarines
sank 810,000 tons of shipping. Simultaneously, British and American shipyards turned out 478,000 tons. The Battle of the Atlantic
was yet to come.

In the winter of 1940 Chamberlain wrote that he had a "hunch"
that the war would end in the spring of 1940. He did not prophesy
a German defeat, but he predicted that the German people would
by that time have concluded that victory was beyond their
grasp. He believed that they would resolve that the continua-
tion of the war would merely increase the national debt, lengthen
the casualty list, and deepen the people's misery.[3]

The German conquest of Denmark, Norway, Holland, Luxembourg, and Belgium, and its penetration of France in April and
May, 1940, exposed Chamberlain's incapacity to assess the international situation. Furthermore, he had been unable to mobilize
the nation for war. Since the opening of the fighting too many
people pursued business as usual, weekends as usual, and the
races as usual. Three months after the beginning of the conflict
England was still plagued by 800,000 unemployed. Almost
nothing had been done to utilize the vast womanpower eager
to render services in the existing crisis. The British expeditionary
forces in Norway were ineptly led and were no match for the
Germans. Even some of Chamberlain's erstwhile appeasers were
vexed with his lack of enterprise. His efforts to defend himself
in the House of Commons led to an uproar of reproach. When
he asked all to sacrifice for the prosecution of the war, Lloyd
George abandoned the last remnants of his appeasement and
bluntly told Chamberlain that his most appropriate sacrifice
would be to surrender the premiership. Leopold Amery, a friend
of long standing, shouted Cromwell's order for the dissolution of
the Long Parliament: "You have sat here too long for any good
that you have been doing. Depart, I say, and let us be done with
you. In the name of God, go."[4]

Chamberlain may not have heard the voice of God, but he
perceived the will of England, and in compliance with it he
proceeded to the Royal Palace, turned in the seals of his office
and proposed Churchill as his successor. George VI would have
preferred Lord Halifax, but his membership in the House of

Lords would have compelled him to live in the twilight zone outside the things that really mattered.[5] He declined, and his intimacy with the appeasers would have made that appointment out of order. In England's deepest agony, the King, on May 10, endowed Churchill with the premiership. Never had the perch on top of "the greasy pole" been so precarious as the one to which Churchill ascended. He was chosen not so much because the people liked him as because they loved England.

He wasted no time in initiating his new duties and powers. On May 10 he hurriedly called conferences and made new appointments, all in rapid succession, until past midnight after which he later confessed, "During the last crowded days of the political crisis my pulse did not quicken at any moment. I took it as it all came. But I cannot conceal from the reader of this truthful account that, as I went to bed that night at three A.M., I was conscious of a profound relief. At last I had the authority to give directions over the whole scene. I felt as if I were walking with destiny, and that all my life had been but a preparation for this hour and this trial."[6] After the close of World War II he confessed that of all the offices he ever held, he enjoyed the premiership more than any other.

In 1893, as a young man, he had mused if only it had been a hundred years earlier, what a splendid time we should have had! "Fancy being nineteen in 1793 with more than twenty years of war against Napoleon in front of one." In 1940 at sixty-six, his extravagant youthful fancy had become a reality, with a bonus attached.

Many, especially among the Conservatives, had thwarted Churchill's aspiration and had exulted in his sorrows. Among them was Neville Chamberlain, who openly had expressed lack of confidence in his judgment. When Churchill assumed the premiership he did not take vengeance on his erstwhile opponents. There were more important matters to attend to than indulging in a personal vendetta. Hitler was the prime enemy, and Churchill mobilized everyone's energies for this objective, even those of Chamberlain, whom he made Lord President of the Council and Leader of the Conservative Party. As Prime Minister, Churchill did not want to square old accounts, but to win the war. He bestowed courtesies upon Stanley Baldwin, who in his heyday had whiplashed Churchill with ridicule. Now, as

Prime Minister, Churchill ignored the past, and on a number of occasions invited his former chief to 10 Downing Street for agreeable discussions. "The courtesies of the one matched the benevolence of the other."[7]

To win the war he created a coalition government representative of all the parties. He appointed Clement Attlee, Leader of the Labourites, Deputy Prime Minister, to preside over the House of Commons and assigned to him the administration of strictly national affairs. Each cabinet member was to be responsible for administering matters relating to his own department. To direct the prosecution of the war the Prime Minister created a War Cabinet over which he presided, and in addition reserved for himself the administration of the Department of Defence. The other members of the cabinet had no other responsibility than "to win the war."

To the execution of this task Churchill brought a confidence in himself similar to that of William Pitt, the Earl of Chatham: "I can save my country and no one else can." And this temper suffused his first speech as Premier on May 13, 1940, to the House of Commons:

You ask, what is our policy? I will say: It is to wage war by sea, by land, and air with all our might, and with all our strength that God gives us; to wage war against a monstrous tyranny, never surpassed in the dark lamentable catalogue of human crime. That is our aim . . . victory, victory, at all cost, victory in spite of terror, victory however long and hard the road may be, for without victory there is no survival, let that be realized; no survival for the British Empire, for the urge and the impulse of the ages that mankind will move forward toward its goal.

But I take my task with buoyancy and hope. I feel sure that our cause will not be suffered to fail among men. At this time I feel entitled to claim the aid of all, and I say "Come then, let us go forward together with our united strength."[8]

With such confident leadership, lord and cockney, mistress and maid, braced themselves for the worst that Hitler could inflict. In memorable exhortations Churchill aroused the noblest and the bravest emotions among his listeners. "With the sound of living history he mobilized the English language and sent it into battle." Being the embodiment of administrative efficiency, unlimited courage, and unusual human sympathy, he inspired his listeners to new levels of dynamism and determination. He summoned them to die in glory rather than to live in shame. He exterminated any feeling of appeasement and defeatism. He entranced English men and women with assurance of victory. Not since the days of Pericles had a leader so transformed the national mettle as did Churchill. The members of the House of Commons, who formerly had booed him, now gave him repeated smashing votes of confidence, and exclaimed, "God knows where we would be without him, but only God knows where we will be with him." As the Earl of Chatham had possessed the power of "putting the State in motion,"[9] so Churchill mesmerized all Englishmen into warriors and ordered each to his station. He made each one feel that the fate of England rested upon him or upon her.

No one knew better than Churchill that it would take more than a blast of eloquence to halt the Germans, and that action was more potent than epigrams. Therefore, five days after his assumption of the premiership, on May 15, 1940, he opened negotiations with Joseph Kennedy, the American Ambassador to London, for transfer of fifty overaged American destroyers to Great Britain in return for ninety-nine-year leases on naval and air bases on the islands of Newfoundland, Bermuda, the Bahamas, Trinidad, St. Lucia, and Antigua, as well as in British Guiana.[10] Four months later, on September 3, this proposal matured into an agreement, and England was the better equipped to cope with the German submarines.

Churchill realized the vulnerability of England's Far East colonies, and without the slightest regard for the political consequences to Roosevelt of such an action, he proposed to the President that the United States should assume a protectorate over Singapore. Since Roosevelt was confronted with his third-term election within a couple of months, he was not disposed to sacrifice himself upon the altar of Churchill's convenience.

The Prime Minister also instituted the strategic bombing of Germany. As justification he cited the fact that a German pilot, by mistake, had bombed a residential area in London. Moreover, a German air squadron of 45 to 50 planes had dropped 94 tons of bombs upon Rotterdam and had laid waste the heart of the city, killing 814 civilians, wounding many more, and making 75,000 homeless. Churchill, acting upon the assumption that this form of *Schrecklichkeit* called for a similar scourge upon the Germans, abandoned the bombing of their cities with peace leaflets and substituted high-explosive saturation bombing.

Before the British had inflicted much damage upon Germany by this strategy, the Germans had driven a wedge between the British and French armies, and were threatening those on the northern flank with capture. In this situation Churchill ordered the evacuation of Lord Gort, the British commander, from Dunkerque to England, on the claim that he was too valuable a prize for Hitler, and this action served as a precedent for Roosevelt's transfer in 1942 of General MacArthur from Bataan to Australia, while his army was left behind. Then upon Churchill's instructions, 228,584 British and 112,546 French soldiers were decamped in 887 vessels of divergent character to England. When the British jubilantly celebrated this achievement as a great victory, Churchill reminded them that wars were not won by retreats.

Churchill, fearful that the French reverses and the Dunkerque incident might incline France toward a separate peace, proposed a union, not only of the two countries, but also of the empires, with a common citizenship. Paul Reynaud, the French Premier, was warmly in favor of the scheme, and tried to induce his cabinet to accept it. The defeatists were of a different mind. On June 16 they forced Reynaud from the Premiership and replaced him with Marshal Philippe Pétain who accepted their views.

They maintained that acceptance of Churchill's proposal would make France a British dominion, while others preferred the status of a Nazi satellite. General Maxime Weygand announced that "In three weeks England would have her neck wrung like a chicken," while Marshal Pétain declared that union with England would constitute "fusion with a corpse." With so violent opposition to Churchill's proposal it was never put to a vote in the French cabinet.

A few days later Churchill received information that France had signed an armistice with Germany. In response to this intelligence he announced, "Now we are alone. I find that very exciting." England was to remain virtually "alone" for another year. Churchill's courage, even then matched his crisis: "Let us therefore brace ourselves to our duties, and so bear ourselves that if the British Empire should last for a thousand years, men will say, 'This was their finest hour.'" To many of his listeners, declamations of this character hallowed heroism and glorified martyrdom.

Churchill believed that France's negotiation of an armistice with Hitler might well result in his acquisition of the French fleet. It, combined with the Italian, and the German, the Prime Minister feared, could threaten British naval supremacy, and therefore endanger Britain itself. He, therefore, submitted three options to the French for the disposition of their fleet:

(1) join the British fleet and continue the war against Germany and Italy: or

(2) steam with reduced crews to some British port.

Upon acceptance of either of the above conditions the ships would be returned to France at the close of the war, and if damaged or sunk, Britain would reimburse the French government for the loss or damage.

(3) Refusal to abide by either of these terms would leave the British government no other choice but to disable them.

The Vichy government rejected the first two options, and Churchill, much to his regret, felt compelled to execute the third provision, and the French vessels in North Africa were disabled by the British fleet.

After France, on June 25, 1940, accepted the German armistice, the Fuehrer found himself triumphant, but without any plan for the future, this being proof, according to the Iron Chancellor, that Hitler was not a great military leader, for the founder of German unification insisted that a successful commander, either in war or diplomacy, should never be caught without alternatives. When Hitler finally adjusted himself to his magnificent victory, he expected Churchill, or some other British leader, to sue for peace. Instead of appearing, hat in hand, along the Wilhelmstrasse, Churchill drew the English together in cheerful defiance, and announced in the House of Commons Britain's determination to continue its resistance against the Nazis. By July 19, because of no British peace feelers, Hitler's patience was frayed. Speaking in the Reichstag, he declared, "In this hour I feel it to be my duty before my own conscience to appeal once more to reason and common sense in Great Britain as much as elsewhere. I consider myself in a position to make this appeal since I am not the vanquished begging favors, but the victor speaking in the name of reason. I can see no reason why this war must go on." Hitler hoped for a humble submission rather than stubborn defiance whose ultimate consequences neither he nor his trusted astrologer could foretell.

When Churchill refused to apply Hitler's syllogisms to his dialectics, the Fuehrer resolved to bomb "common sense" into the Prime Minister's system. On July 10, 1940, Hitler inaugurated his first significant raid on England. From that date until August 18 Goering cascaded bombs on docks, anti-aircraft installations, air fields, and transportation centers along the route from the Channel to London in preparation for the attack upon that city.

When the blitz upon London opened on September 7, Goering expected that within ten days or, at most two weeks, the destruction would be so frightful and dismaying that Churchill and his government would be compelled to sue for peace. To execute this enterprise Goering had mobilized 3,500 aircraft of various types, and in the period from September 7, 1940, to May 11, 1941, showered London with 18,291 tons of high explosives and an almost equal quantity of fire bombs. Among notable structures hit were Buckingham Palace, the House of Commons, the Treasury, Carlton Club, and 10 Downing Street. This downpour of death and destruction left 20,000 dead and 27,000 wounded. September 15 was the climactic day for Germany lost fifty-six planes, more than its daily endurance. By September 27, even Goering had lost confidence in the Luftwaffe's power to subdue England. Heavy bombing continued until November 3 after which it somewhat subsided, but England under Churchill's defense survived the worst that Hitler could impose.

Since the Germans had failed to blitz the Royal Air Force from the skies, invasion of England was an impossibility. They therefore decided to sweep the British ships from the seas. Significant factors doomed this attempt to failure, too, among which was the inability of Hitler, like Canute, to control the waves. Furthermore, Germany did not have enough shipping, for every time it assembled quantities of landing craft at debarking harbors the R.A.F. splintered it. Also, after September 15, autumn storms nullified channel navigation by small craft. So Churchill's strategy, English determination, nature's turbulence, and Hitler's intuitive strategy rescued Britain from German domination and left it as the future keystone of the Grand Alliance which would overthrow Der Fuehrer and all his supporters.

If the British could not be bombed into submission there was the possibility of starving them into surrender. Admiral Doenitz was quite confident of accomplishing this. In 1940 he announced: "I will show that the U-boats can win the war. . . . Nothing is impossible for us." This attempt found expression in the Battle of the Atlantic. Churchill was fully conscious of the dangerous threat which the undersea killers posed. He likened Britain's position to that of a deep-sea diver, who descends into the depths for his necessities. He is sustained by a long air line that ensures him the oxygen that is vital for his survival, and all the while there are hostile fish that frisk about the air line. If they should sever it he would gasp a few times, then gulp and be gone.

In a comparable way England was sustained by long lines of commerce. If a school of hostile submarines should sunder the economic pipelines, Britain would emaciate, shrivel, and collapse. It would have no alternative but to accept the uncompromising terms of its triumphant conqueror.

Churchill was more fearful of the submarine threat than any other weapon, but he rejected Admiral Doenitz's death sentence upon Britannia. He was determined to annul it, despite the fact that England, in 1940, was not so well equipped to defend itself as it had been in 1914.

The British soon had statistical proof of the threat to their lifelines. During the week ending June 8, 1940, England's imports exclusive of oil, amounted to 1,201,535 tons. Six weeks later it had dropped to 750,000 tons. During October, November, and December the weekly average stood at approximately 800,000 tons.[10] The situation was already acutely critical. Increasing German attacks would reduce the weekly imports still more. What further intensified its hazards was the improvement in the lethal capability of its submarines. Furthermore, by the time that Churchill became Prime Minister, Germany had conquered Denmark, Norway, Holland, and Belgium, and France was on the verge of capitulating. These countries outflanked England and their loss made her especially vulnerable to submarine attack. Churchill deplored his predecessor's Treaty of 1938 with Ireland by which England renounced the use of Erin's major ports as military, naval, and air bases in case of war.

Churchill, however, mobilized and exploited whatever antisubmarine weapons the Admiralty could command. Destroyers escorted convoys of merchant ships and herded them into ports. He armed hundreds of merchant vessels and trawlers with guns which increased the inhospitality of the seas for the submarines. The fifty destroyers which he leased from the United States imposed increasing hazards upon the prowlers of the deep.[11] He instituted a vigorous construction program of new destroyers. He installed asdic (sonar) instruments upon as many seagoing vessels as possible, which enabled the skippers to locate undersea wolves. Endangered victims could then shift their course and escape. He was influential in commandeering German and neutral shipping in British ports for carrying service. He also initiated a construction program of cargo vessels for replacement of those sunk. This program, with a similar one in the United States, astounded the world, including Hitler, with its output.

Doenitz had also announced that "an airplane can no more kill a U-boat than a crow can kill a mole." While airplanes sank few submarines, they "made 587 attacks" on them. They escorted 4,947 merchant convoys during which they flew 55,000,000 miles and damaged fifty submarines.

Among the many novel forms of combat that characterized World War II were duels between submarines underneath the ocean surface. "Something more than 20 per cent of the Axis submarines sent down during the war were destroyed by Allied submarines—more in proportion to the numbers engaged than were knocked out by other means, including aircraft."[12]

Improvements in submarine construction and operation increased the difficulty of exterminating them.[13] The Germans created motors that were almost noiseless in operation and therefore difficult to locate. They devised torpedoes which did not leave a trace of air bubbles in their course. Their communication services were improved. German airplanes daily exchanged information with submarine commanders, and the substance of these conversations was relayed to the German Admiralty, which integrated the whole offensive.

This campaign by air and sea took a heavy toll on British shipping, for during the war German submarines sank 4,773 ships which grossed 23,000,000 tons.[14] But what was hazardous for the Allies was perilous for the Germans since they lost 630 of their 1,160 submarines.[15] The mortality of the crews was even greater: 30,000 of the 40,000 in the German submarine service accompanied their vessels to the ocean floor. The British accounted for 70 per cent of the submarine losses while the Americans sank 30 per cent.[16]

Doenitz, who confidently had prophesied victory as a result of submarine depredations, admitted at the end of 1943 that the Allies had defeated his U-boat warfare. This, he said, had been accomplished not through superior strategy or tactics, but by a more effective utilization of science, especially in the field of detection. Much of the credit for this belonged to Churchill, for he had been a member of the National Research Council several years before he entered the cabinet in 1939, where, with the assistance of Professor Frederic Lindemann, he had instituted a program for the development of antisubmarine warfare.

Another measure which reduced the hazards to British commerce was the destruction of German cruisers and battleships that preyed upon allied shipping. The German pocket battleships, with great speed, heavy guns, and thick armor, roamed the seas striking at single ships or convoys and imposed heavy losses. The pocket battleships were hunted down while at the same time improved British antisubmarine fighting imposed a correspondingly heavy toll.

SUMMARY OF THE CONTEST TO CONTROL THE SEAS[17]

Year	German submarines sunk	Allied shipping sunk	New construction British and American	Net gain or loss in tonnage
1939	9	810,000	332,000	− 478,000
1940	22	4,407,000	1,219,000	− 3,188,000
1941	35	4,398,000	1,984,000	− 2,414,000
1942	85	8,245,000	7,182,000	− 1,063,000
1943	237	3,611,000	14,585,000	+10,974,000
1944	241	1,422,000	13,349,000	+11,927,000
1945	183	458,000	3,834,000	+ 3,376,000
	782	23,351,000	42,485,000	+19,134,000

Churchill was almost as determined to shield England from its internal enemies as he was to guard it against its foreign foes.

At the opening of the war, 73,353 persons were examined for their loyalty. Of these 560 were interned, and 6,782 were placed under special restrictions. Among them the constabulary assumed that some were enemies of England and might well perpetrate acts of sabotage, or even worse. During the Blitz, when the British expected German attempts at invasion, Churchill instructed John Anderson, the Secretary of Home Affairs, to make a survey of the loyalty of the aliens within the country, a command which he dutifully executed, but neglected to report the result of his investigation for several days. Churchill then sent him a peremptory request for his findings. The report arrived just as the Churchill family sat down to lunch, and in "his list of detainers, to the delight of the children, amongst the first three, were two of Mrs. Churchill's cousins."[18]

After Churchill's accession to the premiership, he had hoped that the loss of one ally would not be followed by the addition of another enemy, more especially Italy. From the beginning of Mussolini's rule, Churchill had held him in very high esteem. He had admired Il Duce for his "gentle and simple bearing." He had praised him for his statesmanship. He had characterized him as a benefactor, not only of Italy, but of the rest of Europe. He felt especially appreciative for his suppression of Bolshevism in Italy.[19] On September 3, 1938, less than a month before the Munich Conference, Churchill had published an article in *Collier's Weekly* in which he rhapsodized on Mussolini's ability, accomplishments, and character.[20]

Almost immediately after he became Prime Minister Churchill wrote a personal letter to Mussolini requesting him not to enter the war against Britain.[21] It was all to no avail. Mussolini's acquisitive instincts triumphed over his personal sympathies and, on June 10, 1940, he entered Italy in the war on the side of Hitler. He maintained that his attendance at the peace conference was worth a few thousand Italian corpses. Finally, when Churchill learned of Mussolini's assassination on April 26, 1945, he declared that he "was profoundly shocked."[22]

Churchill's major task as Prime Minister was the prosecution of the war, and, for that project he was better qualified than any other British Premier. In character and ability he was superior to any of his subordinates. Furthermore, he was well grounded in military science. He had graduated from Sandhurst Military

Academy; he had read all the standard military works on war; he had participated in wars on three continents, and had written treatises on each one. He, therefore, assumed a confident and positive direction of Britain's military efforts.

Churchill maintained harmonious relations with members of his War Council, partly because they were appointed by him, and also because they were in sympathy with his general strategic principles for the prosecution of the war. In May, 1940, when he became Prime Minister, Sir John Dill was Chief of the Imperial General Staff. Sixteen months later Churchill replaced him with General Alan Brooke whose personality and strategic conceptions dovetailed into his better than did those of General Dill.[23]

General Sir Alan Brooke discovered that Churchill was a very demanding taskmaster. The Prime Minister's restless intelligence harassed him with a succession of strategic plans which demanded more than academic consideration. Most of these had to be rejected, but before their elimination Brooke had to exert all of his persuasive powers. Other plans had real merit and deserved serious consideration, but all of this was very exhausting, even nerve-racking. At times Churchill proposed to initiate an engagement without drafting a specific battle plan.[24] To induce the generals to adopt his campaign proposals, he alternated between cajolery and reprehension, behind which there was always the possibility of an order for compliance, or even worse, loss of command. He even insisted upon his generals' initiation of an engagement before they were ready to launch an attack on the assumption that enemy commanders were as ill prepared as his own officers were. In considering with General Brooke the hesitation of his generals to attack, Churchill maintained that they were too cautious, too loath to engage in battle until victory was assured in advance.[25] He, on the other hand, was under constant pressure from members of Paliament and from the public to proclaim military victories. Failure to do so would threaten his political career. In the early years of the war, he was unduly critical of General Montgomery for not opening a major campaign before he did.[26] One of Brooke's major concerns was to restrain Churchill from initiating offensives prematurely. He frequently inquired of Brooke: "Have you not got a single general in the army who can win battles, have none of them any ideas? Must we continuously lose battles in this way?"[27]

Most successful executives are extremely demanding of their subordinates, and Churchill was no exception; he was inordinately so, for he was driven by a compulsion to rescue England from defeat. He had no desire to impose exhaustion upon his fellow Britons, but if overwork was necessary for the security of his country, their aching muscles, weary bones and jaded brains did not make him slacken the pace. Day after day he kept his own activity geared in overdrive. He saw nothing unjustifiable in accelerating his subordinates' efforts.

In his attitude toward Churchill, Brooke alternated between exasperation and adulation. On November 30, 1942, after having served as Chief of the Imperial Staff for a year, he confessed that he could not endure much longer the exactions imposed.

Despite the high appreciation which Brooke had of Churchill he recognized some of his shortcomings. He maintained that Churchill could not see all the facets of a strategic problem, and that he failed to take into account the bearing of one theater upon the war in another, and to convince him of this defect was both delicate and difficult. "By the end of the third week I thought I was finished and could never compete with my job."[28]

CHAPTER X

Acquisition of Allies

FROM THE MOMENT OF THE ANNOUNCEMENT OF THE HITLER-STALIN Pact of August 23, 1939, Churchill doubted its durability. He perceived fissures in its framework, and he expected these to widen. He realized that the two dictators lacked cordiality toward each other, and that the people of the respective nations disliked one another, that the Germans despised the Russians as *Untermenschen,* and that the Slavs disdained the Germans as a race of snobs, all of which militated against the permanence of the alliance.

Stalin had read *Mein Kampf,* in which the author revealed his lustful yearning for the resources of the Ukraine, the wealth of the Urals, and the oil of the Middle East.

Churchill realized that all of this constituted a combustible combination, and he prepared to take advantage of its explosive potential. When Stalin fell upon Finland, in November, 1939, the British government did not freeze Russian funds in its banks as the United States government did to Russian funds in America, proof that the British government possessed both the short glimpse and the long view. Roosevelt and Churchill, on the basis of their intelligence reports, had warned Stalin of the impending attack, but Stalin interpreted these admonitions as capitalist devices to foment trouble between himself and the Fuehrer, and he therefore did not take these alarums seriously.[1] He felt confident that Hitler would inform him before he would mount an attack.[2] On June 18, 1941, Stalin left for Sotchi where he intended to spend his vacation.[3] He was aware that an attack was "possible, but not imminent."[4] Churchill, in *The Hinge of Fate,* maintains that "Hitler surprised the Russians."[5]

Few people were more astounded than Stalin when the German troops, on the morning of June 22, 1941, invaded his country. In his amazement he remained incommunicado until July 3.

In a sense Hitler should be credited with providing Britain with an ally, for his invasion of Russia brought succor to the island nation. It was, however, British stubborn resistance against the Fuehrer's Blitz that induced him to shift the attack from Britain to the Soviet Union.

Only few if any experienced such a joyous relief as did Churchill over Hitler's invasion of Russia, for in so doing he granted Britain reprieve from mortal danger. With the assistance of Russia, Churchill proclaimed, "We have but one aim, one single purpose. We are resolved to destroy Hitler and every vestige of the Nazi regime."[6] On another occasion he maintained that he "would make a pact with the devil himself if it would save England." He confessed that he had been a virulent opponent of Bolshevism, and for that he would make no apology. "Past animosities," he said, "should not influence England's present policy." He insisted that Russia's danger was England's peril, and that Russia's security would enhance England's safety.

On July 12, 1941 Stalin negotiated with Churchill a mutual assistance pact which committed each nation to fight Hitler to his political and military extinction. Churchill also promised Stalin whatever assistance he could spare, but he reserved to himself the right to decide later on the quantity and the categories of matériel to be sent.

The Soviet leader, hard pressed as he was, and never inhibited by modesty, did not tarry in taking advantage of the offer. He soon drafted an enormous list of items which he urgently hoped Britain would dispatch without delay, an admirable tribute to his appreciation of capitalist efficiency. Though Churchill did not fill all of Stalin's orders and expectations, Britain's shipments were considerable. During the war it sent forty convoys to Russia, valued at £428,000,000. Among matériel dispatched were 5,000 tanks and more than 7,000 aircraft. In forwarding commodities via the arctic route a large number of the ships were sunk by German submarines. The Royal Navy suffered even greater losses. Inasmuch as Britain was also supplying the underground forces in France, Norway, and Yugoslavia, as well as supporting its own forces, the military equipment sent to Stalin represents a huge donation, and an equally great sacrifice.

This did not restrain the Generalissimo from asking for still more, ignoring the fact that England was prosecuting a war of its own, and that its armed forces needed daily replenishments.[7] Stalin's extremity, however, was so acute that he paid little attention to Churchill's rejection of some of the Russian requests and he continued his pleas for shipments of matériel.

When these supplications failed to bring greatly increased deliveries, Stalin became abusive. He derisively compared, to the point of insolence, the British military effort with the Russian. Churchill at first did not respond vexatiously for he was appreciative of the fact that the Russians were enduring blows that might have been concentrated on Britain. But there was a limit to his forbearance, and to calm Stalin, Churchill reminded him that for twenty-one months he had supplied Hitler with stupendous quantities of war matériel, had applauded all of his triumphs yet felt no embarrassment in pressing Churchill for enormous shipments of military equipment. In spite of administering such a blunt rejoinder, to which Stalin was not altogether accustomed, the Britisher rejoiced in having Russia as an active ally, and was reluctant to remind the Soviet leader of his previous intimacy with Hitler for fear of losing him as an associate against his former accomplice.

On July 18, Stalin made his first request for the opening of a second front, either in France, or in Norway,[8] with so much insistence that it approached the nature of a command.[9] Two days later Churchill replied that he saw no possibility of mounting such an offensive. The Channel coast of France, he said, bristled with heavy fortifications whose guns could fire projectiles into England. Behind this artillery lurked forty divisions, eager to extend an inhospitable welcome. Churchill preferred not to subject his troops to such a reception.

There was no denying the desperation of Russia's plight. Three weeks after the invasion, Field Marshal Fedor von Bock had taken Smolensk and was within 200 miles of Moscow. Field Marshal Karl von Rundstedt had captured 660,000 Russians in the Ukraine and had reached the Black Sea. Field Marshal Wilhelm von Leeb was approaching the Gulf of Finland. So deep had the German penetration of Russia become that by the end of September Hitler ordered the demobilization of forty divisions and assigned them to industry.[10]

Hitler's intuition, which led him to assume that Russia was beaten, had neglected to remind his overconfident generals of the Slavic devotion to Mother Russia, and of the inexorable influence of their greatest ally, "General Winter." He reported on the steppes in mid-October in his most ferocious frigidity in fifty years, and held the Germans in an icy embrace so tightly that 14,447 men required amputations, 62,004 suffered serious freezing, and 94,270 light freezing. Furthermore, Russian resistance and offensive action from June to February accounted for 210,572 Germans killed, 747,751 wounded, and 47,338 missing.[11] Since Hitler had assumed that the campaign against the Russians would be over by early autumn he had not provided his troops with winter clothing. Massive snowdrifts prevented shipment of adequate quantities of food, and starving soldiers turned to horse carcasses long since frozen to death.[12] The weatherman and the Russian armies halted the German troops within sight of Moscow, and then the Russian forces launched a counterattack and drove the Germans back as much as one hundred miles in places along the battle line. The Germans escaped disaster by the narrowest margin. But the battle was far from won. The leading statesmen of the world, including Churchill, revised their estimates of Russia's fighting qualities, and shipments of British matériel to the Soviets increased.

So desperate was the situation for Stalin that he issued a second request for a cross-Channel invasion to relieve the pressure on the Russian forces. Churchill was aware that the dispatch of British troops across the Channel might prevent a Soviet collapse, but this would impose skyrocketing casualties which he very much wished to avoid. On the other hand, failure to comply with Stalin's request for a second front might eliminate Russia from the war. Churchill was confronted with a difficult decision. In meeting it he took one of his characteristically long chances and declined Stalin's request. Subsequent developments, in British opinion, justified his decision. By January, 1942, Russia had demonstrated its power and endurance and this led to ever increasing shipments from Great Britain and the United States.

At the outbreak of the war the President of the United States and the Prime Minister of Great Britain were not strangers, for in 1915 they had met at Gray's Inn in London while the latter was head of the Admiralty and Roosevelt was Assistant Secretary of the Navy. Both later claimed that they recalled the incident. Twenty-four years later, on September 1, 1939, Roosevelt initiated a correspondence with Churchill in which he expressed his pleasure over his friend's return to the cabinet, and requested him to "keep me in touch with anything you want me to know."

Churchill seized the opportunity, and thus began one of the famous exchanges of letters in history. The British statesman sent some 950 communications to the President, who dispatched about 800 in return. Churchill did not exchange letters with Roosevelt for idle literary delectation, especially when his country was involved in a struggle which might terminate its existence as an independent nation. He was dominated by an ulterior motive: the enlistment of the United States as an ally in the European conflagration. And Roosevelt was not unwilling to listen. He appreciated far more clearly the significance of the raging conflict than did most members of Congress or their constituents. He was conscious of what the American predicament would be if England should succumb and the Fuehrer would dominate the whole European Continent.

Churchill, although in many ways a man of the nineteenth century, fully recognized his country's dependence upon its child, the United States. He had not forgotten that a million American doughboys had served in French trenches during World War I, and that an enormous flow of American matériel had reached France and England before and during its participation in the conflict. The British and the French, from March to July, 1918, had stared defeat in the face.

As World War II was progressing Churchill shuddered at the prospect of facing the Nazi armies without the support of his American kin. As early as October 16, 1938, while still in the eyes of Brahmin officialdom a political leper, he had broadcast a speech from London to the United States in which he evoked the thesis of identical insecurity. In it he had insisted that both countries at the time were faced with a common danger, and that the way to meet it was by joint effort.[13] He had urged joint action by the United States and Britain, for he believed that this would deter the Fuehrer from engaging in any further aggression.

Five days after he had become Prime Minister he sent an urgent appeal to Roosevelt in which he entreated him to enter the struggle.[14] He warned Roosevelt that if he delayed much longer a later effort might be useless.[15]

The President was not unmindful of the verity of these appeals.

British expulsion from Dunkirk, with the loss of all its equipment, impelled the President into action. On his own initiative and authority he stripped American arsenals of their reserves and dispatched some 500,000 rifles, 1,800 machine guns, and 3,000 field guns to England.[16] It was not without good cause that Churchill referred to Roosevelt as "Our Good Friend."

Churchill may not have known that Cornelius Mann in "Two Famous Descendants of John Cooke and Sarah Warren," in the *New York Genealogical and Biographical Record*, III, July, 1942, 159-66, had traced the lineage of the Churchill and Roosevelt families and had revealed that the President and the Prime Minister were "eighth cousins once removed."[17] Furthermore on a visit to the United States, Lord Randolph Churchill had called upon Franklin Roosevelt's father at Hyde Park.

In the presidential election of 1940 Churchill very much wanted to see Roosevelt continued in the White House, but during the campaign the Prime Minister remained discreetly silent, but as soon as "Our Good Friend" was assured another term Churchill was fulsome in his expression of pleasure. In a telegram he said to the President, "I prayed for your success. . . . I am truly thankful for it."[18]

After these felicitations the Prime Minister soon presented his next petition, which grew out of England's efforts to accelerate production of war matériel. Its prosecution of the war had reduced its gold reserves almost to the vanishing point. Churchill believed that he could establish so intimate an identity of interest with the United States that its government would relieve England of paying for the deliveries. Roosevelt approved, but Congress and the people hesitated. Finally, however, in March, 1941, Congress passed HR 1776 (the Lend Lease Bill), which authorized the President to sell, or lease, necessary war matériel to nations whose policies, he believed, contributed to American security. By the law's termination in August, 1945, the United States had granted $46,040,054,000 in aid of which John Bull received the lion's share.

LEND LEASE AID BY COUNTRY
(March 1941 to October 1946)[19]

British Empire	$30,269,210,000
U.S.S.R.	10,801,131,000

France	1,406,600,000
China	631,509,000
American Republics	321,467,000
Netherlands	162,157,000
Greece	75,416,000
Norway	52,443,000
Turkey	28,063,000
Yugoslavia	25,885,000
Other countries	43,284,000
Aid not charged to foreign governments	2,088,249,000
Total lend-lease aid	$46,040,054,000

The British secured 69 per cent of the total aid and the U.S.S.R. secured 25 per cent. The two countries together were the recipients of 94 per cent of the lend lease aid.

Roosevelt gave Churchill even more significant assurances for on January 10, 1941, Harry Hopkins, on the President's authorization, consoled the Prime Minister: "The President is determined that we shall win the war together. Make no mistake about it. He has sent me to tell you that at all costs and by all means he will carry you through, no matter what happens to him. There is nothing that he will not do so far as he has the human power."[20]

This was gratifying. Churchill's nature, however, was such that anything that would be comforting tomorrow should be enjoyed today. He, therefore found it agonizing to wait while Roosevelt was wrestling with the isolationists.

England's situation was so desperate in 1941 that Churchill could rescue it only by wringing the maximum of aid from anyone willing to contribute. In pursuance of this aim he concentrated upon the United States. In exercising solicitation he was restrained by few inhibitions. No sooner had Roosevelt assured him an abundance of raw matériel gratis than he asked Roosevelt to deliver it wherever it was needed, and then to escort the vessels part of the way across the ocean, and the American government acceded to his request. To expedite deliveries Roosevelt, in January, 1941, dispatched a mission to London to devise the procedures for the reduction of the number of vessels which might be sunk by German submarines. The President was eager to "render all assistance short of war." This was benevolent neutrality in its most magnanimous guise.

Almost inevitably, the United States drifted into World War II. Each of its military acts generated succeeding ones, and its involvement in the conflict was almost as inevitable as the succession of the seasons.

On an afternoon in July, 1941, Harry Hopkins strolled into the gardens at the Prime Minister's residence, and during a pleasant and informal conversation Hopkins conveyed a proposal from Roosevelt that he and the President should meet for discussions in the near future. Churchill endorsed this suggestion with avidity. The date and the place of the rendezvous were promptly arranged: August 9 at Placentia Bay, Newfoundland. The *Prince of Wales*, Britain's largest battleship, was promptly readied for the accommodation of Churchill and his staff. On August 4, escorted by a fleet of cruisers and destroyers, it steamed off toward the west and five days later anchored at its destination. Harry Hopkins, who was on board, maintained that "You'd have thought Winston was being carried into the heavens to meet God."[21]

Churchill arrived at the scene of deliberations with a number of issues which he wished to consider with the President. Since the enactment of the lend-lease program Hitler had attacked Russia and Churchill feared that the United States might concentrate its beneficence on the Soviet Union rather than Great Britain. He also wished to refute the contention of an American general that Britain would not be able to ward off an invasion.

Information had reached the Prime Minister that the President was skeptical about the wisdom of Churchill's Middle Eastern campaign. He was determined to justify this strategy, and his aides rallied dutifully in defense of their master's contentions.

After deliberation on each of these topics the Prime Minister felt that his views had prevailed on each one. He had brought another document with him, and after some emendation by Roosevelt it was formulated into the Atlantic Charter. It comprised eight points:

1. Neither the United States nor Great Britain sought aggrandizement for territorial gains.
2. Neither the United States nor Great Britain would approve territorial changes which did not have the endorsement of the people concerned.

3. Both countries would promote the right of all people to establish the form of government they desired. Furthermore, they favored the restoration of sovereign rights and self-government to those people who have been deprived of them.

4. They favored the fullest opportunity of all people of the world to raw materials and to trade in order to satisfy their desire for a decent standard of living.

5. They favored the fullest collaboration of all people of the world in the economic field in order to assure all people improved labor standards.

6. Following the overthrow of the Nazi regime they favored a peace which would enable the people of all lands to pursue their careers free from fear and want.

7. After the close of the war they would establish a peace that would assure all people freedom to travel upon the high seas and oceans without hindrance.

8. They championed the abolition of force in international relations. They favored the disarmament of those nations which, because of their military power, made the existence of others insecure.

The formulation of point 3 called for several painful compositions, for Churchill was in complete sympathy with its principle of self-government, provided that it did not apply to British-owned territories. Roosevelt was equally determined that it should have universal application. And thus at the very first meeting of the two great leaders their divergent views were revealed in sharp relief: one envisioned a society adjusted to the future, the other, one that was pegged to traces of the past.

Critics maintained that the Atlantic Charter was merely a recapitulation of Wilson's Fourteen Points, but it was more than that. Wilson's declaration was issued thirteen years before the depression of 1929 imposed its tragedy upon hundreds of millions of people. Both Churchill and Roosevelt had witnessed grief and heartache caused by business failure and unemployment, and in Article 5 they urged action against recurrence of these calamities.

The Charter was not a treaty for it was never submitted to the House of Commons nor the Senate for ratification. It was a propagandist's image of a world society based upon justice, peace, security, freedom, and an Allied victory. It did not deny that, for the moment, the Allied cause lacked luster, but it evoked the vision of a rainbow on the horizon which presaged a break in the storm and it appealed to the neutrals to lend a hand in sweeping away the clouds in the murky sky.

It was a counterblast against the dictators. Hitler and Mussolini in resplendent uniforms had met in Rome, Berlin, Berchtesgaden, and at the Brenner Pass where they had "heiled" each other as conquering heroes, as if they already had victory tucked away in their knapsacks. At Placentia Bay Churchill and Roosevelt aimed to inject an element of doubt into the Axis pretensions.

Churchill's quest for moral and material assistance was almost boundless, and part of his genius reposed in his capacity to indulge his desire. American willingness to assist him in his difficult task was generous, and its boosted his and his country's morale, for during the first two years of his premiership England's war record was largely a succession of retreats and defeats.

Month after month elapsed without any serious diminution in isolationism in the United States, but on December 7, 1941, Japan came to Churchill's rescue. As he was tuning in on the evening news, he heard the report that the Japanese had attacked the American fleet at Pearl Harbor. He immediately got this information confirmed by a long-distance call to Roosevelt. In reply, the President said, "We are in the same boat now," and this was true, but Churchill aimed to occupy the rudder-seat. On November 11, he had announced that in the event of a war between the United States and Japan, he would declare war on Tokyo within the hour, and so he did, even before Washington issued its declaration.

The Prime Minister's reaction to the attack on Pearl Harbor was a synthesis of relief, excitement and exultation, and he gave voice to his ecstasy:

So we had won after all! Yes, after Dunkirk; after the fall of France; after the horrible episode of Oran; after the threat of invasion, when, apart from the Air and the Navy, we were almost an unarmed people; after the deadly struggle of the U-boat war—the first battle of the Atlantic, gained by a hand's breadth; after seventeen months of lonely fighting, and nineteen months of my responsibility in dire stress, we had won the war. England would live; Britain would live; the Commonwealth of Nations and the Empire would live. . . .[22]

It is doubtful if any event during World War II, perhaps in his life, gave him the suffused satisfaction that did the American entry into World War II. As the day drew to a close he was "saturated and satiated with emotion and sensation." In that state of elation he "went to bed and slept the sleep of the saved and thankful."[23]

CHAPTER XI

Strategic Military Decisions

WHEN CHURCHILL WOKE UP ON THE MORNING OF DECEMBER 8, 1941, following the bombing of Pearl Harbor he developed a fixation that a meeting with Roosevelt was imperative. His object was not to extend personal condolences to the President for the tragic naval catastrophe in Hawaii, but to thwart any possible American design to concentrate its military efforts against the Japanese and thereby leave England alone to deal with Hitler in the West.

Later there would be considerable basis for his concern, for at the end of 1942 there were as many American troops in the Far East as there were in England, 350,000 in each theater.[1] Of the army aircraft then in operation outside the United States, approximately one-third flew against Japan, and even as late as 1944 there were more landing craft in service in the Pacific than there were in northwestern Europe.[2]

Churchill left England for the Arcadia Conference on December 12, and arrived in Washington on December 22. Discussions between Roosevelt and Churchill commenced almost immediately upon arrival of the Prime Minister and his retinue at the White House.

Churchill's major motive in going to Washington was to secure American approval of his program of defeating Hitler first and then settling accounts with Mussolini and Hirohito later. Roosevelt and his staff endorsed the Prime Minister's general strategy. Once the Fuehrer should have been given passage to Valhalla, Mussolini and Hirohito would soon join him there. On the other hand, a prior defeat of Japan and Italy would still leave Hitler in Central Europe, a threat to anyone upon whom he should focus his greed and rapacity.

To coordinate the military objectives of the two countries, Churchill and Roosevelt confirmed the establishment of a

Combined Chiefs of Staff Committee of the two countries. Actually the Chiefs of Staff of England and the United States had held joint meetings since January, 1941, eleven months before the United States entered the war. World War I had glaringly demonstrated the ineffectiveness of separate commands; this had resulted in a lack of coordination among the British, French and the Americans, in consequence of which their attacks were rarely as effective as they should have been. Roosevelt and Churchill were determined to prevent repetition of past errors.

The Combined Chiefs of Staff drew up a strategic plan for the defeat of the Axis. It provided for:[3]

1. Increased bombardment of Germany. Churchill was then of the opinion that the combined air forces of the United States and Britain could bomb Germany into defeat.
2. Maintenance of a spirit of revolt among the subjugated peoples in German-occupied countries.
3. Acquisition of allies.
4. Assistance to Russia by every means, except a cross-Channel invasion. This might be feasible later, thought Churchill, although he lacked enthusiasm for such a venture.
5. A joint British-American expedition into North Africa, to which Roosevelt gave his approval, chiefly because he believed it was deleterious to the morale of hundreds of thousands of troops to be idle.
6. A possible invasion of the Continent, either from across the Mediterranean, from Turkey into the Balkans, or possibly through landings in Western Europe.

Another benefit which accrued from the creation of the Combined Chiefs of Staff Committee was the enhanced authority of the military chiefs which enabled them to restrain the President and the Prime Minister when they espoused campaigns that were military aberrations. The intention was not so much to limit the authority of Roosevelt as it was to curtail Churchill whose brain emitted a constant flow of military designs for the defeat of the enemies. All of these plans needed screening, for, while some of them were brilliant, others were eccentric, and they were all expounded and defended with vigor and passion. Henry Stimson, the American Secretary of War, maintained that Roosevelt and

Churchill needed "balancing restraint of carefully organized staff service."[4]

In one of the first sessions between Roosevelt and Churchill, at Placentia Bay in August, 1941, the President had indicated to the Prime Minister the advisability of drafting broad plans for the prosecution of the war. Forthwith Churchill produced a document for the organization of the Grand Alliance with which to oppose the dictators. In its original form it comprised the United States, Great Britain and Northern Ireland, the Soviet Union, the Dominions of Canada, South Africa, Australia, New Zealand, as well as Belgium, China, Czechoslovakia, Greece, Luxembourg, the Netherlands, Norway, Poland, Yugoslavia, and various South American countries. These countries were to bind themselves to

1. Employ their full resources, military or economic, against those of the Tripartite Pact and its adherents with which such government is at war.
2. ... Cooperate with the governments signatory hereto, and not to make a separate peace with the enemies.

Thus was formed the military alliance whose members were to strive jointly for Allied victory. Roosevelt, Churchill, Soong, and Litvinov signed this Declaration of United Nations in the White House on January 1, 1942, and the other twenty-two nations affixed their signatures later.[5] Churchill considered this step to be a further assurance that Old Ben would eventually peal out the victory chimes.

For the more immediate future, Churchill with all of his dynamism sponsored plans for Allied control of the Mediterranean Sea. His first move toward that achievement called for the invasion of North Africa to which Roosevelt gave his approval. "Gymnast," its code name, was adopted as the major campaign of 1942.

On December 26, Churchill made a speech to a joint session of Congress. It was one of the better oratorical efforts of his career. The occasion demanded excellence, for it was the first time that he had addressed a foreign legislature. Greatly to the amusement of his audience, he remarked, "I cannot help reflecting that if my father had been an American and my mother British, instead of the other way around, I might have got here on my own." The part of the speech which aroused the greatest applause was the rhetorical question regarding the Japanese attack on Pearl Harbor: "It becomes still more difficult to reconcile Japanese action with prudence and sanity. What kind of people do they think we are?"[6]

It was time for courage, ingenuity, and defiance, for both England and the United States had suffered a series of grievous defeats. The Japanese had overrun Malaya and were pouring into the Philippines. They had taken Guam, Wake Island, and Hong Kong. Much of the Pacific was becoming a Japanese lake. Some Americans feared a Japanese invasion of the west coast of the United States.

When there was little occasion for optimism, Churchill had borne all of the reverses with a gallant and courageous composure. For a dozen years before the outbreak of World War II, he had striven in vain to rouse England to its peril, only to be rewarded with haughty snubs and disdainful indifference from party colleagues. Finally his heart registered a warning and a protest. On the morning of December 27, while in the White House, he summoned Sir Charles Wilson, his personal physician, and reported that during the night he had gotten up to close a window. It fitted snugly in its frame and Churchill had exerted himself to raise it, and almost immediately he discovered that he was short of breath, and this was followed by a pain over his heart.[7] When Sir Charles Wilson, later Lord Moran, arrived, Churchill recounted his experience. Sir Charles listened to the Prime Minister's heartbeats and announced he had experienced no serious attack, that he had merely been working too hard.

Churchill was distressed for fear that Sir Charles would subject him to six weeks of intensive care and insisted that he would not submit to such a routine. He maintained that only he could operate the government, that he must do it, and no one else.[8]

Sir Charles confided in no one the nature of Churchill's coronary disturbance. He feared what such publicity might do to the administration of the British government and what the reaction might be in Germany and Italy, and in Japan. The rulers of these three countries, accustomed to differ on minor as well as major issues, would join in glee over the malady of their common enemy. The more acute Churchill's condition might have become the fiercer the Axis soldiers would have fought, and if Sir Charles did not restrict Churchill's fire-horse pace and if he should die, an avalanche of criticism would have engulfed the doctor. Sir Charles took a long chance, and urged him to shift his pace into lower gear.

But this admonition carried little weight with his patient, for two days later, on December 28, accompanied by Sir Charles, he departed for Ottawa where he spoke to the Canadian Parliament, and conferred with the cabinet. To Sir Charles, he said, "It is a great comfort to have you with me," a rare admission for Churchill.

On January 12 he left the White House for Bermuda where he addressed its Parliament. Four days later he returned by plane, for he knew that Admiral Doenitz had detailed more than twenty submarines to hunt down the *Duke of York* on its return voyage.[9] The air had become safer than the sea.

Churchill left the Arcadia Conference under the impression that he had kept it well under his control, and that most of his hopes had been incorporated into the resolutions.[10] Roosevelt had not tried to thwart his wishes. The President had been agreeable, even gracious, and the Prime Minister still regarded him as "My Good Friend." He maintained that Mrs. Roosevelt "had thought of everything that could make our stay agreeable." With her abundant graciousness and humanity, however, she did not find him a comfortable houseguest.[11]

Churchill was gratified with his achievement in Washington, and he assumed that the House would approve his accomplishments.[12] He was not wrong in his surmise, for despite some criticism in the newspapers, the House of Commons extended him a vote of confidence of 464 to 1. A message from Roosevelt cheered him: "It is fun to be in the same decade with you."[13]

There was little time to glory in successes, for failures crowded in upon him. In less than a month after his return from Washington the city of Singapore, whose fortifications had cost $400,-000,000, had fallen to the Japanese. It had been built as a defense against an attack from the sea, and almost none of its guns could fire landward. Also, its water supply came from the surrounding countryside. The Japanese could have taken the city by closing a valve, a fact they did not ignore. The loss of Singapore deprived the British of an important naval base in the Far East and compelled the navy to fall back 4,000 miles to Madagascar for stores and repairs.

Shipping losses added to the tragedy. During 1942 German submarines sank 7,750,000 tons of shipping, more than forty per cent of the total loss of the war.[14] Had this rate of sinking continued, the Anglo-American war effort would have been placed in serious jeopardy.

After Churchill's departure from Washington, Harry Hopkins, General George C. Marshall, the Chief of Staff of the Army, Henry L. Stimson, Secretary of War, and General Dwight D. Eisenhower, Chairman of the Office of Planning Division, expressed their lack of enthusiasm for the Prime Minister's North African and Mediterranean projects. While they admired Churchill as a statesman and were charmed by his personality, they did not endorse his strategy of subduing Germany by prosecuting minor campaigns hundreds of miles from the central theater. All of them feared that Russia would collapse in 1942 unless an Anglo-American army crossed the Channel and diverted a considerable German force from the East to the West.

After serious, reflective, and thorough consideration of Churchill's enthusiasm for distant expeditions, the American military leaders decided to oppose such a strategy. They disagreed with Churchill's thesis that victories on a different and distant continent would contribute materially to the defeat of Germany.

At the Arcadia Conference, General H. H. Arnold, Chief of the Army Air Force, had informed Roosevelt and Churchill that victory over Germany could be achieved by hitting it "Where it would hurt the most, where she is strongest, right across the Channel from England, using the shortest and most direct route to Berlin."[15] American officers, almost without exception, disapproved of sideshows. Ten days after the adjournment of the Arcadia Conference, General Dwight D. Eisenhower decried the inactivity of the Allied armies. He insisted that if Russia was to be kept in the war, an Anglo-American army would have to strike at Western Europe at the earliest moment.[16]

Roosevelt was not deaf to the opposition that was stirring in army circles against the projected North African campaign, nor was he ignorant, or indifferent, to the General Staff's recommendations for a cross-Channel invasion of France. He shared the views of Hopkins and Marshall of the possibility of Russia's collapse unless Germany should be compelled to execute a diversionary movement from the Eastern to the Western front, and in the event of a Russian collapse he appreciated the frightful consequences to the other allies. A supreme effort, a crisis sacrifice if necessary, should therefore be made to prevent such a disaster.

To convince Churchill of the urgency of such an effort, Roosevelt sent Hopkins and Marshall to London. They arrived there on April 8, and Churchill, fully conscious of their purpose, gave them a cordial welcome. On the day of their coming he conceded them two hours in which to present their proposals, which he said were in accord "with the classic principles of war." Then he proceeded to enumerate the difficulties of executing their plan. Men and materials would have to be allocated to prevent a juncture of Japanese and German forces in the Middle East, for such an eventuality would seriously jeopardize Allied military efforts. There was also another difficulty involved in executing the project: the preparation for it would be revealed to the German scouts by the increased war matériel and activity at the docks. This information would lead them to strengthen their coastal defenses and this again would make landings costly in human lives. While Churchill pointed out these difficulties, he did not definitely veto the proposal.[17]

Hopkins and Marshall accepted Churchill's endorsement of the proposal with greater enthusiasm than they did his enumeration of the difficulties of its execution. They returned to Washington in the belief that he had accepted their project and so reported to Roosevelt. The President had great confidence in both Marshall and Hopkins, and looked with favor upon the plan.[18] In order to promote it further, he asked Stalin to send a high-ranking official to take part in discussions on the most efficacious means by which the United States could render assistance to the Soviet Union.

In response to this suggestion Stalin sent Molotov to the West. He stopped off in London May 21-26 for talks with Churchill. When Molotov introduced the subject of a second front in France in 1942, Churchill was reluctant to commit himself definitely to any pledge, but urged Molotov upon his return from Washington to call on him for further consideration of this possibility.

With this farewell lodged in his memory, Molotov on May 29 left for Washington, where he was graciously received by Roosevelt. After consideration of some minor problems connected with the prosecution of the war, Molotov finally pointed a direct question to the President: Could the United States and Britain land an army in France in 1942 large enough to compel Germany to withdraw forty divisions from the Eastern front?[19]

Roosevelt referred the question to General Marshall, who also attended the meeting, and he assured the President that a second front in France in 1942 could be established.[20] Since Molotov was aware of the suspicious nature of his master he asked the President for a written statement of his pledge, and this the President granted. This assurance constituted a written commitment. A Presidential press release covering this interview with Molotov declared: "In the course of conversation full understanding was reached with regard to the urgent task of creating a Second Front in France in 1942."[21]

When Molotov returned to London from his conference with Roosevelt he called on Churchill, as he had promised he would do. The Russian Foreign Commissar hoped to secure an equally unequivocal pledge of an Anglo-American landing in France as that given him by Roosevelt. In that he was disappointed, for at the conclusion of a protracted discussion with Churchill the Prime Minister handed him an aide-mémoire which bluntly served notice on the Russians that they should not expect a cross-Channel invasion in 1942 unless it should appear "sound and sensible," and he reserved for himself the prerogative of passing judgment on the merits of prospective crossings.

Churchill had specific reasons for his opposition to a cross-channel invasion at that time. Aside from a shortage of landing gear, the approximately forty German divisions in France, would, he believed, annihilate the nine-division force projected as a cross-Channel army. Furthermore, depredations by German submarines would impose heavy losses. One convoy from Northern Ireland to Murmansk had lost 23 of its 34 vessels.[22] So hazardous had the course become that England and the United States had terminated their deliveries to Russia for a period despite the protests by Stalin.

If the cross-Channel invasion should end disastrously, as it might, the consequences would be calamitous not only in regard to the course of the war, but also to Churchill's career. Two British expeditions in World War II, in which he had been intimately involved, one in Norway, and the other in Greece, had been ingloriously expelled. A third fiasco would almost inevitably have concluded his premiership.

While there was some validity to Churchill's opposition to an invasion of France, his case was weakened by the extent of British shipments of men and matériel around the Cape of Good Hope to Egypt from June, 1940, to June, 1942, during which time they delivered 6,000 planes and 4,500 tanks over a course of 12,000 miles. The width of the English Channel was only twenty miles all within aerial protection. Since the British were able to send 1,130 planes on May 30-31, 1942, to bomb Cologne, American military leaders felt confident that Britain possessed adequate air power. Any British shortage in landing craft was due to the failure of assigning them a high priority.

Nevertheless, Churchill was not going to become involved in a cross-Channel operation in 1942, perhaps never. This did not elevate Secretary of War Stimson's or General Eisenhower's appreciation of Churchill's strategic ability. Furthermore, they believed that he was determined to make them accept his military plans against their own judgment. This led them to consider the possibility of abandoning the European theater to him and turning their own efforts against Japan. The possibility of such an eventuality disturbed him, and to thwart it he sent Lord Mountbatten to the United States. He arrived in Washington at the end of May, 1942, capitalizing on his charm and persuasiveness to induce the American Chiefs of Staff and President Roosevelt to abandon their cross-Channel project. As a substitute he asked them to consider an invasion of Norway, and if this were not to their taste, he proposed the conquest of North Africa. He pressed the latter project with as much vigor as he could for he knew that Churchill favored this plan. Some Americans were susceptible to this approach, for they believed that if Hitler should take Dakar he would gain a base for the conquest of South America. Lord Louis Mountbatten added that by taking North Africa themselves the Allies would deny Dakar to the Fuehrer.

The American Chiefs of Staff listened to Lord Louis but clung to their convictions. They maintained that Molotov had been given a pledge and that it should be redeemed. As Roosevelt listened to this discussion he was keenly disappointed, for England and the United States had thousands of men who were ready for action but were merely marking time. He wanted them to exchange blows with the Germans. He still viewed the Russians as being in a precarious position. Anglo-American delay in extension of aid might result in a Russian military debacle. England and the United States would then have to face a Hitler fortified with Russia's resources.

Mountbatten had failed to shake Roosevelt and his military chiefs who shared his views. All of them maintained that the Russians were engaging and killing more German soldiers and destroying more German matériel than all the other twenty-five nations combined.[23] On that account it seemed imperative to Marshall that no effort be spared in preventing a Russian military disaster.[24]

For three weeks Mountbatten strove unsuccessfully to divert the American military chiefs away from the cross-Channel project. Churchill began to fear that the Americans might concentrate their efforts against the Japanese, and to prevent this he came to the United States on June 19, 1942; discussions between the President and the Prime Minister began almost immediately upon his entrance into the White House.

Churchill knew that Roosevelt abhorred the idleness of a vast horde of soldiers. The President maintained that dormancy seriously impaired their fighting spirit, and the longer the inaction the greater the stagnation. Churchill had just the corrective for this: North Africa.

Since Mountbatten had already swayed Roosevelt toward that point of view, he was a little more susceptible than he might otherwise have been. And since Churchill had a unique charisma, it was difficult to be impervious to either his appeal or his injunction. Even Admiral Fisher, the crusty old seadog, had confessed: "I am sure I am right, I am sure I am right, but he is always convincing me against my will. I hear him talk and he seems to make difficulties vanish. . . . "[25] And Admiral King, who had no love for Churchill, acknowledged after having listened to him that if the Prime Minister had asked him for his "favorite watch he would cheerfully have surrendered it."[26] After having been subjected to such a radiant personality and such lucid arguments, Roosevelt changed his mind about a North African campaign.

Marshall and his Chiefs of Staff, however, were not disposed to surrender either their watches or their convictions. They still recognized the obligation they had assumed by their pledge to Molotov. They still believed that unless they came to Russia's rescue it would succumb. Nor would they agree to Churchill's military schemes of defeating Germany by victories in Bardia and Benghazi; they demanded blows against Bremen and Berlin.[27]

The justification for this insistence was heightened by German successes during the summer of 1942. Hitler's troops were surging into the Caucasus, and his submarines were establishing new records for tonnage sunk. Allied shipping losses exceeded construction by the ratio of five to two. This was the critical period of the war, for Russia was teetering on the verge of collapse and Hitler trembling on the edge of victory. If ever Russia needed diversion of German troops to the West, this was the time.

In the summer of 1942 Churchill was not seeking additional adventure. During his sojourn in Washington Roosevelt informed him of General Rommel's capture of Tobruk.[28] This, combined with military and naval disasters in the Far East, depressed Churchill's popularity to a new low level. On his return from Washington he faced a Parliament some of whose members were clamoring for his surrender of the Defense Ministry. An attempted vote of censure, however, was overwhelmingly rejected, but among the malcontents doubt and dissent were still smouldering.

The national mood being what it was, Churchill was not disposed to ruffle the House of Commons still more, and after consultation with his Imperial General Staff, Sledgehammer, the cross-Channel invasion, on July 25, was rejected by the British government.[29] That body insisted that it offered no chance of success, chiefly because of the superior German force in northwestern France, and the shortage of landing craft. Furthermore, they would not be able to put it into operation until late autumn when the English Channel, though narrow, was difficult to negotiate with small craft. Another factor which the Prime Minister held against the cross-Channel project was that it might turn into a catastrophic defeat. Failure would interfere with the prosecution of an invasion in 1943.

Americans were deeply disappointed that the British should have taken so significant a decision without consulting them.

Harry Hopkins voiced the mood of the American Chiefs of Staff: "I am damned depressed."[30]

At a British Chiefs of Staff meeting in London on December 8, 1941, the day following the attack on Pearl Harbor, Churchill was asked if he planned to continue the cautious approach to the American leaders that he had pursued before the Japanese attack and when American opinion was still in flux on the question of entering the war; he replied with a leer, "Oh, that was the way we talked to her when we were wooing her; now that she is in the harem, we talk quite differently."[31]

The American military leaders almost instantaneously observed the shift from the "Romeo" to the Marlborough mood, and they reacted expeditiously. They became inclined to accept his views only if they coincided with their own. Henceforth they did not regard him as infallible, and they made little effort to hide their hostility when they could not agree with his designs.

Churchill did not let this alter his military strategy. He was all the more resolved to exploit Roosevelt's yen to establish an Anglo-American front against the Germans some place, and so effectively did he promote this idea that Roosevelt announced, on July 24, 1942, his decision to send an army, in collaboration with the British force, into North Africa. Roosevelt believed that this would not necessarily preclude a cross-Channel attack in 1943.

The American Chiefs of Staff thought otherwise, and strove to prevent the North African campaign. It deprived them of their master plan.[32] General Eisenhower maintained that Torch, the North African project, could well go down "as the blackest day in history."[33] He considered it "strategically unsound as an operation either to support Roundup (then the code name for cross-Channel invasion) or as a means of rendering assistance to Russia." If it were to be carried out it should be executed on the assumption that Russia would inevitably be defeated and that North Africa would constitute a favorable base of operations against Germany in the struggle that would follow.[34] In his *Crusade in Europe* he did not endorse Torch, but emphatically favored "the attempt to seize a small bridgehead on the northwest coast of France."[35] Furthermore, he believed that the involvement in North Africa would preclude a cross-Channel landing in 1943.[36]

Marshall contemplated resignation as Chief of Staff of the

Army rather than having any part in Torch.[37] Before its initiation General MacArthur called it "absolutely useless."[38] Roosevelt rarely ignored the decisions of his staff officers but in this case he overruled his generals and ordered them to prosecute Torch. Churchill was pleased, for he had eluded the prosecution of a cross-Channel landing, and he had maneuvered the Americans into an area of combat from which they might not be able to extricate themselves until Germany should have been greatly weakened, or defeated. Furthermore, he was strongly inclined to believe that a cross-Channel operation would not be necessary. Russian attacks from the east, American thrusts from the south, and air attacks cascading bombs from a thousand planes would, he believed, make the Germans consider peace preferable to all this terror. Churchill felt no pangs of conscience in not satisfying the Russian hope and expectation of an invasion of northwestern France. And yet, for a short moment on December 3, as he conferred with General Alan Brooke, his Chief of the General Staff, he confessed: " . . . We must establish a Western Front, and what is more, we promised Stalin we should do so when we were in Moscow." General Brooke interrupted him, "No, *we* did not promise."[39] Churchill yielded to his subordinate.

The year 1942 ended disastrously for Hitler. On October 23 General Bernard Law Montgomery launched his attack at El Alamein against the army commanded by Marshal Erwin Rommel, and within ten days the losses of the Desert Fox totaled 59,000 killed, wounded, or captured. Of these 34,000 were Germans. Of his original army of 96,000 men only 34,000 remained.

On November 8, 1942, an Anglo-American force of 150,000 men disembarked from 500 transports escorted by 350 naval vessels at Oran, Algiers, and Casablanca. In the action one ship was sunk, but not a single life was lost. Torch had begun to blaze but it soon began to sputter as the heavy winter rains transformed the unpaved clay roads into gummy ruts. Not until May 7, 1943, did these forces, and Montgomery's Eighth Army from the east, compress the German and Italian troops into Tunis where they held out until May 13, and then 267,000 of them surrendered. Among them were sixteen German and ten Italian generals.

On the Russian front the German drama developed into an even greater tragedy for the Fuehrer. Early in November the German Sixth Army of twenty German and two Rumanian divisions under the command of General Friedrich Paulus was surrounded by Russian forces at Stalingrad. When Paulus requested permission to break out and retreat, Hitler screamed, "I won't leave the Volga! I won't go back from the Volga!" He ordered Paulus to remain and assured him that he would sustain him by air. Goering, eager to reinstate himself in the good graces of the Fuehrer, volunteered to execute the project. Russian marksmanship reduced the receipt of food and arms to a trickle. Hitler then sent General Erich Fritz von Manstein to release the Sixth Army from its fearful embrace, only to be beaten off with frightful losses. On January 30, 1943, General Paulus surrendered with 91,000 soldiers, the remnants of the army of 285,000 men that he had had two months earlier. Henceforth with rare exceptions, the Germans were on the defensive.

Hitler's bane was Churchill's bonus. Stalin had demonstrated that Russia was not in immediate distress. Anglo-American strategy, therefore, need not be formulated on the basis of preventing a Russian collapse. For that reason Churchill could devote his time and energy not merely to resist a possible German invasion but to the advancement of British interests.

A major one of these was the restoration of British dominance in the Mediterranean Sea. That accomplishment, he thought, would demoralize Italy, and facilitate the intervention of Turkey with its forty-five divisions on the Allied side. This would open the Dardanelles for the shipment of war matériel to Russia. With the Turks on his side, whose army he aimed to equip with modern weapons and competent English officers, he envisaged a Balkan front which would be a serious embarrassment to Hitler after the loss of one army at Stalingrad and another at El Alamein. Later in the event of a cross-Channel invasion, Hitler would be a less ferocious enemy.

Even before these Allied victories both Roosevelt and Churchill realized the necessity of holding another conference in which to consider plans for the prosecution of the war. Casablanca was chosen as the site, and the date for the opening session was set for January 14, 1943.

The Prime Minister and the President, aided by their respective staffs formulated their major projects for the ensuing campaigns:[40]

1. Liquidation of the submarine menace.
2. Increased bombing of Germany.
3. Increased shipment of matériel to Russia.
4. Greater American effort in the Pacific.
5. More active operation of the British in the Mediterranean.
6. Incitation of the people in occupied countries to rebel.

Churchill wanted to eliminate Italy from the war, and to occupy the islands of the Mediterranean, but consideration of these projects was deferred until a later date. His repeated expressions of interest in establishing complete control of the Mediterranean fortified the suspicion of American officers that he was determined to block a cross-Channel landing to France, except on his own terms.

Churchill's and Marshall's interpretation of an invasion of Germany were by no means identical. Churchill's design embraced numerous small incursions in diverse regions to confound and confuse the Germans, already then possessing too few troops to meet all these intrusions. Marshall's invasion plan called for a massive and powerful invasion force designed to paralyze opposition and to win the war. Churchill favored a flexible strategy which would leave England and the United States capable of shifting their attack to take advantage of German weakness at a given point. As the war progressed, American production and mobilization increased in volume and variety, and by 1943, it exceeded the British. With superiority in materials and men Americans eventually exercised increasing influence and power in the formulation of strategic decisions.[41]

One of the major problems at Casablanca was to reconcile these divergent military plans. Roosevelt had favored the inclusion of Stalin at the Casablanca Conference, for he believed that personal confrontation would be conducive to the sublimation of different points of view. Churchill, on the other hand, did not pine for the presence of Stalin. The Prime Minister at times found it sufficiently perplexing and exhausting to deal with Roosevelt alone. To include Stalin would compound the complexities of the negotiations. The Soviet leader had been invited to participate, but he had declined on the ground that his presence was needed in Russia. Later he realized that his absence was a mistake for Churchill and Roosevelt, he believed, acted as if they were the Almighty's impresarios in pursuit of their own goals.

Owing to the fact that Hitler had been thrown on the defensive by his defeats at El Alamein and Stalingrad, the question of the nature of the terms that would be imposed upon the dictator countries was widely discussed in both capitalist and Communist countries. Among the people deeply concerned with the question in the West were the Prime Minister and the President. On January 7, 1943, before Roosevelt left Washington for the Casablanca Conference, he had informed his advisers that he intended to proclaim at the Conference a rousing slogan: "Unconditional Surrender," as the basis for peace, and upon his arrival at Casablanca he had counseled with Churchill on the matter. Churchill, on January 20, 1943, inquired of his cabinet its opinion of the slogan. Both the President and the Prime Minister, therefore, had given the question of terms for the dictator countries considerable thought. Consequently, on January 24, when Roosevelt met the representatives of the press, and one of its members inquired if unconditional surrender terms would be imposed upon the defeated,[42] he replied with spontaneity in the affirmative, and as long as he lived he made no apologies for his response.

Churchill, who was present, endorsed Roosevelt's statement.[43] He later declared that any difference of opinion between himself and Roosevelt would have been injurious to the effectiveness of the prosecution of the war. The Prime Minister later wanted Italy excluded from the "unconditional surrender" terms, because he believed that easier terms would have insured an earlier collapse of the Italians, and this, he thought, would stimulate a desire to submit among the Germans. On the other hand, the continuous repetition of "unconditional surrender," he believed, "would prevent the process of disintegration in Germany."[44] He was afraid that the term would congeal German opinion into unyielding resistance and thus prolong the war. To prevent such an evolution, he announced on February 22, 1944, in the House of Commons that the term "unconditional surrender" did not imply that the German people should be subjected to harsh humiliation or enslavement. The Germans, he said, should be left with no justification for grievances. They were not to be the victims of vengeance.

Churchill did not underestimate the significance of the Anglo-

American victory over the Italo-German forces in North Africa. He rated its importance with that of the Russian triumph at Stalingrad. The losses of the Germans and the Italians in the surrender at Tunis in May, 1943, were enormous both in men and matériel. Thirty per cent of their supply ships had been sunk. Finally, after four years of tortured anxiety and waiting, victory was inclining toward the British. The public, through newspapers and the radio, expressed its gratification. King George sent Churchill gracious congratulatory commendation.

For Churchill the Fascist-Nazi surrender at Tunis was not only a military victory, but also a personal and political triumph. Henceforth the opposition in the House of Commons was silenced. When the oracle held forth even Lady Astor muffled her snarling criticism. This enabled him to formulate and impose his military strategy with little regard for the reaction in the House of Commons.

With his authoritarian personality, fortified by military victories, Churchill became increasingly dominant, if not domineering, in his relations with members of Parliament and even with members of his cabinet. According to Mackenzie King, the Canadian Premier, he "bullied Attlee" and treated other members of the cabinet like a lot of schoolboys frightened by the headmaster.

Churchill envisaged greater victories, and additional notes from George VI. To effectuate these, he and his staff induced the Americans to cooperate with them in the conquest of Sicily, after which, to the painful disappointment of Marshall, Eisenhower, and Stimson, Churchill then inveigled Roosevelt into approving an invasion of Italy. Until the Americans and the Russians at Teheran agreed on future steps Churchill could always claim shortage of landing gear or some other item as justification for postponing Overlord, the cross-Channel invasion of France.

Arrangements were made whereby a British army was to advance up the east coast of the Italian peninsula, and an American army to proceed along the west coast. Churchill had hoped to accelerate the advance of these troops, defeat the Italian and German forces, and then unite the Anglo-American units, invade Yugoslavia, and proceed up to Vienna. This grand design remained unrealized, for German resistance stiffened, and the Appenine Mountains were not designed for winter campaigning.

The Anglo-American advance was reduced to an average of a mile a day, and the leg of Italy was 365 days long. The languid northward pace of the Allied army led Aneurin Bevan, Churchill's proverbial disputant, to insist that Italy was not Europe's soft underbelly, but its backbone.[45] Bevan regretted that the advance was so slow and confessed, "Indeed, I am bound to say, if the House will forgive the metaphor, that the Allied Command have approached the Italian mainland like an old man approaching a young bride, fascinated, sluggish, and apprehensive."[46]

Long before this objective reached fulfillment, Roosevelt, Churchill, and Madame and Marshal Chiang Kai-shek met from November 23 to 26, 1943, at Cairo, chiefly to consider the military situation in the Far East. Japan had occupied all the Chinese seacoast towns and was strangling China. There was acute danger of Chinese economic suffocation and military collapse. This probability disturbed Roosevelt, for he realized that in such an eventuality Japan would be able to mobilize all of China's resources against the United States. The President wanted to succor China by opening a transport route from the Bay of Bengal to Chungking in southwestern China.

With this project Churchill had no sympathy. This was an Asiatic enterprise. His concern was the defeat of Hitler to which he subordinated all other campaigns. An attack in the Bay of Bengal would necessitate the use of landing craft which he, with Marlborough determination, wanted to reserve for his Mediterranean, Aegean, and Balkan operations. With persistence and dynamism he still strove to induce Turkey to enter the war. With courtesy and perseverance its leaders deflected his appeals.

All the members of the Cairo Conference were of one mind, however, on the subject of reducing the status of Japan. They drafted a communiqué which called for the loss of all the territories which Japan had incorporated since World War I. Formosa, the Pescadores Islands, and Manchuria should be restored to China. Korea "should also become free and independent."

Almost as soon as the Cairo Conference adjourned on November 26, 1943, Roosevelt and Churchill, with their staffs, proceeded to Teheran where they found Stalin already present. Churchill immediately took up residence at the British Embassy, and Roosevelt at the American. The President had not been there more than fifteen minutes when Stalin called on him and informed him that there was a plot afoot to assassinate him. For the sake of his comfort and security he invited Roosevelt to reside in the Russian embassy where the meetings were to be held. To Churchill's annoyance, Roosevelt accepted. The following day Stalin asked Roosevelt to have lunch with him and he accepted. Churchill not wanting to be completely isolated asked the President to have lunch with him the next day but Roosevelt declined for fear that Stalin and his commissars would construe this as Anglo-American conspiracy. Churchill did not appreciate Roosevelt's rejection of his invitation and announced that he "could take rebuffs as well as the next one."

Roosevelt was eager to convince Stalin that the conference would not be dominated by an Anglo-American cabal. To that end the President inquired of Churchill whether he might twit him about his smoking, drinking, his pink baby-faced countenance and various eccentricities, to all of which Churchill yielded assent; and Roosevelt entered into the venture with American enterprise and Dutch perseverance to the point that Churchill angered and his face reddened. Stalin at first seemed uninterested but eventually burst into loud laughter. Roosevelt then knew that he had scored a diplomatic success through this simulated personal intimacy.

Later in conversation with William Bullitt, the President declared that he believed that Stalin was primarily interested in the security of the Soviet Union, and that if the United States and Britain would convince him of their peaceful intentions Stalin would conduct himself like a gentleman among gentlemen.

Churchill did not concede that much confidence in Stalin's virtue. The President, nevertheless, believed that he had the confidence of Stalin to a greater degree than Churchill did, and on that account he insisted that he could negotiate more effectively with Stalin than could the Prime Minister.[47]

In spite of this divergence this conference yielded more pleasure to the participants than any other during the war. Stalin appeared in a new marshal's uniform, and Churchill presented him with a gold sword in commemoration of Russia's victory over the Germans at Stalingrad.

In previous conferences with Roosevelt, Churchill had enacted the big-brother role, but by the end of 1943 Britain's physical inferiority denied its Prime Minister the role of an equal or superior to his diplomatic colleagues. They had fixed tenure assured in a democratic constitution, or embodied in a dictatorship. Churchill on the other hand, was the leader of a House of Commons holding sway over a vast empire. He was, therefore, vulnerable to forces to which both Stalin and Roosevelt were immune. What made Churchill's position all the more hazardous was that Roosevelt was in sympathy with the separatist tendencies within the British Empire, and Stalin wasted no tears over the Prime Minister's sorrows.

The most significant problem that came under consideration at Teheran was the opening of a second front in northern and western France. In previous meetings Churchill had been able to postpone the date, or evade the issue. With Stalin supporting Roosevelt, Churchill had to accept the decisions of the majority. The conference adopted a resolution which called for an invasion of France in May, 1944.

Stalin was pleased. After many delays and deferments it now seemed to him that assistance from the West was to materialize. To clinch the matter he inquired whether a commander of the expedition had been selected; when an embarrassed negative was given. Stalin inquired bluntly if it was not about time to do so. Both Roosevelt and Churchill were in a predicament, for Churchill had assured Brooke that he would get the nod, and Roosevelt had pledged the command to Marshall. Both the President and the Prime Minister, for different reasons, had to abjure their commitments. Churchill came to realize that the French might be more inclined to resist a British commander than an American; Roosevelt, upon reflecting upon his dependence upon Marshall, realized how much he was needed in Washington.

Marshall, being the key man in the whole war effort, was vitally necessary where he was. Both Marshall and Brooke were disappointed, but neither one ever uttered a complaint, and each continued to execute his duties as if he had experienced no remorse. On February 7, 1943, Churchill had called on Eisenhower in Algiers to assay him with a view to his appointment as commander-in-chief of an Anglo-American expedition in Europe. Eisenhower passed the qualifying test. Early in December, 1943, in Tunis, Roosevelt took Eisenhower for a ride in an automobile and the President said, "Well, Ike, you are going to command Overlord,"[48] and that settled the matter.

Eisenhower was relieved of his Mediterranean command and returned to the United States for consultations with Marshall, Stimson, and the President in preparation for directing the cross-Channel invasion of France.

After the designation of General Eisenhower as Commander-in-Chief of the Allied forces of invasion, the Teheran Conference considered the basic problems confronting it.

Chief among these was the Polish. It was no easy matter to delineate Poland's boundaries. At the Conference which closed World War I Clemenceau, Lloyd George, and Wilson, none of whom wasted love on the Bolsheviks, designated the Curzon Line as the western boundary of the Soviet Union. This was acceptable to everyone except the Poles.

During the Civil War in Russia (1917-1921) the Poles advanced into Russia, and, with generous British and French assistance, defeated the Bolsheviks, and, on March 18, 1921 imposed the Treaty of Riga on Russia. It advanced the Polish frontier more than 100 miles east beyond the Curzon Line. So it remained until defeated the Bolsheviks, and, on March 18, 1921, imposed the Fourth Partition on Poland, the territory east of the Curzon Line falling to the Soviet Union.

At the Teheran Conference it was realized that the Poles would demand territory east of the Curzon Line. Stalin confuted that claim by the statement that the region had been assigned to the Bolsheviks in 1919 by Wilson, Clemenceau, and Lloyd George, and that he could do no less for his country than his enemies had arranged. Roosevelt, at the moment, was hamstrung politically for, with an election in the offing, he could not afford to sacrifice millions of Polish votes in order to do justice to Russia or to ingratiate himself with Stalin. Churchill was equally embarrassed, for though he would have liked to do as much for Stalin as Lloyd George had done for Lenin, he felt under some obligation and gratitude to the thousands of Poles who had fought, not only for Warsaw, but also for London during World War II.[49] In the end the diplomats of 1943 evaded all binding commitments by endorsing Russian claims to the territory east of the Curzon Line, and consoling the Poles with the possibility of reimbursement by the acquisition of German territory in the west. Further consideration was given to this question at the Yalta Conference in February, 1945, at which time Churchill maintained that Russia's territorial demand on its western borders was not unreasonable. His benevolence toward Poland sprang not only from a sense of justice, but also because he wanted that country to be sufficiently powerful to offer resistance to its two neighbors.

By the time of the Teheran Conference, German defeat was pretty well assured, unless something very remotely possible should happen. Therefore, the three negotiators eschewed conflict among themselves and postponed definitive solutions until Germany's surrender. Since parts of Russia had been devastated, it was not surprising that Stalin proposed stern terms. He insisted upon the death penalty for 50,000 top German military and civilian leaders. Churchill was aghast at this figure. Roosevelt interjected a compromise figure of 49,000, but this was not the quality of humor that Churchill appreciated. He left the room. He later declared that he favored disarming Germany, but he also quoted Burke to the effect that a whole nation could not be indicted. Punish the criminals, he urged, and then forget the hatred.

With regard to territorial adjustments after the war Churchill favored the separation of Prussia from the other German states and its establishment as a completely separate political entity.

The Teheran Conference added little if anything to the stature of Churchill. Throughout the sessions he found himself in quasi-isolation, for Stalin and Roosevelt had greater mutual sympathy for each other's aims and objectives than they did for Churchill and his points of view. Both believed that he was more interested in advancing England's imperial plans than in promoting Germany's defeat. He always maintained that wars were fought for the realization of political objectives, and already as 1943 was drawing to a close he was adjusting England to its prospective international interests. His profoundly deep interest in occupying the Balkan area was not so much to assure those countries democratic institutions as to prevent the establishment of Soviet domination there. When American troops landed in southern France on August 4, 1944, he denounced the venture as "sheer folly." He confessed that he had fought "tooth and nail" to prevent the campaign. Then he rued the fact that those ten divisions were not made available for his Balkan designs.[50]

To him the advance of the Russians into the Balkans was a serious peril for all Western Europe. "Good God," he said, "can't you see that the Russians are spreading across Europe like a tide; they have invaded Poland, and there is nothing to prevent them from marching into Turkey and Greece,"[51] and, as he reflected upon their objective after that, he shuddered.

Upon dissolution of the Teheran Conference, Roosevelt and Churchill departed for another session at Cairo. They arrived there on December 2 and remained in session until December 6. Stalin at Teheran had assured Roosevelt that as soon as Hitler should have been defeated he would enter the war against Japan. To Churchill this was a great relief for Allied use of Chinese bases for bombing of Japan would no longer be necessary since bombing planes could take off from bases in Eastern Siberia for attacks on Japan. Churchill was, therefore, more averse than ever to an Anglo-American campaign in Burma, and that was its deathblow.

Churchill again renewed his attempt to induce Turkey to enter the war, but Inönü remained graciously adamant against participation; Churchill sustained another blow. There was one more in store for him; since Turkey refused to enter the war, the American Chiefs of Staff refused to provide landing craft for an invasion of Rhodes.

Each disappointment had exacerbated his predisposition to pneumonia. An incipient cold afflicted him at Teheran, and Lord Moran in vain exhausted his medical ingenuity to check it. The Prime Minister's condition grew progressively acute and he was soon the victim of another attack of pneumonia.[52] On December 10, 1943, he was removed to Carthage where he recuperated. On January 14, he was flown to Gibraltar where he boarded the *King George V*, and a few days later he was back in London. For almost two months England had fought the war without his direction, a credit to the system which he had developed, and to the loyalty and competence of his subordinates.

CHAPTER XII

Cross-Channel Invasion

DESPITE CHURCHILL'S EAGERNESS FOR AN INVASION OF SOUTHEAST-
ern Europe, the entry into northwestern France occurred on
June 6, 1944, at which time 326,000 men in 4,000 ships and several smaller vessels landed on the coast of Normandy. Within
twenty-five days American and British merchant vessels had
delivered more than 500,000 tons of supplies.[1]

To facilitate the occupation of the invaded territory 11,000
British and American airplanes had bombed bridges, railways,
and highways so thoroughly that the transit of German troops
from Ghent to Normandy at one time required nine days because
of the circuitous routes which they had to follow. Churchill
called the invasion "the most complicated and difficult that had
ever taken place." To accomplish the feat British and American
engineers had constructed two artificial docks, each weighing
75,000 tons. These were towed across the Channel during the
night of June 5 and 6, and rammed into the French shore in such
a manner that the unloading of supplies began almost immediately upon the arrival of the troops. Within twenty-four hours
250,000 men had landed on the beaches. By June 12 sixteen
allied divisions occupied parts of northwestern France.[2] One
hundred seventy-seven thousand vehicles had been landed in
France.[3]

Hitler also contributed to the success of the invasion, for he
had forbidden Field Marshal Gerd von Rundstedt, the German
commander in the west, from utilizing two available tank divisions against the invaders, for the Fuehrer wished to learn the
nature of the invasion before engaging them. Furthermore, after
having given this order he went to bed, and before doing so he
gave orders that he was not to be disturbed until three o'clock
in the afternoon. Upon waking he issued an order to his commander to liquidate the invasion that very night.[4]

Before the departure of the expedition Churchill had developed so much enthusiasm for the enterprise that he was determined to join it. To prevent his doing so required all the authority that inhered in General Eisenhower, the Combined Chiefs of Staff, the British government, and the royal prerogative. The Prime Minister, however, consoled himself by reporting to Stalin on June 6 that "Everything has started off well."[5] The Soviet leader acknowledged, on the same day, his great pleasure with the inauguration of the landings.

Four days later, on June 10, General Montgomery informed the Prime Minister that the situation was sufficiently stable for him to receive guests, and Churchill, accompanied by Field Marshal Jan Smuts, landed, without incident, on the French shore. Montgomery's army by that time had already driven the Germans eight miles inland. Churchill took a lively interest in surveying the bridgehead, sat down to a delectable lunch, returned to the destroyer which had conveyed them across the Channel, and "slept soundly on the four-hour voyage back to Portsmouth."[6]

On June 14 Churchill dispatched an account of his visit to the war front to Marshal Stalin. The Prime Minister now gave the Marshal the kind of report which for three years he had yearned to receive. Though tardy, it was highly welcome. Churchill also apprised Roosevelt of his trip to the battle front. He opened his report by informing the President, "I had a jolly time on the beaches and inland," and concluded, "How I wish you were here!"

One reason for his jubilation was that casualties in the cross-Channel project had not been so high as he had anticipated. American casualties during the first twenty-four hours of assault were reckoned at 6,603, of which number 1,465 were killed, 3,184 were wounded, 1,928 were missing, and 26 were captured. The Canadians suffered 946 casualties of which 335 were killed. British casualties have been reckoned at between 2,500 and 3,000.[7] During the first ten days of the invasion, 15,000 Americans were either killed, wounded, or missing in action, not enough to "redden the English Channel with the blood of American and British youths," as Churchill had feared.

June 6, 1944, was a day of double jubilation, for in addition to the successful cross-Channel landing, General Alexander reported his capture of Rome. Though the expulsion of the Germans from the Eternal City came almost eight months after it had at first been expected, the event lightened the hearts of all Englishmen, and, not least, that of Churchill.

The mood of exultation created by these two military triumphs was followed by the news of a new and awesome death-dealing weapon. As early as November, 1939, the British intelligence service had learned that the Germans were doing research on rockets for military purposes.[8] The research was centered in Peenemünde, a city on the Baltic coast of Germany. The British did not ignore these reports, for in May, 1942, they had dispatched aerial photographers to secure pictures of these locations. These pictures authenticated the reports of a mysterious activity in the research center there. In October the Germans launched their first missile, and this was soon followed by others. Accounts of these achievements reached Downing Street and aroused Churchill's concern.

What disturbed him still more were reports from reconnaissance flights of ominous structures which resembled ski slides. In an effort to secure as much information as possible about these edifices, the British made an aerial survey of the coastal regions opposite England. Through this effort they located ninety-five of the ninety-six towers which had been erected. The most plausible explanation of these structures was that they were launching sites for missiles. These threatening edifices aroused not only Churchill's interest but also his anxiety. His instinct for self-preservation led him to order the towers blasted to splinters and left that assignment to the British and American air forces. They opened their efforts with an explosive drenching of Peenemünde. On the night of August 17, 1943, 571 British bombers dropped their destructive cargoes upon the experimental station and warehouses. Since it was not a good night for bombing the damage was not so great as had been desired, and yet it resulted in considerable demolition, enough to induce the Germans to change the location of production and experimentation to caverns in the Harz Mountains. Flight training centers were moved to Poland.

The price of the first bombing of Peenemünde was not a bargain-counter figure, for the British lost forty planes, while others limped back to England seriously wounded. But Churchill derived consolation from the enterprise for the bombing imposed a delay in production of missiles.[9]

During one of the German practice launchings a bomb failed to negotiate a proper ascent and landed in the Bug River, where the Germans left it. The following night Polish engineers rescued it, made a technical autopsy, and one of them took all the details to England. There the British acquired definite information about their peril.

As Defense Minister, Churchill inaugurated two measures to minimize the holocaust in store for his country. The approach to London, which would be the main target of the missiles, was divided into three zones. The first of these comprised a balloon network immediately surrounding the city. Beyond this was a belt of anti-missile batteries which were to blast away at the approaching missiles. Above and beyond all this hovered an array of thirty fighter planes which were on continuous guard against the intruders.[10]

The Prime Minister's next measure to minimize the anticipated onslaught was a continuous aerial bombardment of launching sites; this bombardment frequently resulted in serious damage, and, therefore, delayed inception of the attack on London.

The V-1 bomb, the first type to land in England, was twenty-four feet in length and had a wingspread of seventeen and one-half feet. Its warhead weighed 1,870 pounds, and it traveled 350 miles an hour. Because of its relatively slow speed it warned its victims of its approach and also enabled fighter planes to pursue them and shoot them down.

Despite Allied bombing of launching sites the Germans finally, on June 13, inaugurated the missile attack on London by dispatching four V-1s across the channel. Three of them went astray and only one reached the outskirts of the capital. The British at first, perhaps to bolster their morale, regarded the bomb as a minor nuisance, an aerial clown. But two nights later 300 V-1s fell upon the city and dissipated any facetious interpretation of the weapon.[11] Ten weeks later a million Londoners had evacuated their city while millions of others shuddered at the thought of being subjected to another blitz, and the Germans gloried in the effectiveness of their *Vergeltungswaffe* (vengeance weapon).

Their delight, however, was of short duration, for the skill of the British in combating the bomb was remarkable. By late August they were shooting down 97 per cent of the missiles,[12] and on September 1, 1944, the last V-1 bomb was fired across the Channel.

The Germans, however, were justified in feeling some gratification, for their V-1 weapons had wrecked almost a million homes. Furthermore, the Allied effort against the V-1 had cost them 100,000 tons of explosives and the loss of 450 planes. All of this was diverted from their military effort against other installations in Germany. Furthermore, the Anglo-American effort to neutralize the V-1 had compelled them to divert several squadrons of fighter planes from participation in the fighting on the Continent. A surprisingly large quantity of matériel and technical equipment had been deflected from other war needs.

The British enjoyed but brief respite in their triumph over the V-1 bomb, for within a week after the cessation of its flight, on September 8, 1944, the Germans instituted the flight of the V-2, a rocket. It was forty-six feet in length and five and one-half feet in diameter. It carried a warhead of 2,000 pounds of liquid oxygen. Because it flew in the stratosphere at a speed of 3,000 miles an hour, no allied weapon could destroy it. The only means of eliminating it was the destruction of its launching site or its storage. Its maximum range of 220 miles enabled it to take off from sites farther removed from the Channel than those of the V-1. Since its speed was greater than that of sound, its approach was inaudible.

CASUALTIES CAUSED BY FLYING BOMBS AND ROCKETS
ON THE UNITED KINGDOM, 1944-1945[13]

	Number		Killed by		Seriously injured by	
	Bombs	Rockets	Bombs	Rockets	Bombs	Rockets
Totals	5,890	1,054	5,835	2,855	16,762	6,268
In London	2,563	517	5,373	2,642	15,258	5,670
Elsewhere	3,327	537	462	213	1,504	598

During the worst of the bombing General Eisenhower inquired of the Prime Minister whether he should change his battle plan and divert troops from their initially assigned regiments in order to expedite the capture of launching sites. Churchill replied in the negative.

The Allies were delayed in their advance into France when their tanks attempted to negotiate the crossing of the hedgerows and became stalled with their thin bottom surfaces exposed to the rifle fire of the German soldiers. This took a heavy toll of the tank drivers. This situation perplexed the whole American officer corps. After three weeks a sergeant finally solved the problem by welding prongs to the forward part of the tanks which enabled them to tear openings in the hedges through which they could then pass.

Eisenhower's forces in early August comprised twenty American divisions, thirteen British, three Canadian, one Polish, and one French.[14] In southern France an army of 100,000 men under the command of General Patch threatened the German forces in that region. This led Hitler to order their evacuation, and to take Marshal Pétain with them. Churchill had vigorously opposed the dispatch of Allied troops into this sector for he was eager to utilize them in the Mediterranean and Aegean seas.

The Allied forces had prosecuted so aggressive an attack against the Germans that the latter were badly shattered.[15] By the end of July Eisenhower believed that victory was almost within his grasp.

On August 25 the Allies took Paris, and brought General Charles de Gaulle to the French capital. He was no favorite of Roosevelt, but Churchill had supported him and his cause. The French acknowledged him as their leader.

Some months before that even Hitler had designated General Dietrich von Choltitz to command the German garrison in Paris, and had ordered him to destroy the city rather than surrender it to the Anglo-American forces. Because of his past ruthless conduct he was known as "The man who never wavered in the execution of an order," but as the armies of Great Britain and the United States approached Paris, he refused to apply the torch to it. He surrendered the city not to the Anglo-American forces but to the French Government with General de Gaulle as its head.[16]

With the capture of Paris the Allied army officers believed that German defeat was near. All that was needed for the collapse of the Nazi forces in the West, they assumed, was an aggressive attack which would deny the Germans the opportunity to regroup. Unfortunately for the British and American forces, they needed to regroup too. Furthermore, they needed vast quantities of supplies in almost all categories. Owing to the inadequate French transportation facilities these shortages were not made up for several months, and this enabled the Germans to regroup and reinforce their armies, and to resist.

Eisenhower had hoped to defeat the German armies before they should retreat and find refuge behind the Siegfried Line. In this both he and the British Chiefs of Staff were disappointed. They were reluctant to puncture this wide defensive wall, for it frowned defiance against all such efforts. They, therefore, attempted on September 17 to execute a vast air lift of three divisions into Holland, but courageous and dramatic as this was, it ended in failure.

Eisenhower, therefore, had no alternative but to pierce the Siegfried Line. Along some of its length it was studded with seventy pillboxes to the mile, and some of these were large enough to accommodate from ten to twelve men. These were guarded by sharp-toothed tank traps and mine fields. Interspersed among all these obstacles were thousands of field pieces of all calibers to a depth of twenty-six miles.

On September 15 the Americans launched their drive against Aachen, one of the key points in the line. On October 16, after 85 per cent of the houses had been destroyed, the German commander surrendered. This, however, was merely a dent and not a rupture in the wall. The limited success did not dishearten the attackers. During the autumn the Allies exploited their destructive talent to puncture the German defensive line, but they failed to penetrate it.

German efforts to defend the line of fortification had been expensive; the total losses since June had been 400,000 killed or long-term wounded. These casualties seriously diminished German human and material resources.

Faced with this situation, Marshal Gerd von Rundstedt, commander of the German forces in the West, recalled a Clausewitzian aphorism: "He who is hard pressed will regard the greatest daring as the greatest wisdom." German intelligence had discovered that a seventy-five mile sector from Trier to Monschau was defended by only three divisions, and these of inferior quality. This situation induced Rundstedt to execute another Clausewitzian maxim. He announced to his troops: "We gamble everything now, we cannot fail." A bold plunge might insure victory, he thought. Continued resistance would inevitably end in collapse.

Rundstedt's objective was to capture Antwerp, and if that action should succeed, he aimed to envelop the whole northern Allied army. On December 16, 1944, Rundstedt with an army of 250,000 men, 1,200 tanks, and hundreds of jet planes, initiated a surprise attack. "All hell broke loose" on a forty-mile front, and the Germans advanced fifty miles. To check this drive Eisenhower summoned 1,000,000 men, 3,000 tanks, and 10,000 planes. By January 15, 1945, these forces had driven the Germans back to their former position fewer in number and weaker than they had been before they initiated their drive.

The British press severely criticized Eisenhower for having a front line so weak that the Germans could force it back so effectively and so far. Furthermore, most Englishmen endorsed General Montgomery's strategy in preference to Eisenhower's. General Rundstedt's military strategy, weak though the German forces were in comparison with the Anglo-Americans, corroborated in their minds Montgomery's strategic contentions. The English public supported their own compatriot as against a foreigner.

Rundstedt's serious threat to the American line emboldened Montgomery in his criticism of Eisenhower. He contended, "It was always clear to me that Ike and I were miles apart when it came to the conduct of the war."[17] Montgomery insisted upon a massive and powerful thrust through the German line in a narrow sector, followed by sweeping flank attacks to paralyze and defeat the enemy.[18] Eisenhower, on the other hand, favored the less dramatic and safer approach of attacking all along the line of the enemy until it should have become so weak that it could no longer resist.[19] He was also conscious of the possibility of the capture by the Germans of an army that had penetrated their line. Such a defeat would be catastrophic. Montgomery insisted that Eisenhower's approach was wasteful of human and material resources.[20]

Churchill, with his fondness for drama, was sympathetic

toward Montgomery's strategy; within a week after Montgomery had taken Eisenhower to task, the Prime Minister, in a corroboratory vein, registered his disapproval of Eisenhower's strategy to President Roosevelt. He opened his attack on Eisenhower's strategy with an appreciation of the Allied army's accomplishments since D-Day, its capture of Paris, Metz, and Strasbourg. Having thus glazed the victim of his attack with courtesies and compliments, he launched an assault against Eisenhower's strategy: the Allied forces had not yet reached the Rhine, the landing of fourteen divisions in southern France constituted military stupidity, the absence of great victories in France had bred frustration in Italy.[21]

With the moral and diplomatic support of his Prime Minister, Montgomery became all the more vehement in his criticism of Eisenhower. So abominable did Eisenhower regard Montgomery's conduct that he issued Monty a blunt challenge to the effect that if he felt that he, Eisenhower, was so incompetent as he maintained, then the relationship between the two should be referred to "higher authorities for any action they may choose to take, however drastic."

A few days later Eisenhower received Montgomery's abject reply in which he assured Ike of his high appreciation of his ability and pledged himself to unquestioned loyalty. He closed his letter with "Your very devoted and loyal subordinate."[22]

However, Montgomery's devotion to his Prime Minister, and his own conceptions of strategy took precedence over his loyalty to his immediate commander, for he persisted in agitating in favor of a powerful thrust through the German line.

CHAPTER XIII

Formula for Peace

IN THE MIDST OF ACRID CONTROVERSY OVER THE MILITARY STRATEGY to be followed by the Allied Armies on the western front, Churchill, Roosevelt, and Stalin felt the need of another conference to make preparations for the peace that glimmered on the horizon. This conference at Yalta, Crimea, served not only to consider past differences, but also to introduce new bones of contention. Throughout the conference, Churchill witnessed his influence declining, not because he personally had lapsed, but owing to his country's diminutive size in comparison with his mammoth allies. The vastness of the British Empire added little force to his arguments. Furthermore, Roosevelt and Stalin, by this time, held similar views on many world problems. This the President revealed in an undated letter to Stalin during the early period of the conference. In it he avowed, "I am determined that there shall be no breach between ourselves and the Soviet Union."[1] In a second letter during the same period he said, "I hope that I do not have to assure you that the United States will never lend its support to any provisional government of Poland that would be inimical to your interests."[2] Partly because of these letters Churchill titled the concluding volume of his war memoirs: *Triumph and Tragedy*.

The Prime Minister was more eager for the assembling of the conference than either Roosevelt or Stalin was, chiefly because he wanted important decisions concluded before the Soviet Union's forces should have occupied territory in Western Europe. Contrariwise, the Marshal wanted the conference delayed until his forces should have spread over vaster regions that he coveted. Roosevelt, heavily involved in his fourth presidential election, followed by the inaugural, refused to be hurried. Churchill, therefore, had to wait upon the convenience of others, a singularity at odds with his character.

During the early years of the war, Churchill's and his allies' main concern had been escape from defeat. Toward the end of 1944 they had to assume responsibility for victory. This compelled them to seek a world devoid of Fuehrers and Duces, totalitarianism and oligarchism, master races and helots, a world fit for human beings in which they could live and develop their personalities and capacities free from want and fear.

Churchill could ignore the promotion of his country's interests no less than the other leaders. He aimed to restore England to the best of its past, among that, imperialism. Above all he wished to secure a peace that would assure England as much power, prosperity, and prestige as possible.

Churchill was conscious of his task at Crimea. What saddened him was his awareness that though he transcended his diplomatic colleagues in ability, their countries exceeded his in size, productivity, and power. England's prodigious war effort had reduced it from its role of a super power. He was, however, rarely without expedients. In this situation he aimed to capitalize upon the fraternal benevolence of his "good friend" in Washington. But he discovered that Roosevelt's knight-errantry was no longer so readily available as it had been earlier. Consequently, even before Churchill's departure for the conference he was mournful about his presence there.

He, nevertheless, appealed to the President for a meeting of the two before their sessions in Crimea. Roosevelt declined, chiefly because he did not want Stalin to arrive at Yalta with a fixation that he would be confronted by an Anglo-American cabal. On January 20, the President did send Harry Hopkins to London to collaborate with Churchill on the main issues to be raised at the conference. Roosevelt also sent his Chiefs of Staff to meet their British confreres at Malta several days before his own arrival there. This was some consolation to Churchill, although meager, for neither Hopkins nor Marshall was to participate in the negotiations or in the final decision-making.

On February 2, Roosevelt arrived on the cruiser *Quincy* at Valletta, the chief Maltese harbor, for discussions with Churchill. It was the day before they were to set out on their flight to the diplomatic gathering.

When Churchill met Roosevelt, the Prime Minister thought the President looked "frail and ill." Roosevelt was not only sick;

he was a dying man. Because of this he was not properly briefed for the diplomatic sessions. The State Department had provided him with adequate files of information on the subjects that would be considered at the conference,[3] but he had made no attempt to use them.[4] The laborious and exhausting effort to assure himself another term in the White House had depleted his energy.

The Russians had exerted themselves to provide comfortable accommodations for their foreign visitors. This was no small achievement, for as the Germans had retreated they had ransacked and looted all human habitations. Discarded material they had put to the torch. Among the structures that had escaped demolition were the palaces of Vorontzov, which was assigned to the British delegation, the Yuzupov Palace, which the Russians had reserved for themselves, and Livadia Palace, built in 1911 for the Tsar, which they assigned to the Americans. In it the sessions were held. To prepare the buildings for occupation the Russians had flown all of the equipment of three Moscow hotels to Yalta. Rooms were crowded. Five American generals occupied one room, and ten colonels another. Harry Hopkins, bedfast with illness, was given a room of his own from which he scarcely emerged during the entire conference. Churchill later maintained that "every effort was made by our host to ensure our comfort."[5] Stalin did not neglect his responsibility as host, for on the day after the British arrived, he called on Churchill and the two had an agreeable discussion about the progress of the war.[6] Even though Stalin had an aversion to British or American troops on the Balkans or in Russia, he now asked Churchill to transfer a few divisions from Italy to Yugoslavia and Hungary. For two years the Prime Minister had begged Roosevelt and Marshall for just such an expedition and to his profound regret, it had been denied him.[7]

The delegates to the Yalta Conference had not assembled primarily to draft plans for the defeat of Germany, for by the opening of 1945 that was already quite well assured. Roosevelt, Churchill, and Stalin had convened in the role of caretakers of a disorganized continent following the anticipated defeat of the Fuehrer.

According to Churchill the most important problem was the reconstitution of Poland, for it lay at the vortex of a Europe physically, politically, and socially seriously injured. Its restoration involved the manipulation of many sensitive and perplexing problems whose attempted solution would arouse meager appreciation and might easily inflame angry passions.

Churchill felt under a deep obligation to Poland, for Britain had gone to war in 1939 to protect it against German aggression, and the British had done very little, if anything, to shield it. When the Germans struck, ten thousand Polish airmen managed to escape, first to Rumania and later to France, where they fought in behalf of the Third Republic. When Paris surrendered the Poles fled to England and there they rendered valorous and valuable service to the R.A.F. in resisting the Blitz. Churchill was appreciative.

He had additional reasons for feeling under some obligation to Warsaw, for one hundred and fifty thousand Poles had fought shoulder to shoulder with the British in Italy and later in France. On that account he was eager to assure the Poles a reward for their sacrifices, "a home where they could organize their own lives as they wished." He maintained that he had no material interest in Poland.[8]

Churchill was also motivated by political factors. He abhorred the prospect of expansion of Russian influence into Western Europe. Toward the end of the war, even while he was fighting Hitler and his Nazism, he was resisting Stalin and his Communism. The Prime Minister hoped to preserve Poland as a democratic, capitalist bastion against Marxist penetration. To achieve that he supported the Polish Government-in-Exile, in London, in its endeavor to return to rule in Warsaw on democratic principles, after the expulsion of the Germans.

In this attempt Churchill met vigorous opposition from Stalin and the Lublin Government within Poland. Its members had endured and survived persecution for five years, and insisted that they reflected the wishes of a majority of the Polish people more accurately than could the government in exile, which had been out of intimate touch with the people for the duration of the war and had dwelt in personal comfort and security. The members of the London Government were unable to appreciate the change in the minds and the moods of the Polish people. Stalin embraced this view. From February 4 to 11 the forensic tug of war went on between Stalin and Churchill. After an extended dialectical skirmish Churchill reluctantly agreed to a compromise which provided for a provisional government that should comprise representatives from both factions. This was later to be succeeded by "free and unfettered" elections. There was considerable difference in the Churchill and the Stalin interpretation of what constituted "free and unfettered" balloting. Furthermore, the presence of a Russian army of 1,600,000 soldiers in Poland was not conducive to "free and unfettered" voting; in consequence, Poland became increasingly Communist oriented.

Another problem which Churchill realized would demand settlement was the boundaries of Poland. He knew that Russia would demand the reestablishment of the Curzon Line as its western boundary. Stalin repeated his contention that the Russian people would insist that he should do as much for Russia as Lloyd George, Clemenceau, and Wilson had done in 1919. Churchill did not attempt to refute this claim. But Russia's gain in this matter would be Poland's loss and it would have to be compensated for from some other source. The Poles demanded East Prussia and the region as far west as the Oder and Neisse Rivers. Churchill approved their demands as far west as the Oder River, but not to the Western Neisse.[9] He wanted a Poland large enough to defend itself against encroachment by either Russia or Germany, and he also insisted upon a Germany powerful enough to guard Western Europe against expansion toward the west. He also maintained that the influx of 6,000,000 East Germans into West Germany would result in overcrowding. Stalin, on the other hand, maintained that this augmentation would merely compensate for those who had been killed in the war. Neither Stalin nor Churchill would accept the other's contention. Poland occupied the territory as far west as the Oder-Neisse, and the definitive boundary was left unresolved until March 1972 when Poland and West Germany agreed that those rivers should constitute the boundary between Poland and East Germany.[10] By this treaty Poland acquired 40,000 square miles of former German territory east of the Oder-Neisse Rivers.

At Yalta Stalin reserved for Russia the northern part of East Prussia. Since the Russian troops were already in occupation of the region, there was little that Churchill could do about it. At Yalta he hoped to delay the establishment of definitive boundaries of the constituent states of the region.

In line with this objective he opposed partition of Germany into five states as advocated by Roosevelt. With some hesitation he considered the creation of two German states, one with Prussia and Berlin as the core, and the other comprising Austria and the South German States. He wanted a Germany strong enough to thwart Russian advance into the West. His object was not so much to impose penalties for the past as to provide safeguards for the future.

All the countries which had been victims of German aggression were eager for reimbursement for the destruction inflicted on them by the Germans. The Russians and the French were especially desirous of compensation, while Norway, Denmark, and the Low Countries had also accumulated accounts for which they expected atonement. Roosevelt would limit American reimbursement to the confiscation of German assets in the United States. Churchill reminded his Yalta colleagues that Britain had also suffered losses from the sky and from beneath the waves. He maintained that it would be impossible for Germany to satisfy the demands of all the claimants. He reminded Stalin that after World War I Germany had dispensed only about one billion pounds in reparation, and that most of this had come from American loans.[11] He admitted that the destruction within Russia had been so immense that justice demanded some repayment. The question was in what form. Though Churchill was no expert in finance, he realized that the transfer of marks would produce unfortunate consequences. And yet he did not want to place a premium upon international robbery and vandalism. On that account he favored a reparations bill of $20 billion, half of which was to be assigned to Russia, and the rest to lesser claimants, and that these obligations should be met within ten years.[12]

The question then arose in what form these payments were to be made. Churchill ruled out monetary transfers, with which Stalin and Roosevelt were in agreement. Stalin proposed the confiscation of 80 per cent of the German heavy industry, i.e., "iron and steel, metal working, engineering, chemicals, electrical engineering, etc." All military production and aviation as well as synthetic petroleum should be prohibited completely. About 20 per cent of German heavy industry would be left, and this would be enough for the real need of the German economy.

Churchill did not think that Germany would be able to meet

these demands.[13] Furthermore, he feared that the imposition of too burdensome an obligation might lead the Germans to find escape in the adoption of a Communist regime. This he believed would be worse than nonpayment of reparations.

He also insisted that France was entitled to a share of the reparations, chiefly because of the destruction by the British and the American planes preceding the invasion. Stalin took issue with this proposal. He reminded Churchill that the French had fought like cowards at the beginning of the struggle, and that at no time since their surrender in 1940 had they maintained a military force as large as those of the Lublin Poles or Yugoslavia. He did not think that France was entitled to either assistance or distinction.[14]

Because of these sharply contrasting views Roosevelt proposed that a committee should be appointed to consider the problem, and to submit a report on the subject. Churchill approved, and so did Stalin, and the decision was delayed until the meeting at Potsdam six months later.

Churchill was also appalled and shocked by a toast of Stalin's in which he proposed the execution of thousands of Germans and demanded reparations paid in labor by German prisoners of war.

Churchill raised the question of the division of Germany into zones of occupation by the victorious nations at the close of the fighting. This was arranged without any vigorous dissent from any of the conferees. But when Churchill proposed that France should be assigned a zone, Stalin dissented. Only after Roosevelt had supported Churchill did the Marshal yield a point and concede France a zone, on the condition that it should be carved from the British and American zones. Churchill raised no objection to this.

Stalin, however, discovered that one concession made to Churchill generated another request, and it was not long in coming; the Prime Minister wanted France represented on the Administrative Council of the zones. This ignited another clash between the Prime Minister and the Marshal. The President again saved the day for Churchill by supporting him.

Churchill was very insistent upon this point for Roosevelt had announced that all American troops would be evacuated from Europe two years after the close of the war. This would leave England alone to wrestle with the bear, a prospect which he did not envision with equanimity. To guard against such an eventuality he wanted France on the Administrative Council. For the same reason Stalin wanted it excluded. France was finally conceded a seat on the Council.

Churchill reversed England's policy toward Russia's rights in the Dardanelles. During the premiership of William Pitt the Younger (1783-1801) the British adopted the practice of denying Russian ships of war passage through the Straits, and, with the exception of one brief period, they had maintained that policy until the end of World War II. The latest affirmation of the closure of the Straits was embodied in the Montreux Convention of 1936.[15] At the Crimea Conference Stalin insisted that "It was impossible to accept a situation in which Turkey had a hand on Russia's throat." Churchill voiced no dissent, and the three diplomats agreed that the Straits should thenceforth be open not only to commercial vessels but also to ships of war.[16]

Another subject which came before the Conference was Russia's involvement in the war against Japan. To Secretary of State Hull, in Moscow in 1943, Stalin had volunteered participation, and again at the Conference of Teheran the following month he had proffered Russian assistance. At neither time did he stipulate his price. At the Crimean Conference he presented his bill in advance of deliveries: the recovery of Sakhalin and the Kurile Islands; the restoration of Russian interests and rights in the Chinese Eastern and South Manchurian Railroads; the port of Dairen should be internationalized, and the naval base of Port Arthur should be restored to Russia; Russia's interests in Outer Mongolia should be respected. Stalin was to enter the war against Japan within ninety days after the close of the European phase. Roosevelt was to inform Chiang Kai-shek of the terms of this agreement and secure his approval,[17] which he did. To these conditions Chiang raised no violent objection, partly, it has been suggested, because it would have been futile to have done so, and also because he was involved in serious difficulties with the Communist Party within China. Also, Russia's demands constituted merely the restoration of its position in the Far East before the Russo-Japanese War of 1904-1905.

At the time of the negotiation of the Stalin-Roosevelt agreement for Russian intervention in the Far Eastern War, Americans generally gave their assent.[18] Even members of the armed forces generally approved the document. The common assumption was that the war against Japan would persist for at least a year after the defeat of Germany, and that it would impose a million casualties unless Russia could be induced to detain the powerful Japanese Army in Manchuria. There was yet no assurance that the atomic device would be available in time to influence the war.

When Roosevelt told Churchill of the contents of the deal with Stalin, the Prime Minister, who had taken no part in its formation, made no objection to it.[19] And when Churchill revealed its terms to the House of Commons there was scarcely a murmur of protest. Likewise, when Roosevelt divulged its provisions to Congress, its members were equally quiescent.

The American people were greatly relieved at the prospect of an earlier end to the war, and at a lower casualty cost. *The New York Herald-Tribune* called the Yalta Agreement "a remarkable document." Rarely has gratitude been so transient. As soon as victory was in closer focus the enemies of the President, and to a lesser degree, of the Prime Minister, lashed out at them and the agreement as if they had betrayed the honor of their countries.

The conference had begun on February 4, and closed on the 11th. Churchill would have preferred a few more sessions for, as he said, the reorganization of the world. Roosevelt, however, contended that his appointments with sovereigns of the Middle East prevented this. Churchill pressed him to remain and reminded him that "even the Almighty took seven days to organize the world."

Shortly before the opening of the conference Churchill envisioned the future with optimism, but as the sessions closed he was less radiant.[20] Even years later when he wrote *Triumph and Tragedy* he confessed "Our hopeful assumptions were soon to be falsified."[21]

CHAPTER XIV

The End of the War

THE CRIMEAN CONFERENCE HAD BEEN CONVENED IN ANTICIPATION of an early German collapse. After the German Sixth Army's surrender at Stalingrad and the subsequent general retreat, the remaining German forces no longer displayed their former haughty and arrogant self-confidence. The Fuehrer, formerly so exultant, could no longer conceal his despondency. Successive defeats imposed by the Russians, whom Hitler formerly had classified as "swamp animals," had infused traces of humility in his vain soul. Even he, in September, 1943, in conversation with Goebbels, confessed that he had no clear picture of a German victory.[1]

In contradistinction, the Allies grew increasingly hopeful as their image of triumph was turning into the fabric of reality. Their problem was no longer how to escape defeat but how to administer the *coup de grace,* and how to deal with the prostrate foe.

On March 7, 1945, the American army crossed the Rhine at Remagen. Within two weeks other American forces had negotiated similar passages at various places, and by April 11 more than a million men and 1,250 guns were on the eastern bank. By March 18 they had compelled 325,000 German troops in the Ruhr Pocket to surrender. Among them were thirty generals. After March 19 the Germans fought more like a fanatical mob than an organized force. There was no longer an integrated front in the West; fighting was fluid, a skirmish here, and an encounter there. American forces swept forward, and by April 12 the Ninth Army under General Simpson had advanced 250 miles in two weeks, and had also crossed the Rhine.

Montgomery who was operating farther north than the American Army, in the middle of March was 250 miles from Berlin. He arrived on the Elbe on April 11.

[186]

Meanwhile, the Russians, with an army of 1,250,000 men and 22,000 guns, on January 12, had begun their winter drive, and by February 15 they had reached the Oder 35 miles from Berlin;[2] here the German armed forces offered stubborn resistance, and slowed the Russian advance.

Even before these developments a war of words had resumed between the British and Americans on the issue of the capture of Berlin. On September 14, 1944, Eisenhower had declared, "There is no doubt whatever, in my mind, that we should concentrate all our energies and resources on a thrust to Berlin."[3] This was four months before the Conference of Crimea assembled and resolved to partition Germany into four zones, each to be under the administration of one of the Allies, the eastern zone being assigned to Russia. Within it was Berlin, 110 miles east of the zone's western border.

The assignment of Berlin to the Russian zone altered Eisenhower's attitude toward the city's capture. He decided not to seize the German capital. On March 28, without discussing the matter with the British Imperial General Staff, Eisenhower dispatched a note to Stalin in which he informed the Marshal that he would make no effort to capture Berlin.[4] This generated a verbal assault from Churchill and from his Chief of Staff, Alan Brooke.[5] Churchill, despite Berlin's assignment to the Russian zone, strove desperately to force Eisenhower to take the city and the territory as far as he could east of the capital. He was determined to thwart, as far as possible, Russian westward influence and expansion.[6] Furthermore, he felt that if the Russians should take Budapest, Vienna, and Berlin, their egotism would know no bounds. He was afraid that it would enhance their influence in West Germany and all Western Europe. He dreaded the possibility of Russian expansion with much the same aversion that he had deplored Hilterian aggression in the 1930's.[7]

In discussing the Communist issue with General Bradley on March 6, 1945, at the Allied Army Headquarters in Reims, Churchill insisted, "We shall never sit by quietly and permit a minority to force its will upon a helpless group anywhere." He cautioned General Bradley to beware of the guile of Uncle Joe. He discussed Allied, i.e., American criticism of his policies and insisted that he had "the hide, horns, and tusks of a rhinoceros," and assured his listeners that he would be as ferocious in defense of his policies as the African two-ton mammal was in the protection of its interests.[8] Eisenhower maintained that to have yielded to Churchill's insistence to take Berlin would have constituted a usurpation of the rights that each occupying country possessed in its zone. On the other hand, no resolution had been adopted at Yalta prohibiting one ally's invasion of the other's zone in pursuit of the enemy, nor had any commitment been made that Berlin's capture was reserved for the Russians. However, it may have been assumed that military etiquette and courtesy among the Allies should have inhibited one from encroaching upon the other's zone. Churchill contended that Russia's violation of international agreements during the war, specifically in the Balkans, constituted justification for the West to protect its interests wherever they were jeopardized.

Another factor which restrained Eisenhower from capturing Berlin was the danger of clashes between Russian and American forces as they would approach each other in the vicinity of the German capital.[9]

Furthermore, if the Americans had captured the city they would have been compelled to surrender it to the Russians almost immediately, anyway. This led Eisenhower to ask Bradley how many casualties the capture of Berlin would entail: Bradley replied 100,000. The Supreme Commander could not rationalize so bloody a sacrifice in behalf of Stalin, nor could he summon any justification for it to the American public.

Churchill had no intention of taking the city and excluding the Russians from it permanently, or even for an extended interval. He wanted it as a bargaining chip with which to negotiate concessions from the Russians in other areas and on other issues.

In a letter to Montgomery, on March 31, 1945, Eisenhower declared that as far as he was concerned Berlin had become "nothing but a geographical location."[10] His purpose, he said, "was to destroy the enemy's forces, and his power to resist."[11] He had made his resolve on the basis of widespread reports that fanatical Nazis were escaping to the Bavarian Alps where they would conceal themselves in caverns stocked with food, medicines, and deadly weapons, and from there prosecute a vicious guerilla war indefinitely, in their determination to rescue Germany from its enemies.[12] Eisenhower believed that it was more important to neutralize southern Alpine pockets of resistance than to capture northern cities.

Since Churchill and Montgomery took no stock in this, the Prime Minister in one of his very last messages to Roosevelt, appealed to him to divert Eisenhower from his southern campaign.[13] It was all to no avail. Marshall and the President supported Eisenhower, and Churchill had one more reason for disappointment with the close of World War II.[14]

On April 16 the Russians opened their attack on Berlin, and within a fortnight it had become a heap of rubble. Rarely in all history had so large a city been subjected to such terror and horror. Most, if not all its people, preferred submission to continuance of their torment.

Even Hitler ultimately concluded that prosecution of the war was hopeless. Proof of this fact was not needed, but it was emphasized by the report which arrived, on April 29, that Italian partisans had captured Mussolini and his mistress near Switzerland as they had tried to escape; and that both had been shot and their corpses had been subjected to execrable and humiliating indignities. Hitler still had a vivid imagination. On that same day he drafted his last will in which he designated Doenitz as his successor, after which he committed suicide.

Some days later, on May 2, the Russians captured Berlin with some 150,000 German soldiers. On May 7 General Jodl for Germany surrendered unconditionally to General Bedell Smith for the Western Allies at Reims. On the following day in Berlin Field Marshal Wilhelm Keitel on behalf of Germany surrendered unconditionally to Air Chief Marshal Tedder for England and Marshal Zhukov for the Soviet Union. The Reich which was to have endured for a thousand years fell short of its goal by 988 years, and Churchill contributed as much, or more, than anyone else for exposing the fallibility of the Fuehrer's reckoning.

Churchill, on the other hand, had realized his objective. In his first speech as Prime Minister, in the House of Commons, he had announced his goal: "Victory, victory at all costs, victory in spite of terror, victory however long and hard the road may be; for without victory there is no survival."

The war in Europe was over, but the conflict in the Pacific continued. Even after the defeat of Germany Japan resolved to continue the contest; the United States was not inclined to overlook Pearl Harbor; China was not disposed to disregard fifteen years of encroachment; Great Britain would feel uneasy in its Far Eastern possessions without humbling and weakening Japan. Unanimity, therefore, prevailed among the Allies to inflict defeat upon the Land of the Rising Sun.

Churchill, in agreement with Roosevelt and General Marshall, assumed that the subjugation of Japan would require at least a year of fighting and a million casualties unless some new weapon could be devised to shatter the fanatical intransigence of the Japanese military hierarchy.

Even before 1939 certain scientists had been conducting research on atomic energy. In Germany Otto Hahn and Lise Meitner made notable progress in 1939 by splitting the uranium atom and discovering the possibility of a chain reaction. Hahn did not fully appreciate the import of their achievement,[15] but Lise Meitner did, and she hastened to Denmark to inform Niels Bohr of their accomplishment. Bohr comprehended the significance of their success and escaped from occupied Denmark to neutral Sweden. From there the British flew him to London, and later he took passage to the United States and joined the scientists there at work on the atomic project.

Among the scientists the startling news of fission spread with the speed of underground telegraphy. Soon Eugene Wigner, Leo Szilard, Edward Teller, all Hungarians, V. Weiskopf, an Austrian, and Enrico Fermi, an Italian, as well as Sir James Chadwick, an Englishman, joined Niels Bohr and American scientists, among them Robert Oppenheimer. All of them eventually came under the Manhattan Project directed by Vannevar Bush and Leslie Groves, and after four years of cooperative research developed the atomic bomb. In July 16, 1945, the bomb was detonated. Though it weighed only thirteen pounds, its force was equivalent to 20,000 tons of TNT, four times greater than its developers had anticipated.[16] The development of this explosive had cost the United States 2.2 billion dollars or about $18 per man, woman, and child.[17]

On July 17, 1945, President Truman and Prime Minister Churchill, who both were in attendance at the Potsdam Conference, were informed about the explosion. Truman told Stalin of the new scientific weapon, and he seemed distantly interested. During the discussion which followed, the question was never raised as to whether the bomb should be used against the Japanese. Three weeks before the bomb was dropped the British Government had endorsed the use of the bomb. No responsible person associated with the prosecution of the war voiced any dissent against the use of the bomb. All the British and American leaders, however, would have preferred a peaceful surrender of the Japanese without recourse to nuclear persuasion.

In order to escape the unconditional surrender terms, the Japanese had approached Moscow in the hope of securing an intercession in their behalf. Stalin had remained noncommittal, and not even he divulged the Japanese note until after the Alamogordo explosion.

In this situation the United States, Great Britain, and China dispatched their surrender terms to Japan. These were a recapitulation of the Yalta-Cairo provisions, providing for unconditional surrender with the loss of all territory annexed since 1900. Japan's fighting forces were to be disarmed and returned to their homeland. Furthermore those guilty of cruelties and brutalities would have to stand trial.

Japan rejected these terms. This left no option for President Truman and Prime Minister Attlee. They would have to drop the bomb. Though Churchill was no longer Prime Minister, he favored the use of the bomb, for he believed that its explosion on a Japanese city might end the conflict and thereby prevent Russian participation in the Asian theater of the war.

On August 6, an American B-29 dropped a uranium bomb on Hiroshima and imposed a devastating destruction of property and loss of life.[18] This, however, did not induce the Japanese warlords to sue for peace. Because of their determination, the American Air Force on August 9 sent a second plane over Nagasaki,[19] and dropped a plutonium bomb on that city. The two bombs killed 120,000 persons, and wounded an enormous number, but even this new violence was not enough to induce the Japanese army to sue for peace. The Emperor, therefore, exercised his royal authority and requested an end to the conflict on the terms of unconditional surrender prescribed by his opponents with one exception: there was to be no interference with the status of the Emperor, to which Truman, Stalin, and Attlee gave their approval, and the war came to a close.

CHAPTER XV

Twilight and Curtain

AFTER HAVING HELPED TO RESCUE GREAT BRITAIN FROM DEFEAT, Churchill assumed that the British people in appreciation would vouchsafe him continuance in office, for he was not a "Cincinnatus eager to return to the plow." Since there had been no election in Britain for ten years, there was a general assumption that another one was due. The question was when. Churchill at first favored one in October.[1] Clement Attlee, leader of the Labour Party, preferred its postponement to the end of the war, but members of the Labour Party generally opposed delay.[2] As Churchill assessed prevailing opinion he reacted promptly and vigorously. On May 25, 1945, he dissolved the coalition government over which he had presided for five years and formed a caretaker government solely of Conservatives. On June 15, he dissolved the House of Commons, and announced a parliamentary election for July 5. This left only twenty days for the campaign. So brief a period enabled him to capitalize on his popularity incidental to his triumph over Hilter, while the brevity would prevent the opposition from organizing and popularizing its program. Churchill was not only a statesman, but also a politician.

At the opening of the campaign, Attlee believed that he and his followers "would make a good showing, but that they would be defeated." Churchill did not take issue with this contention. The Prime Minister had reasons for facing the election with confidence. Because of his unique contribution to victory during the war, he had repeatedly won smashing votes of confidence, and even in May, 1945, he had been endorsed almost unanimously by the members of the House of Commons.

Churchill rarely prosecuted any enterprise in a languid manner, and in the election of 1945 he did not deviate from his customary zeal. He participated in the electoral campaign much as if he were engaged in suppressing a general strike. He denounced Labour's doctrines as despicable and their devotees as execrable. He identified socialism with the most rabid phase of communism.[3] A socialist victory, he said, "would impose a Soviet regime which would involve queuing, rationing, lethargy, and inefficiency." He maintained that any confidential matter of the British government would without delay be transferred to Moscow. Furthermore, he warned that a Labour victory in England would induce a Communist landslide on the Continent which would be inimical to the best interests of Great Britain. He inveighed against the leaders of the Labour Party, who, during the war, had been in the coalition with him, loyal and patriotic colleagues. During the campaign he treated them as if they were prospective commissars of the British soviet system.

During the war he had been a national hero. In the election he stooped to partisan hack. Throughout the war his speeches had rung with exemplary eloquence and grandeur. In the election campaign a good many of them were ordinary harangues.

Likewise, his former enthusiasm for Mussolini and Franco exacted a price in electoral votes. His addiction to imperialism, even in imperial England, by 1945 had become a political liability, since most Englishmen had lost the Edwardian enthusiasm for empire and its advocates.

Furthermore, the Conservative Party could not then escape the blame for frustration and irritation which the war had engendered. Peace afforded the opportunity for voicing these annoyances.

Churchill's real liability was his affiliation with the Conservative Party. In the preceding election, in 1935, it had won by a landslide, and it had governed, not primarily in England's interest, but to promote the prosperity, comfort, and security of the nobility and the well-to-do. Whatever it had done for the masses was with some justification regarded as bribes to keep them submissive; it had not sought alleviation of their hardships or enlargement of their opportunities. On the other hand, the Conservatives had striven to preserve as much security, privilege, and luxury for the upper orders as they believed twentieth-century England would tolerate.

In the nineteen-thirties an element of the British population, chiefly among the Conservatives, had viewed Hitler with admiration. To them he had seemed a hero, a man they could trust. During World War II, however, the Fuehrer's ferocity, terror, and ruthlessness dispelled whatever basis they may have had for their appreciation of him.

While British admirers of Hitler could abandon their esteem of the Fuehrer, they could not, in the public mind, dissociate themselves from their past; and Hitler's suicide, when defeat stared him in the face, liquidated the last remnants of the "golden opinions" any Englishman may have cherished for him. Politically, those who had lauded him reaped the backlash of his last act of disrepute, and this was registered in the balloting booths.

The British people had not forgotten Churchill's heroic gallantry in his opposition to the Conservatives' coquetry with peril. They admired him for his magnificent patriotism, resolute perseverance, and inflexible courage from 1930 to 1940. But their main objective in balloting was not to bestow favors for the past, but to inaugurate improvements for the future.

Furthermore Labour had no confidence in the postwar plan of Lord Woolton, the Conservative Minister of Reconstruction. In form it bore some resemblance to Labour's program, but workingmen, and many intellectuals, lacked confidence in the Conservatives' integrity to execute it with fidelity. They viewed it as political bait rather than a genuine blueprint for the future. Labour preferred its own prescription for the days ahead.

Clement Richard Attlee (1883-1967), leader of the Labour Party, was a graduate of Oxford University, a social worker turned politician. When World War I broke out he renounced his pacifism, joined the army, fought at Gallipoli, in Mesopotamia, and in France. At the close of the war he was a major. In 1922 he entered the House of Commons from Limehouse. He held posts in the Labour Governments of 1924 and 1929. He entered Churchill's cabinet in 1941 and became Deputy Prime Minister in 1942, which assignment he held until 1945.

Labour based its appeal upon public ownership of the Bank of England, inland transportation, fuel and power industries, and the iron and steel industries. It insisted upon state supervision and control of monopolies and cartels, prices, housing, and the export program. It favored the ultimate nationalization of the land. It pledged itself to impose compulsory school attendance to the age of sixteen, to provide free medical care, and social insurance from the cradle to the grave. It would improve the relations among the nations of the world by eliminating war as a device for the settlement of international differences.

By mutating these objectives into legislation Labour hoped to make the working class the ruling class.

During the election campaign Churchill made forty speeches which were marked by invective, vilification, and generalities.[4] In very few of them did he come to grips with the postwar problems that intimately concerned the people, and on that account many did not believe that he would foster their interests.

During the war the whole population had cooperated for a common cause, and had produced military equipment and civilian needs in prodigious quantities.[5] Many British citizens wished to perpetuate this efficient cooperative system rather than that which had prevailed before the war, and they insisted that this could best be done under a Labour government.

In the campaign Attlee's speeches revealed a dignified restraint in line with the best English precepts. He endorsed his party's program with earnestness and energy.

During most of the campaign Churchill felt confident that he would be returned to 10 Downing Street, and this view was shared by most of the political sages. Among the few who dissented from this assumption was Aneurin Bevan, later Minister of Health in Attlee's government, who predicted the actual results. The oracles, however, had erred in their reckoning, for the voters flung aside the Conservatives in one of the greatest landslides in British political history,[6] for Labour won 393 seats, which was more than their wartime voting strength.

RESULTS OF THE ELECTION

Parties	Seats before July, 1945	Seats after July, 1945	Popular vote in July, 1945
Conservatives	358	202	9,030,000
Labour	162	393	12,000,000
Liberals	18	10	2,280,000

While the Labour Party comprised primarily members of the lower classes, it also embraced a significant middle-class element, since its parliamentary representation included "49 university professors, 44 lawyers, 26 journalists, 15 doctors and dentists." Two hundred and twenty-nine of the socialist members of the House of Commons belonged to the Fabian Society, the intellectual elite of the Labour Party, and many of them were at ease among the finest intellects in England. Those who had come from a middle-class background, the professions, or business exceeded by nearly 25 per cent those representing trade union interests or having a working-class background. Labour elected twenty-one of the twenty-three women who won seats in the House of Commons.

The election revealed that Churchill's party had been repudiated by the country which he had saved, and he disclosed his profound disappointment with the voters' verdict and their lack of appreciation of his magnificent service. Absorbed in his grief, he mused, "This is democracy." "In a moment of victory, in one foolish afternoon," he said, he had lost the Premiership.[7] Temporarily, his milk of human kindness curdled. To Lord Moran he confessed, "It would have been better to have been killed in an airplane accident, or to have died like Roosevelt."[8]

Instead of executing a leisurely evacuation of 10 Downing Street, he made an abrupt exit. He resolved "not to remain for an hour responsible for the country's affairs." At four o'clock on July 25, the day on which the election results were publicized, he appeared at the Royal Palace and tendered his resignation to the King. "No sooner was the peril over," he said, "than they turned me out."

To the public, however, he issued a gracious farewell in which he expressed regret at being denied the opportunity to remain in office until the conclusion of the conflict. He respected the sovereignty of the majority and abided by its verdict. He paid high tribute to his colleagues in the War Cabinet, and expressed gratitude for the "unswerving support" and the many expressions of kindness which had been bestowed upon him by his fellow citizens.[9]

Clemmie, his wife, was conscious of the fact that the electoral defeat was a devastating blow to Winston, and, full of compassion, she attempted to console him: "It may well be a blessing in disguise," she said, to which he replied, "At the moment it seems well disguised."

The wound inflicted by the electorate's repudiation seared the inner recesses of his being, and though he succeeded in obliterating the psychic trauma, it never completely healed. After July 25, 1945, Churchill summoned his doctor, Lord Moran, more frequently for medical consultation and treatment than he had formerly done.

The King, in recognition of the great service which Churchill had rendered throughout the war, was also eager to soothe his anguish, and asked him to accept membership in the Order of the Garter, founded in 1348. Churchill declined. Later he confessed that since the electorate had given him the boot, he abjured the Garter.

Even though he had been deprived of the premiership, he could take comfort and consolation from the fact that his removal as First Minister constituted a repudiation of the Party rather than a censure of himself. In retrospect, he could view his administration of the government as a superb performance, superior to that of any of his contemporaries, and, perhaps, any of his predecessors. To his fellow Britons he did not remain so much a personality as a symbol of England at its very best. His benign and whimsical display of the V-sign sent the multitude into outbursts of adulation, and Churchill into a glow of happiness.

Before the announcement on July 25 of the results of the parliamentary election, Churchill had gone to Potsdam to attend the last of the great war conferences. Two other heads of state in attendance there were United States President Harry Truman and Russia's Premier Joseph Stalin. The first plenary session was held on July 17, and the final one, with Prime Minister Attlee representing Great Britain, on August 2, 1945.

None of the participants was well prepared for the diplomatic sessions. Truman was a novitiate in diplomacy for he had only recently assumed his duties as President, and Stalin had been well occupied with other Soviet problems, while Churchill had devoted his time and energy to the election campaign.

Of the three, Churchill was the most benevolent and dispassionate toward the defeated. "Hate died with their surrender," he insisted. According to him, the main purpose of the conference was not to inflict punishment upon the defeated but to evolve an era of peace and creativity. The future, he contended, called for clemency and understanding. He had exemplified his approach forty-five years earlier in his negotiations with the Boers. He wished to utilize the same principle in his treatment of the Germans, especially in situations in which it would not jeopardize British interests. He strove to prevent an environment that might produce another Hitler and World War III.

Churchill made a point of meeting Truman before Stalin would interview him. The Prime Minister wanted to immunize the President against the Communist virus. Churchill realized that small as England was in comparison with Russia, he alone could not defend his contentions against Stalin. He needed an ally and he attempted to entice Truman to function as his advocate.

By the time of the opening of the Potsdam Conference Hitler had been dead for ten weeks and Germany was prostrate. Berlin was, therefore, powerless to be obstructive. On that account each member of the conference could be more assertive of his contentions than during earlier meetings. Because of this, clashes and collisions were more frequent than in previous meetings. In this atmosphere Churchill was condemned to a more subdued role than was customary for him because Roosevelt was no longer there to support him, and Truman, though inclined to be pronunciatory, was not yet so emphatic in his verbal dueling as he was to become. Churchill, the ablest of the three and representing the smallest country, was, therefore, left without an effective second in the forensic fencing. He was unhappy in the adverse circumstances in which he found himself.

The most significant question which confronted the conference was the Polish problem. Churchill very much wanted to establish that country as a democratic bastion against the westward expansion of Communism. Stalin, on the other hand, strove to organize a tier of buffer states on Russia's western border that would be loyal to Moscow in the event of any future war. Contrariwise, Churchill felt a deep sense of obligation to the Poles. Britain had committed itself to defend the country against attack, and at no time during the entire war had England been able to materialize its pledge.

Nor had Churchill been able to protect the Poles against those whom he considered the country's own Philistine elements, the Communists. During the war they had established themselves in strategic Polish centers, and there these Marxist emissaries had exercised greater political power than Churchill's panegyrics on democracy.

Churchill was conscious of his handicap; he acceded to that which he could not control and approved terms which provided that the Poles should have a government based upon "free and unfettered" elections. This enabled Churchill to tell the Poles that he had done the best he could for them, and Stalin was able to impose his own political prescription, for neither Churchill nor Truman would resort to force to impose his constitutional preference. The Prime Minister had one more reason for concluding that tragedy was the price of triumph.

Churchill was also interested in the boundaries of Poland, for he wanted that country sufficiently large to resist Russian intrusion and adequately liberal to resist the diffusion of Communism. In 1917 he had attempted to extirpate Communism in Russia. In 1945 he hoped to limit its expansion. He could not alter the eastern boundary of Poland, for already in 1919 Lloyd George, Clemenceau, and Wilson had delineated Poland's eastern border along the Curzon Line, and this had been confirmed by the Soviet-German treaty of 1939. Churchill endorsed Poland's reimbursement in the west for its loss in the east, but he did not want the amount to be so extensive as to cripple Germany, since he already envisioned it as the keystone of opposition to a westward incursion of Soviet Russia. He approved of the Oder and Eastern Neisse Rivers as the western boundary of Poland. Stalin designated the Western Neisse as the boundary. The question was left to be decided in a later peace treaty with Germany. In the meantime Poles had surged into the disputed territory, and they, under authorization of the Warsaw government, controlled the region. To evacuate them would involve a major enterprise.

One of the cardinal policies of Britain for almost 200 years had been to deny Russian ships of war passage through the Dardanelles. Moscow had been compelled to comply with this because of the preponderance of the British navy. Tsars and Soviets alike had complied in angry disappointment. By 1945 the British Lion realized the folly of antagonizing the Russian Bear, and at Potsdam Churchill withdrew British restrictions to Russian navigation not only through the Dardanelles but through other seaways from which Britain had barred them.

While Churchill was eager to safeguard democracy and free

enterprise in Eastern Europe, Stalin was equally avid to promote Communism in the West, more specifically in Spain. On this issue Truman came to the support of Churchill, and Stalin's attempt to establish a Communist oasis in the West withered.

Similarly, Churchill strove to preserve democratic institutions in Italy. For his part, Stalin spared no effort to install Marxism in the land of Mazzini, Garibaldi, and Cavour. Before World War II Churchill had genuinely admired Mussolini, and had appealed to him in a personal letter not to join Hitler in making war upon Britain, but to no avail. The effort to subdue Italy and its Nazi legions was an exhausting struggle for the British and American forces, which Churchill could not easily dismiss from his memory. Nevertheless, so far as he was concerned, Potsdam was not a place to wreak revenge, but to establish peace, and to guard the West against the spread of Communism. On his own initiative and authority, he temporarily restored the House of Savoy and democratic institutions in Rome.

Upon losing his lease on 10 Downing Street where he had been the chief tenant for more than five years, he made a search for new quarters and located one at Hyde Park Gate, almost a mile from the House of Commons. He purchased the house immediately adjoining his residence in which his historians and secretaries could pursue their projects. He also leased a suite of rooms in the Savoy Hotel in order to be in closer proximity to the House of Commons. This became the scene of lavish entertainment, jovial and significant association of sophisticated and competent characters in all walks of life.

In 1922 Churchill had bought Chartwell, a house southeast of London, and the surrounding eighty acres for £5000. Almost immediately he commenced remodeling it to meet his needs. From 1922 to 1940 the Churchill family spent most of its time there. During the war years he had not risked dwelling there for fear that it would be a target for German airmen.

In 1945 Churchill decided to sell Chartwell. When a group of close friends learned of this, they decided to buy it and give it to the National Trust on condition that it should be preserved for the nation, and that the Churchills should be permitted to live there undisturbed during his lifetime.

Churchill's immediate objective after his electoral defeat in July, 1945, was to recover from the blow. To accomplish this he operated on the principle that the most efficacious way of healing an emotional wound was to supplant it with enjoyable experiences, and, acting upon this hypothesis, he took a renewed interest in horse racing. He maintained a stable of horses whose occupants were almost as spirited as himself. Colonist II, during his racing career, had won ten times his purchase price. Churchill had six others, although not as fleet-footed as his swiftest one. Momentarily this obliterated his desolation, but the massive psychological wound remained sensitive.

One other diversion, traveling, dissipated a host of disappointments. From ocean liner, railway coach, and airplane he disgorged his regrets over seas and continents, always accompanied by two detectives, two secretaries, and his valet. And when he wearied of these emotional absorbents, he got out his easel, paint and brushes, and duplicated nature's beauty upon his canvas.

When these expedients failed to expunge his disappointment, he, with six secretaries and four professional historians, concentrated on the writing of his war memoirs, sometimes at the rate of 8,000 words a day. Idleness in his habitation was as rare as indolence in a beehive. This labor of love further reduced the remnants of his despondency.

Contributing articles to magazines also served to distract him from his dejection. *Life* paid him a pound a word for the serial rights to his war memoirs which led him to remark, "I am not writing a book but developing a property."[10] He had superior talent in either pursuit.

The defeat of the Conservative Party in the 1945 election transferred Churchill from the majority to the minority leadership of the House of Commons. A subordinate position in any field was never to his liking, since it was irksome for him to follow anyone else's directions. His major objective in his new role was, therefore, to recover his previous one, and he made his aim clear immediately after his defeat, for he announced, "We shall return, as sure as the sun rises in the east."

While no one regarded this statement as an idle proclamation, Churchill did not expect to implement it immediately, for Labour had come to office with a large and disciplined majority. He knew that its members possessed a cohesion which defied any attempt to dislodge them. During the early years of Attlee's premiership,

Churchill pursued a temperate policy. His attendance at the sessions of the House of Commons was infrequent and irregular. His varied activities, including the writing of his war memoirs, visits to other countries, and speaking engagements, accounted in part for his absences. However, he rarely missed a Thursday session, at which time Herbert Morrison, the Majority Leader of the House of Commons, announced the parliamentary program for the ensuing week. Members of the Conservative Party did not think that this was often enough to keep him informed on the proceedings of the House. Another deviation from the customary role of a Minority Leader was his public speaking without first consulting the Conservative shadow cabinet, in consequence of which his statements too often were at variance with the policies of the Party. Furthermore, he did not take time to inform himself of committee reports. Because of these factors, some members of the Party would have been relieved by his resignation as Minority Leader. That role was contrary to his innate character and personality.

Churchill's paramount concern after World War II was anxiety for England's security. His abhorrence and fear of the Soviet Union was very obvious.[11] Even before the close of the war, Russia had demonstrated its titanic power. Its army had halted the advance of the Herculean Hitlerian horde, and then had driven it back to its own premises, and in so doing had dispelled any assumptions of its impotence. Since not even the Wehrmacht could halt its advance, there obviously was nothing to stop its drive in any direction if it should exploit its stamina. During the last few months of the war, Churchill envisioned Soviet incursion of Western Europe following the defeat of the Nazis.[12]

In 1899 Lord Salisbury in the Venezuela Dispute finally turned the issue over to the United States with assurance that he would accept the American verdict as a definitive solution. This was the beginning of British avoidance of critical differences with Washington. As the years sped by in the twentieth century, England became increasingly dependent upon the United States, and Churchill accelerated this tendency not only during his premiership, but following it. He was aware that England alone was no match for a major opponent, and he voluntarily paid a handsome price to preserve American goodwill. Repeatedly he deferred to Washington's preference or insistence. In his dependence upon the United States he made Britain an American satellite.

One country in particular, the Soviet Union, aroused Churchill's anxiety and increased his dependence upon the United States. His antipathy toward Moscow after 1917 was profound, more so than that of any other responsible Englishman, and his hostility remained vigorous until Hitler, on June 22, 1941, invaded the country. Churchill then experienced relief, elation, and ecstasy, without diluting any of his loathing toward Communism or repugnance toward Stalin. And during the war he evinced no real affection for either one.[13] He learned to respect Stalin for his ability, and to admire his armies for their competence. His obsession during the war to prosecute a Mediterranean campaign, and his desire to capture Vienna before the Russians should reach that city cannot be interpreted as anything but a profound anxiety regarding the Soviet Union's motives.

Churchill revealed suspicion of, and antipathy toward, the Russians even while London and Moscow were engaged in subduing their common enemy. During the Battle of Stalingrad, in 1942, he developed plans to prevent "Russian barbarism from overrunning Western Europe."[14] In March, 1945, while Russian armies were battering Berlin, he again manifested his distrust when, as the German soldiers were surrendering arms, he dispatched an order to General Montgomery to have them stack their weapons in such a manner that they could easily be reissued to those who had formerly fired them, if the Russians, after the capture of the city, should surge into Western Europe.

Churchill had frequently confided to Lord Moran, his doctor, his anxiety over the possibility of a Russian advance into Western Europe. When the doctor, in October, 1946, inquired when they might do so, Churchill replied, "In two or three years, perhaps sooner."[15] England alone could not prevent such an incursion. Nor could any European country mobilize an army sufficiently strong to resist a Soviet invasion. Protection of Western Europe, therefore, depended upon acquisition of an ally that could neutralize what Churchill assumed as the aggressive intentions of Moscow, and in his view only one country could do so, the one in possession of the atomic bomb. At Fulton, Missouri, on March 5, 1946, in his "Iron Curtain Speech," he appealed to

Americans, "with words that breathed and ideas that burned," to fuse their strength with West European forces to resist the Philistines of the East. While Americans had almost unlimited admiration for Churchill, they, then, lacked fervor for adventure beyond their shores. Churchill subsequently maintained that though the response to his speech was hesitant and indecisive, the United States had materialized the substance of his plea.

Clement Attlee, like Churchill, was conscious of Britain's weakness, and equally aware of Soviet strength. The Labour Prime Minister feared that Moscow might precipitately take advantage of its might in Greece and Turkey. Therefore, early in March, 1947, Attlee appealed to the United States to assume the burden of obstructing Soviet penetration in the two small states.

President Truman responded with reflex action, and induced Congress to donate $400,000,000 with which to salvage the two countries from their destitution and possible Russian absorption.

Almost simultaneously, General George Marshall, then Secretary of State, proposed to render similar assistance to other countries vulnerable to Soviet infiltration, and Congress with equal avidity enacted this suggestion into law. The organization set up to administer the Marshall Plan and successor agencies was soon functioning, and the American government until 1970 dispensed military aid under the Marshall Plan, Mutual Security Act, and the A.I.D. (Agency for International Development);[16] the Western European states secured amounts as follows:

Austria	$1,079,000,000
Belgium-Luxembourg	651,000,000
Denmark	260,000,000
Finland	42,000,000
France	4,123,000,000
Germany	2,849,000,000
Iceland	66,000,000
Ireland	146,000,000
Italy	3,028,000,000
Netherlands	761,000,000
Norway	229,000,000
Portugal	136,000,000
Spain	1,040,000,000
Sweden	99,000,000

United Kingdom	6,570,000,000
Yugoslavia	1,930,000,000
European Atomic Energy Community	54,000,000
European Coal and Steel Community	51,000,000
European Payments Union	238,000,000
Others and unspecified	508,000,000
	$23,865,000,000[17]

Churchill was impressed by the American rescue policy. Already in May, 1951, he declared in the House of Commons, "Look at the money they have given to Europe. Look at the money they have given to this country during the Socialist rule. I doubt if we should have the utopia which we enjoy without their aid. Where should we be without their assistance to Europe?"

While Churchill rejoiced over United States aid to various countries after World War II, he was keenly disappointed by Roosevelt's statement at the Yalta Conference that all American troops would be withdrawn two years after the close of the conflict. Contrary to this policy, however, and mainly because of American fear of Russian penetration into various parts of the world, American troops have been dispatched to 43 countries which the Soviet Union might occupy. By 1970 the United States maintained "375 major and 3,000 secondary bases abroad" manned by 1,001,000 men. In 1969, 291,000 of these were stationed in Europe.[18]

Churchill never passively observed an unfolding drama when it in any way involved him or his country. He renewed his supplication for European unity and American assistance. He confessed that Europe was quite incapable of defending itself, and that it would remain so for several years.[19]

But even with all the assistance that the American aid had provided, Europe remained jittery from consciousness of its weakness and its realization of Russian strength. Since the war the Soviet Union had incorporated the eastern provinces of prewar Poland, Eastern Karelia, Tuva, Estonia, Latvia, Lithuania, Bessarabia and Northern Bucovina, Petsamo, northern East Prussia, the Kurile Islands, Southern Sakhalin and Ruthenia, a total of 262,533 square miles with a population of 22,162,000, all of which, with few exceptions, had belonged to Russia in 1900. It had, by 1950, imposed a satellite status upon Poland, Rumania, Bulgaria, Czechoslovakia, and to a slight degree upon Finland, all of which comprised 469,347 square miles with a population of 73,619,000. Churchill found it difficult to rationalize all these Russian moves as a search for its security. He overlooked the fact that "fourteen times since 1800 hostile troops have crossed the western border; Minsk has suffered precisely 101 foreign occupations; Kiev has been sacked so often that its citizens have lost count, and every invader since the time of Genghis Khan has sent spies and fifth columnists ahead of his troops."[20]

What further contributed to the suspiciousness of the Russians was the action of various countries from 1917 to 1920, when Japan, France, England, Germany, Italy, Yugoslavia, Czechoslovakia, and Poland sent armies into Russia to help the White Russians in their attempt to defeat the Bolsheviks. Furthermore, these countries imposed a blockade of Russian ports. They also denied the Russian people shipments of food and drugs to reduce the violent famine and sickness. The Russians have found it difficult to overlook this interlude in their history. And Churchill's action did not add to his stature.

To dispel the prevailing mood of helplessness in Europe, Churchill already in 1946 contemplated a European Union with which to meet possible aggression, and in agreement with this apprehension Ernest Bevin, Labour's Foreign Secretary, negotiated, on March 4, 1947, the Treaty of Dunkirque between England and France. While it was directed, at the time, primarily against Germany, Churchill soon shifted its target to Moscow.

Further to protect the West against the East, Bevin on March 17, 1948, negotiated the Treaty of Brussels. Its membership comprised France, Britain, The Netherlands, Belgium, and Luxembourg. Each member pledged itself to come to the assistance of any component if it should become the victim of aggression. It also created a permanent consultative Council whose members were to meet periodically.

Though Churchill was pleased with the establishment of this aggregation of powers, he realized that it was no match for the Soviet Union. The West, he believed, was still at the mercy of the Eastern Giant. To redress the balance of strength, he sounded the alarm with speeches in Western Europe, Canada, and the United States, and these aroused the West to organize, on April 4, 1949, the North Atlantic Treaty Organization. It comprised Canada, France, Norway, Denmark, The Netherlands, Belgium, Luxembourg, Iceland, Italy, Portugal, the United States, and Great Britain. Subsequently three other countries, Greece, Turkey, and West Germany, were admitted to membership. The purpose of the organization was to obstruct the Soviet's westward drive. In reflecting upon the North Atlantic Treaty Organization, Churchill maintained that the Russians "fear the friendship of the West more than its hostility."[21]

Though the NATO countries had a population of 370,000,000, Churchill still lacked adequate assurance of safety. He, therefore, during his final premiership (1951-1955), sponsored the formation of the European Defense Community, but French refusal to ratify it consigned it to the diplomatic dump.

Churchill was disappointed. He was still determined to help strengthen the solidarity of Western Europe, and he gave his full support to the establishment of the Western European Union which became effective after its ratification in 1955. It also provided for mutual defense in case of attack.

These security pacts did not hypnotize Churchill into a sandman's repose. He was fully aware that peace pacts are fatuous unless reinforced by soldiers, tanks, and bombers. He, therefore, mounted the platform, utilized the press, and prevailed upon Parliament to prosecute a rearmament program, even before England had recovered from the last embroilment. Prior to his assumption of his last premiership in 1951, he urged enlargement of the fighting forces. This had been induced by the Czechoslovak coup d'etat in 1949, the Berlin blockade, and the North Korean invasion. In response to these developments, the British government in January, 1951, enacted a rearmament program which called for the expenditure of 4,700 million pounds over a period of three years. In prosecuting this program, Britain spent a higher percentage of its income than did any other Western nation, 7.4 per cent to 5.9 per cent in the United States. The American monopoly of atomic weapons and the loyalty of the dominions reassured Churchill as to the future.[22]

Churchill, however, wanted the support of West Germany too. On March 28, 1950, though still out of office, he announced in the House of Commons, "I see no reason why the British, French, American, and Germans should not stand in line together on honourable terms of comradeship as part of a combined system of defense."[23] He wanted a European army commanded by a European general or marshal responsible to a European council. The House of Commons, on Churchill's endorsement, enacted compulsory military training to provide the troops. He pleaded, "Why should not the Rhine become a street where Europeans meet rather than a ditch dividing hostile camps?"[24]

Further to bolster the West, he sponsored the rearmament of Western Germany. To no small degree he was responsible for the unification of the three West German zones and the establishment of a central government at Bonn.[25] West Germany, ten years after the Potsdam Conference, was accorded membership in the family of nations, largely through Churchill's influence, all of this in order to strengthen the West against a possible thrust from Moscow.

Because of the efforts at consolidating the West, fervently sponsored by Churchill, the Soviet Union could not escape a sensation of danger, and on April 13, 1949, Andrei Gromyko voiced his conviction in the U. N. General Assembly that the West was consolidating its strength against the Soviet Union:

"The circumstances which accompanied the preparation of the North Atlantic Treaty, as well as the composition of the parties for this treaty, show that this new military bloc of states situated on both shores of the Atlantic Ocean is aimed against the U.S.S.R. This is borne out by the fact that the North Atlantic Treaty, similar to the Western Union, denotes the creation of a limited grouping of States and excludes the participation of only one great power—the Soviet Union.

"It cannot be regarded as fortuitous that the initiators of the North Atlantic Alliance take such interest in the inclusion in it of States bordering on the Soviet Union. . . . This pursues the aim of securing the possibility for creating on the territory of those states military bases including air bases for attacking the Soviet Union. . . .

"Inasmuch as the North Atlantic Treaty is aimed against the U.S.S.R., it contradicts the aims and purposes of the Anglo-Soviet Treaty of 1942."

Churchill's ardor, therefore, to create security for Britain aroused apprehension and anxiety in the Soviet Union. An increasing number of people, not only in the Labour Party but in other countries as well, became disturbed by the tremulous mood he was stimulating.

* * * * *

While England's status as a world power declined after World War II, its primacy as an empire collapsed. The hypocrisy of "taking up the white man's burden" had been exposed and discredited, and mother countries too exhausted to suppress uprisings had resigned themselves to what they could not prevent.

Even before 1939 it was obvious to Britons with eyes to see, ears to hear, and hearts to feel that England's imperial swan song would soon echo around the world. Roosevelt was already beating the time to the melody, and Churchill grimaced in pain at the aria.

One of the sharpest differences, if not the sharpest, between Churchill and Roosevelt arose from the President's repeated and urgent proposals that England should concede independence to India. Churchill tolerated a generous amount of pressure from Roosevelt, but there was a limit to his endurance. When the President insisted too firmly upon independence for India, Churchill maintained that he had not become His Majesty's First Minister in order to liquidate the British Empire. He refused to regard India as a nation. He contended that it was "an abstraction. . . . It is no more a nation than Europe, or the equator." To Churchill, Empire approached the inviolable. To alter or alienate it was unpardonable folly. And for Ramsay MacDonald, who, in 1930, proposed commonwealth status for India, he had a profound repugnance.

As Prime Minister during World War II, Churchill could not let his imperial predilection completely dominate his policy, nor could he ignore India's claims, for to do so would intensify its insistence upon dominion status. Furthermore, if he did not grant its demands, Japanese troops, already in the region, might champion its cause. Churchill, therefore, in March, 1940, two months before he became Prime Minister, reversed his attitude, during England's darkest hour, and announced that as soon as possible after the war Britain would concede dominion status; that India should enjoy the same freedom and rights as the other dominions, and that it should be accorded the authority to draft its own constitution.

Two years later when the Indian Congress and the Muslim League had failed to formulate satisfactory constitutional arrangements with each other, and the Soviet Union and the United States had become allies of Britain, while Germany and Italy had been forced to take the defensive, Churchill postponed further consideration of the Indian problem until the close of the war, when Britain would be in a more favorable position to deal with a dependency.

The Labour Party which assumed office in July, 1945, lacked enthusiasm for Empire, and, on February 20, 1947, Attlee, in the House of Commons, announced that the British government would confer independence on India and that it would leave the country to its people.[26] This grant, he said, was extended on condition that the country should be divided into two states: India and Pakistan.

It is with deep grief that I watch the clattering down of the British Empire with all its glories, and all the service which it has rendered mankind. I am sure that in our hour of victory, now not so long ago, we had the power to make our solution of our difficulties which could have been honorable and lasting. Many have defended Britain against her foes. None could defend her against herself. We must face the evils that are coming upon us and that we are powerless to avert. We must do our best in these circumstances, and not exclude an expedient that may help mitigate the ruin and disaster that will follow the disappearance of Britain from the East. Let us not add to the pangs of sorrow so many of us feel, and the taint of near shame.[27]

In spite of his conviction, Churchill wrote Attlee and assured him that the Conservative Party would facilitate the enactment of the constitutional change for India.[28] Attlee on the following day answered Churchill's communication with equal courtesy.[29]

Churchill found it difficult to reconcile himself to the loss of this significant domain which had meant so much to England, and with which his family had been closely associated. Seventeen months after Attlee's announcement of the independence of India, Churchill observed in a spirit of regret and resignation:

Our imperial mission in India is at an end. We must realize that. Some day justice will be done by world opinion to our record but the chapter is closed. . . . We must look forward. It is our duty.

Whatever part we may have taken in the past, we must hope and pray for the well-being and happiness of all the people of India, and of whatever race, religion, social condition or historical character they may be. We must wish them well and do what we can to help them along the road. Sorrow may lie in our hearts, but sorrow and bitterness must be purged from them, and in our future more remote relations with India we must rise above all prejudice and partiality—and not allow our vision to be clouded by memories of glories that are gone forever. And in this temper we shall find true guidance—and indeed, only hope—in strict and faithful adherence to the underlying principles of justice and freedom which are embodied in the United Nations Organization. . . .[30]

☼   ☼   ☼   ☼   ☼

On November 2, 1917, Arthur Balfour, Foreign Secretary of Great Britain, issued what became known as the Balfour Declaration in which he assured the Jews of a "National Home" in Palestine at the close of the war. "National Home" was a new and vague diplomatic term. It was open to various interpretations, and previous pledges to the Arabs increased the complexity of the relations between the two peoples. What complicated the situation still more was Balfour's assurance that nothing should be done that was not "compatible with the freedom of the existing population, both economic and political."[31] Already in 1921, when Churchill was Secretary of State for Colonies, he perceived that if the Jews should outnumber the Arabs in Palestine they would insist upon administering the government of the domain.[32] In 1922, 11 per cent of the Palestinian population was Jewish. By 1929 it had risen to 29 per cent, and with the advent of Hitler to the chancellorship the influx of Jews into Palestine was greatly accelerated; by 1947 there were 608,000 in the country in which 1,203,000 Arabs resided.[33] Since the former were aggressive, industrious, and intelligent, Churchill, in 1920, maintained that a Jewish state "under the protection of the British Crown" would be of great advantage to Britain.[34]

Since Churchill regarded himself as a consistent friend of the Jews, President Weizmann wrote him in August, 1940, offering him 50,000 troops.[35] Churchill declined the offer for fear that Mohammedans all over the world would take countermeasures against the British. Four years later, with the Nazis and the

Fascists on the defensive, Churchill accepted the overture of the Jewish Agency for Palestine.[36]

After almost six years of fighting, peace came in 1945 to the world, but this tranquility did not embrace Palestine, a British Mandate since 1919, for there the Jews and the Arabs began fighting each other. The Arabs loathed the Jews for their restless activity. They denounced the Israelis for elevating the wages of the fellaheen (farm laborers) which compelled the Arab magnates to follow suit, and this reduced their resources for lavish and luxurious living. The Arabs feared the immigration of additional Jews in consequence of which the bloody turmoil between the two peoples would increase in volume and violence.

Many Englishmen, among them Churchill, were weary of the conflict and regretted their failure to maintain peace in the region over which they had some jurisdiction. On January 31, 1947, Churchill, then out of office, proposed in the House of Commons that Britain dissociate itself from its legal ties with Palestine, and surrender its mandate to the United Nations Organization. The Attlee government accepted this recommendation, and in May, 1948, the new state of Israel was established.[37] By that time the Palestinian problem had cost the British taxpayer £80,000,000. "This," Churchill said, "was one of the least successful disengagements from Empire since Yorktown."

❈   ❈   ❈   ❈   ❈

By mid-century enormous changes had occurred in the oil industry of the world, and this had been followed by an intensified wave of nationalism over the oil-rich areas, including Iran.[38] This movement awakened the people's pride in their country, and aroused opposition to their exploitation by foreign financial operators. When Iranians learned that American lessees in Venezuela and Europeans in Saudi Arabia before World War II had been paying royalties of 50 per cent, the Iranian minister of finance, with insistence, demanded an increase in oil royalties from the Anglo-Iranian Oil Company. Upon its refusal to comply, the Majlis (National Parliament) on May 1, 1951, nationalized the company in which the British government possessed large investments.[39]

Churchill, still out of office, deplored England's inability to impose a Palmerstonian reproof upon the Iranian government.

A number of factors inhibited it from doing so. Difficulties in Egypt, embarrassments in Malaya and Burma, and disturbances in other parts of the Empire made the lion roar like a kitten. Churchill insisted that "judged by every standard of conduct the Persian Government has been outrageous," but he added, "This must not lead us to ignore what is fair and equitable in the Persian case...." He also insisted that the Anglo-Iranian Oil Company was earning 150 per cent in profits and paying only 30 per cent to Iran.[40]

Britain could not allow this case to persist, for if it did, Churchill maintained, Moscow might intervene and supplant the British there. Originally the Anglo-Iranian Oil Company had refused to operate under a nationalized administration, in consequence of which dissent enormous quantities of oil had remained in the bowels of the earth.[41] Since this was a loss that neither the Company nor the Iranian exchequer could endure, both sides decided to arbitrate, and production was resumed. Finally on August 5, 1954, when Churchill again was Prime Minister, an agreement was reached between Iran and the consortium according to which definitive terms were reached under which the company was to operate.[42] Churchill reconciled himself to these terms, for he prized the flow of oil more than he did the glory of a futile triumph.

* * * * *

One of the significant instances of mutilation of empire occurred in the separation of Egypt from Britain. A succession of treaties between Cairo and London from 1882 to 1936 had defined the legal relationship between the two countries. To the small Egyptian aristocracy and the wealthy middle class, both suffused with a rabid sense of nationalism, each document seemed more abominable than the previous one, and the 1936 instrument aroused the most vociferous condemnation. By it Britain had pledged itself to execute the following terms by 1956:[43]

1. Terminate the military occupation of Egypt.
2. Enroll Egypt in the League of Nations.
Egypt committed itself to:
1. Aid Britain in case of war.
2. Respect Britain's right to defend the Suez Canal.

The two agreed to:

1. Continue joint administration of the Sudan.

British Governors-General of the Sudan continued to assure the Egyptians that the English sojourn there was only temporary, and that they had come, not to rule, but to serve. This affirmation of philanthropy carried little conviction among the Egyptians. A cynical skepticism was injected in the hearts of the residents along the Nile.

After World War II, shouts of "Up with Egypt, down with England," rang through the streets of Cairo, Alexandria, and other cities. It even echoed from Egypt's Foreign Office, for on August 26, 1950, while Churchill was in opposition, Mohammed Bey served notice on Sir Ralph Stevenson, British ambassador to Cairo, that Britain must evacuate Egypt and the Sudan at once, so as "to ensure complete independence of both as one integral whole."

Churchill, fervent imperialist that he was, even when he was out of office, deeply regretted Britain's expulsion from Egypt. On November 6, 1951, by this time back at 10, Downing Street, he announced in the House of Commons that he was determined to maintain his country's "rightful position in the Canal Zone in spite of the illegal and one-sided Egyptian violation of the Treaty of 1936."[44] Egypt ignored this announcement and demanded the removal of British troops that guarded the Suez Canal.[45]

Churchill was also disappointed with Egypt's attitude in financial matters. During World War II the British had brought £400,000,000 worth of commodities in Egypt on a pledge to pay for them after the war.[46] This had enabled the Egyptian upper class to enjoy a higher standard of living than almost anyone else in the world.[47] Churchill further maintained that since England had shielded Egypt from German conquest and exploitation, this should cancel whatever financial obligation that could be assessed against London.[48] The Egyptian finance minister, however, did not regard himself as that kind of accountant. The daughter moralized her mother, something new in British imperialism.

Egyptian insistence upon Britain's meeting its financial obligation, and its urgency for the establishment of its independence compelled Churchill to admit that the most England could hope for was a recognition of its right in the Canal Zone.[49] And yet he had some reservations about even this expectation for he added a word of prudence: "Here again, I think that time, within certain limits, and restraint and forebearance, may give the best chance of the crisis being successfully surmounted."[50] This mood and his cerebral hemorrhage, on June 23, 1953, facilitated the Egyptians in their escape from British suzerainty.[51]

One problem, however, remained: that of British troops in the Suez Canal Zone. On that subject negotiations between Cairo and London proceeded, and the British agreed to withdraw their forces as quickly as possible. The British, however, reserved the right to maintain 4,000 technicians there to insure the efficient operation of the canal equipment. But this did not diminish Churchill's regret over England's loss of the Gate to the Far East. Nor could he feel benevolent toward John Foster Dulles, the American Secretary of State, for his thwarting British and French efforts to recover their mastery of this strategic route.[52] Churchill regarded Dulles so dominant in directing American foreign policy that Eisenhower was "no more than a ventriloquist's doll."[53]

Churchill's determination to obstruct the Soviet Union in the West was equaled by his resolve to restrain it in the East. He helped to realize the latter objective in the Korean War of 1950-1953. After President Truman, acting upon his own initiative, had rushed American troops to the assistance of the South Koreans, he petitioned the United Nations Organization for its endorsement and support of his action. Churchill, though not Prime Minister at the time, endorsed Premier Attlee's dispatch of two British battalions to Korea despite the fact that England was already involved in its own difficulties in Malaya, Hong Kong, and the Middle East. But Churchill had an ulterior motive for endorsing British support of the United States in the Korean War: that was to maintain the goodwill of Washington, and in support of that objective Britain sacrificed 1,200 lives.[54]

Churchill took a vigorous stand against the prosecution of the war beyond the 28th parallel. Likewise, when Truman threatened to utilize the atomic bomb against the North Korean forces, Churchill spoke with emphasis against it. At one point in the war Attlee, while Prime Minister, flew to Washington to dissuade Truman from bombing mainland China. He was aware that the North Koreans were prosecuting the war supported by China and Russia.[55]

Churchill's reason for opposing war with China was that he appreciated the difficulties of waging a campaign at such an enormous distance. Furthermore, he did not want to leave the European continent defenseless against a possible Russian invasion. He was also convinced that too many lives had already been sacrificed to Mars. Because of these factors he was in agreement with Omar Bradley, who maintained that a war with China would be "fighting the wrong nation in the wrong war, and in the wrong place."[56] During his final premiership, ending in 1955, Churchill, contrary to American inclination, extended recognition to China, not because he approved of Marxism, but in order to expand the markets for British exports.

* * * * *

The Labour Party had come to power in 1945, and by 1951, according to Harold Laski, had effected the most comprehensive peaceful revolution in English history, a revolution by consent through the ballot box.[57] This had also been accomplished during the critical shift from war to peace. The reforms were widely appreciated. But some of the lower classes had expected immediate and comprehensive deliverance from the hardships and inequities of the past while most of the middle class and the nobility demanded guarantees against what they considered the horrors of the future: additional socialism. The disaffection of these groups reduced Labour's representation in the House of Commons. It had also been weakened by internal dissension. Furthermore, death had taken a heavy toll on its leaders: Ernest Bevin and Sir Stafford Cripps, among others, had died and had been succeeded by less significant personalities. In the election of 1950 Labour's representation fell to 315 while it raised the Conservatives to 297. The Liberals secured nine seats.[58] Henceforth Labour would govern on borrowed time, and it ran out eighteen months later, in 1951. In the election of that year the Conservatives won 321 seats, Labour 295, the Liberals six, and a scattering of others received three. Despite the Conservatives' majority in seats, Labour polled 231,000 more popular votes than did the Conservatives.[59]

Churchill at seventy-seven had won his "last great prize."

In 1900, he had begun his political career as "a child of the House of Commons." In the evening of his life he had become its grandfather. During the intervening years he had fought eighteen election campaigns, more than any other member of the House of Commons had ever done.

At his advanced age Churchill no longer operated in mental or physical over-gear, but few men of his age could have followed his pace. Because of his reduced vitality he delegated an increasing amount of responsibility to his subordinates. He had a high appreciation of Anthony Eden's intelligence and integrity, but he never treated him as a boon companion, as he did Brendan Bracken or Lord Beaverbrook. Eden nevertheless was his favorite political son to whom he entrusted the Foreign Office and left him a wide range of authority and action. Only on rare occasions did Churchill review a problem or a situation with him.

Rex Butler was no favorite of Churchill's but he had confidence in his ability and character, and to him he assigned the Chancellorship of the Exchequer. Except for an unfortunate incident in his career he might well have become Prime Minister. He was an authority in economics and finance, in which fields Churchill was no genius. He, therefore, left the Treasury and all questions involving funds to Butler, and there were few that did not have a pecuniary angle. Similarly, other cabinet chiefs were given enlarged jurisdiction in administering their departments, and this relieved the Prime Minister of detailed labor and provided him with time and energy for supervision.

Churchill's final premiership lacked the excitement and dynamism of his earlier one because the era was not fraught with the danger and perturbation of his previous administration. Furthermore, the populace yearned for quiescence, repose, and amenities. Churchill did not find it as fascinating to provide these as it had been to shield his country from Nazism and to capture Hitler. The postwar period, therefore, seemed less fascinating and inspiring than rescuing his country while its future hung in the balance.

Furthermore, Churchill was less competent to deal with complicated and involved subjects than he had been previously. Dr. Moran, his personal physician, reveals in his *Diaries* that before Churchill's assumption of his last premiership he had suffered a heart attack and a couple of mild strokes.[60] Thenceforth he could not escape the consciousness of his uncertain future.

His daily consumption for years of alcohol and cigars had also finally impaired his physical and intellectual energy. Even before his stroke his doctor had reduced his consumption of brandy and cigars. His nightly reliance after October, 1944, upon sedatives to insure sleep, according to Dr. Moran, assured him nocturnal repose at a price levied against his nervous system.

From his entry into the ministry in 1940 until the close of World War II, Churchill had distributed proposals to his cabinet colleagues for the improvement of the administration of their departments. But from the incipiency of his last premiership he offered few suggestions for the conduct of their offices.

After 1953 he spoke less frequently in the House of Commons, as well as throughout Europe. *Hansard's Debates*, however, reveal that his major speeches commanded the admiration of his listeners. But he was also more often severe and sharp in his retorts to those who differed with him. When Mr. Wigg, a member of the House of Commons, asked Churchill whether General Montgomery, upon leaving the army, had retained documents relative to the management of his forces, Churchill replied: "No, sir. Field Marshal Montgomery has not left the Army, so the question is ill-formed, as well as ill-natured."[61] On another occasion when Ronald Chamberlain, in November, 1949, disapproved of one of Churchill's statements and shouted "Rubbish," Churchill responded, "The right honorable Gentleman seems to have nothing in his head but rubbish." When the House registered its disapproval of Churchill's riposte, he apologized.

Age did not mellow Churchill's disposition toward Marxism, yet during his last premiership he took no steps to "repeal the twentieth century," and with one exception, the denationalization of the steel industry,[62] the Conservatives perpetuated the socialist establishment. Churchill viewed "Britain as a community, as a living partnership between the living and the dead," and he believed that socialism could be woven into the framework of this pattern without discarding all of the characteristics of capitalism.[63]

Industrial production in Socialist England during the nineteen-fifties was sluggish, lower than in France and Germany.[64] The output per man in England was also lower than in France and Germany. The production in England from 1953 to 1958 increased 14 per cent while that in West Germany and France increased 51 and 54 per cent respectively.[65] The chief reason for the lower rate of production in England was its deficiency of raw materials. This compelled it to import all of its petroleum, tobacco, and cotton; 80 per cent of its wool; 30 per cent of its iron ore; and vast quantities of its food products. Twenty-five per cent of its exports defrayed the cost of these imports. A further economic handicap was that most of its foreign investments had been drafted for the prosecution of the war. All of these factors were hindrances that weighed with equal difficulty on Conservatives and Labour.

Production increased a little more rapidly during Churchill's second premiership than it had under the Socialist administration, chiefly because the country was then a little farther removed from the exhausting demands of the war. But not to be discounted in the search for British economic recovery were the American grants and loans of $6,570,000,000 extended to Britain from 1945 to 1968. Furthermore, the razing of the old factories and their replacement by new ones with modern efficient equipment accelerated output.

These factors, and a number of others, elevated the standard of living in Britain. Many commodities which had been scarce or unavailable after the war were, by 1951, fairly easily obtainable.

Even before the inception of World War II, scientists in almost all of the advanced countries had prosecuted research on the atom. Early in the war Roosevelt and Churchill entered into a compact according to which the Prime Minister agreed to abandon major nuclear research in England, and to transfer its distinguished scholars to the United States where they would cooperate with the Americans in developing an atomic bomb, on the basis of a full flow of information between the two countries.

This agreement was faithfully observed by both parties to the contract until late in 1942 when the flow of scientific information from the United States ceased. Leading scientists in England protested to Churchill, and at the Casablanca Conference, in

January, 1943, he considered the matter with Roosevelt, who reminded the American scientists of their obligation to their British colleagues on the project. The American scientists finally justified their refusal to transmit their research findings to the British on the grounds that they had strong suspicions that one of their fellow scientists, Klaus Fuchs, was "leaking" American research data to foreign recipients. When this became known to members of Congress, it finally, on August 1, 1946, passed the McMahon Act prohibiting the release of atomic information from the United States.

By that time the whole episode had aroused British sentiment against the United States. This was further accentuated later by John Foster Dulles's authoritarian relations with Anthony Eden and his associates which chilled British public opinion toward Washington. Churchill, although disappointed, did not let this affray deflect him from his intimacy and cordiality with President Truman, for in the period from 1945 to 1955 he visited the United States five times. Churchill also remained on cordial terms with Eisenhower after the latter's election to the presidency. The Prime Minister visited Eisenhower even before he assumed his duties as President, not so much ٤o convey his congratulations and good wishes as to orient him in support of British policy.

The British, including Churchill, were concerned for fear that the world leaders no longer considered Britain one of the major powers, and to convince themselves, and the world, of their majestic might they needed an atomic bomb. Without informing Churchill of their action the Labour government began the development of such a weapon, and on October 3, 1952, Britain exploded its first atomic device on Montebello Island. Following this achievement, American secrecy in atomic matters toward Britain could no longer serve any purpose, and Congress, in August, 1954, lifted the ban on atomic research and development so far as Britain was concerned.

During his second premiership, from 1951 to 1955, Churchill developed an amicability toward his country's former allies and enemies. A number of factors account for this conversion, one of which was the death in March, 1953, of Stalin. During the Commissar's reign, he inspired all with either fear or animosity, or both; his departure instilled a concord and compatibility among large sections of the human race. Even Churchill responded to this altered environment, but he still retained his distrust of the Soviet government. It induced him to sponsor the unification of the three West German political divisions. He argued in favor of West Germany's entry into the North Atlantic Treaty Organization; he even approved the remilitarization of West Germany.

But as he took these precautions he also proposed normalization of relations with Moscow. He appealed for a world conference on disarmament over which he wished to preside. One of his last significant aspirations was a long, if not permanent, world peace.

He did not believe that congenial relations between East and West could be established by the negotiation of a single treaty. Those relations could be accomplished, he believed, perhaps by a succession of minor conferences which would eventuate in a series of treaties which in turn would reestablish normal relations without any fanfare.

A manifestation of his earnestness was Britain's reduction, in 1953, of its length of a man's military service from eighteen to twelve months, and also a decrease in its appropriations for its armed forces.

Another factor which may have contributed to Churchill's mellowness during his last years was the marked decline in Communist Party membership throughout Western Europe since 1946, ranging from 31 per cent in Italy to 65 per cent in Belgium.

As the active chapters of Churchill's life were closing, there were consolations. In 1953 he was awarded the Nobel Prize for literature. In 1954, when he was seventy-nine, he accepted membership in the Order of the Garter—an honor which he had refused in 1945. Nine years later he was granted Honorary Citizenship of the United States. Only one other foreigner, Marquis de la Lafayette, had been awarded similar distinction. Honorary degrees came from universities of all the continents of the world. It is doubtful if any other person in the world had ever been the recipient of so many public honors.

Though Churchill was fervently devoted to democracy, royalty intrigued him; kings and queens, princes and princesses had a peculiar fascination for him. He esteemed them largely because of their traditionally exalted eminence and idealization. He envisioned the world as a stage upon which mankind contested for the highest stakes, motivated by evil or idealism.

Elizabeth II constituted a special appeal for him. On Coronation Day, June 2, 1953, he contributed to her "a kiss and a tear."

Chatham, Sheridan, the Younger Pitt rate high among British statesmen, for with courage and ability they had held off England's enemies, but their tasks had been simpler than Churchill's, for in their time England's fleet was invincible, the waters surrounding the island were destitute of submarines, its skies devoid of Messerschmidts, flying bombs, and rockets. In 1940 Britain was vulnerable to all these hazards, and to defend his country Churchill had to neutralize these lethal instrumentalities, and this he did. For this, superabundant praise is not superfluous.

Churchill with all of his merits also had his defects. On November 10, 1946, he announced in the House of Commons, "I have passed more social legislation than any man before." For a brief period prior to World War I he was an apostle of David Lloyd George, but that episode closed in 1910. Following that year he aimed to preserve society essentially as it was. He desired no major social, political, or economic innovations in English life, even though enormous inequities existed. During neither of his premierships did he inaugurate significant reforms. At no time did he prosecute or enact a British New Deal as Roosevelt had done in the United States. For the upper classes to experience complete satisfaction and enjoyment, a modest and submissive lower class was an absolute requirement. Churchill accepted reforms once they had been passed. He made no attempt to disavow or repeal Liberal enactments that had entered the statute books.

On his eightieth birthday, on November 30, 1954, all England celebrated the occasion more jubilantly than any other birthday in English history, with perhaps the exception of the Jubilee Period honoring Queen Victoria. The occasion evoked a panorama of all his successes and triumphs, and depicted him as the hero of each. The event was marked with benevolence and harmony. The Queen and members of her family were among the celebrants and contributed to the birthday fund, while thousands of other admirers made generous donations. Compliments and congratulations converged upon him from all parts of the world.

The event was celebrated in Westminster, which was crowded with admirers while thousands of others remained outside. All were deeply moved by the band's rendition of a selection to the lilt of "Land of Hope and Glory." This was followed by speeches which extolled Churchill's grandeur, and he punctuated them with tears of gratitude. For the moment the speakers jettisoned all differences and disappointments of his career, and left him with only the cheerful memories of the great events in his majestic course. All of this adulation justified Churchill's own high appreciation of his significant career, and as the years rolled by his memory of this celebration lightened his burden of aging.

During the last period of his life Churchill was more than ever conscious of his historical significance, and while he was still intellectually competent he planned every detail of his funeral. It was not to be a farm-cart parade as Lloyd George had prescribed for his own departure, but a noble and majestic pageant designed to commemorate his Homeric career. His compatriots approved his design, and, even more, accorded him a state funeral, the first such tribute to a commoner since Gladstone's obsequies in 1898. In compliance with his wishes his remains were interred at Blenheim, where his progenitor, the Duke of Marlborough, reposed. Even in death Sir Winston appreciated distinguished companionship, and during centuries to roll by he wanted succeeding generations to know that the Duke had an illustrious descendant.

Notes and References

CHAPTER I

1. Geoffrey Bocca, *The Adventurous Life of Winston Churchill* (New York, 1964), p. 27. Hereafter cited as *The Adventurous Life of Winston Churchill.*

2. Randolph Churchill, *Winston Churchill, Youth 1874-1900* (Boston, 1966), I, p. 51. Hereafter cited as *Winston Churchill, Youth 1874-1900.*

3. Peter Mendelssohn, *The Age of Churchill* (New York, 1961), p. 70. Hereafter cited as *The Age of Churchill.*

4. Leonard Wibberley, *Life of Winston Churchill* (New York, 1956), p. 16.

5. Robert Lewis Taylor, *An Informal Study in Greatness* (Garden City, N. Y., 1952), p. 71. Printed by permission of Doubleday & Co., Inc.

6. René Kraus, *Winston Churchill* (Philadelphia, 1940), p. 34.

7. *Ibid.*, p. 46.

8. Charles J. V. Murphy and John Davenport, "The Lives of Winston Churchill," *Life*, XVIII (May 21, 1945), 94.

9. *Winston Churchill, Youth 1874-1900*, pp. 19-20.

10. Lewis Broad, *Winston Churchill, A Biography* (New York, 1958), p. 50.

11. René Kraus, *op. cit.*, pp. 18-19.

12. *Winston Churchill, Youth 1874-1900*, p. 16.

13. Ralph G. Martin, *Jennie, The Life of Lady Randolph Churchill, The Romantic Years* (Englewood Cliffs, N. J., 1969), pp. 340-41.

14. *The Age of Churchill*, p. 22.

15. *Winston Churchill, Youth 1874-1900*, pp. 18-19.

16. *Ibid.*, p. 22.

17. René Kraus, *Young Lady Randolph* (New York, 1943), p. 180.

18. *Winston Churchill, Youth 1874-1900*, pp. 93-99. Winston Spencer Churchill, *A Roving Commission, My Early Life* (New York, 1930), p. 25. Hereafter cited as *A Roving Commission.*

19. *Winston Churchill, Youth 1874-1900*, p. 43.

20. *A Roving Commission*, p. 5.

21. *Ibid.*, p. 31.

22. Justin McCarthy, *Political Portraits* (New York, 1903), p. 2.

23. J. L. Garvin, *The Life of Joseph Chamberlain* (London, 1933), I, pp. 152-53.

24. Walter E. Houghton, *The Victorian Frame of Mind* (New Haven, 1957), pp. 183-95.

25. *Parliamentary Debates*, Third Series, CCCX, col. 62, January 27, 1887.

26. *Ibid.*

27. *Parliamentary Debates*, Fourth Series, XCIV, col. 399, May 16, 1901.

28. Arthur Balfour, *Retrospect* (New York, 1930), p. 140.

29. *Parliamentary Debates*, Third Series, CCCX, col. 58, January 27, 1887.

30. *Winston Churchill, Youth 1874-1900*, pp. 80-82.

31. Sir Herbert Maxwell, "Lord Randolph Churchill," *Living Age,* CCV (April 6, 1895), 35.

32. *The Life of Lady Randolph Churchill,* pp. 56-57, 321-35.

CHAPTER II

1. *A Roving Commission,* p. 19.

2. *Winston Churchill, Youth 1874-1900,* pp. 272-78.

3. *A Roving Commission,* p. 76.

4. *Winston Churchill, Youth 1874-1900,* pp. 255-56.

5. *Ibid.,* p. 267.

6. *Ibid.*

7. *Ibid.,* p. 276.

8. *A Roving Commission,* pp. 163-64.

9. *Ibid.*

10. *Winston Churchill, Youth 1874-1900,* p. 412.

11. *Ibid.,* p. 428.

12. *Ibid.,* pp. 316-17.

13. Lord Elton, *Gordon of Khartoum, The Life of General Charles Gordon* (New York, 1955), pp. 368-69.

14. *Winston Churchill, Youth 1874-1900,* p. 371.

15. *Ibid.,* p. 410.

16. Violet Bonham Carter, *Winston Churchill, An Intimate Portrait* (New York, 1965), pp. 26-27.

17. Sir Leslie Shane, *Men Were Different* (London, 1937), p. 13. With permission of Sir Leslie Shane and the publisher, Michael Joseph, Ltd.

18. *The Age of Churchill,* p. 153.

19. Edgar Holt, *The Boer War* (London, 1958), p. 74.

20. *Winston Churchill, Youth 1874-1900,* p. 437.

21. *Ibid.*

22. *Ibid.,* p. 491.

23. *Ibid.,* p. 493.

CHAPTER III

1. *A Roving Commission,* p. 354.
2. *Winston Churchill, Youth 1874-1900,* p. 524.
3. *Ibid.*
4. Paul Glad, *McKinley, Bryan and the People* (Philadelphia, 1964), p. 22.
5. Randolph Churchill, *Winston Spencer Churchill, The Young Statesman 1901-1914* (Boston, 1967), p. 2.
6. *Parliamentary Debates,* Fourth Series, LXXXIX, 408, February 18, 1901.
7. *Ibid.,* col. 412.
8. *Ibid.,* col. 415.
9. *Ibid.,* XCIII, 1564, May 13, 1901.
10. *Winston Spencer Churchill, The Young Statesman 1901-1914,* p. 18.
11. *Parliamentary Debates,* Fourth Series, CXXIII, 193-94, May 28, 1903.
12. *Ibid.*
13. *Ibid.,* CXXXVII, 579, July 4, 1904.
14. *Ibid.,* CXXXVIII, 514-15, July 19-20, 1904.
15. *Ibid.,* CLIII, 1238, March 14, 1906.
16. *Ibid.,* CLVII, May 14, 1906.
17. *Winston Spencer Churchill, The Young Statesman 1901-1914,* p. 184.
18. *Ibid.,* p. 76.
19. Violet Bonham Carter, *Winston Churchill, An Intimate Portrait,* p. 89.
20. *Winston Spencer Churchill, The Young Statesman 1901-1914,* p. 75.

CHAPTER IV

1. Lord Moran, *Churchill Taken from the Diaries of Lord Moran* (Boston, 1966), p. 387. Hereafter cited as *Diaries.*
2. Winston Churchill, *Savrola, The Tale of Revolution in Laurania* (New York, 1956), p. 124. Hereafter cited as *Savrola.*
3. *The Age of Churchill, Heritage and Adventure, 1874-1911,* p. 576.
4. Randolph Churchill, *Winston Churchill, Youth 1874-1900,* p. 513.
5. John Milton, *Paradise Lost,* Book I, Line 263.
6. Kay Halle, comp., *Irrepressible Churchill, A Treasury of Winston Churchill's Wit* (Cleveland, 1966), p. 117.
7. *Ibid.,* pp. 264-65.

8. Carl Eric Bechhofer Roberts, *Stanley Baldwin, Man or Miracle* (London, 1937), p. 360.

9. *The Age of Churchill, Heritage and Adventure*, p. 71.

10. *Winston Churchill, Youth 1874-1900*, p. 341.

11. Allen Churchill, *The Roosevelts* (New York, 1965), p. 229. Permission of Harper and Row and the author.

12. Lewis Broad, *The Years of Preparation* (New York, 1965), pp. 181-82.

13. R. W. Thompson, *The Yankee Marlborough*, p. 283. With permission of the author.

14. Barbara Tuchman, *The Guns of August* (New York, 1962), pp. 264-65.

15. *The Adventurous Life of Winston Churchill*, p. 24.

16. *Winston Churchill, Youth 1874-1900*, p. 341.

17. The Earl of Swinton, "In Parliament and Cabinet," *The Atlantic Monthly*, CCXV (March, 1965), 56. With permission of *The Atlantic Monthly*.

18. *Diaries*, p. 350.

19. *Ibid.*

20. William Shirer, *The Rise and Fall of the Third Reich, A History of Nazi Germany* (New York, 1960), pp. 911-13.

21. Raymond Daniell, "Man of Blood, Sweat and Tears," *The New York Times Magazine* (December 28, 1944), p. 3.

22. Alan Moorehead, "The Great Man's Last Trip to the Commons," *Life*, LVII-1 (August 7, 1964), 31.

23. *A Roving Commission*, p. 113.

24. *Winston Churchill, Youth 1874-1900*, p. 151.

25. *Savrola*, p. 85.

26. *Ibid.*, p. 86.

27. *Diaries*, p. 444.

28. *Winston Churchill, Youth 1874-1900*, p. 392.

29. John Spencer Churchill, "Painting for Uncle Winston," *The Atlantic Monthly*, CCIX (January, 1962), 66.

30. Clement Attlee, "Best Wartime Chief Britain Ever Had, Attlee Says," *Milwaukee Journal*, February 9, 1965.

31. *Ibid.* By permission of *Milwaukee Journal*.

32. *Diaries*, p. 330.

33. *The Yankee Marlborough*, p. 305.

34. Winston Churchill, "The Controversies of Teheran," *Life*, XXXI-2 (October 22, 1951), 103.

35. Foster Hailey, "Churchill Way: Two Days in One," *The New York Times Magazine* (November 26, 1950), p. 55.

CHAPTER V

1. G. D. H. Cole and Raymond Postgate, *The British People, 1746-1946* (New York, 1946), p. 340.

2. *Parliamentary Debates,* Fourth Series, CLXII, 731, July 31, 1906.

3. *Ibid.*

4. Randolph Churchill, *Winston S. Churchill, The Young Statesman 1901-1914,* pp. 158-59.

5. *Ibid.*

6. G. P. Jones and A. G. Pool, *A Hundred Years of Economic Development in Great Britain (1840-1940)* (London, 1940), p. 267.

7. Simon Nowell-Smith, *Edwardian England 1901-1914* (London, 1964), p. 181.

8. *The British People, 1746-1946,* p. 118.

9. John Cook, "Vagrants, Beggars and Tramps," *Quarterly Review,* CCIX (October, 1908), 408.

10. J. Ellis Barker, "The Land and the People, and the General Election," *The Nineteenth Century and After,* LXVI (September, 1909), 399.

11. Barbara Tuchman, *The Proud Tower, A Portrait of the World Before 1914* (New York, 1966), p. 26.

12. R. J. Minney, *The Edwardian Age* (London, 1964), p. 66.

13. *Ibid.,* p. 142.

14. *Winston S. Churchill, The Young Statesman, 1901-1914,* p. 30.

15. *Ibid.*

16. Bentley B. Grant, "Winston Churchill Versus the Webbs: The Origin of British Unemployment Insurance," *The American Historical Review,* LXXI (April, 1966), 854.

17. *Ibid.,* pp. 855-61.

18. Hugh Massingham, "Sir Winston Spencer Churchill," *The Atlantic Monthly,* CCXV (March, 1965), 51. With the permission of the publisher and the author.

19. *Winston S. Churchill, The Young Statesman,* p. 314.

20. *Parliamentary Debates,* Fifth Series, XXI, 1042, February 15, 1911.

21. *Ibid.,* XIX, 1350, July 20, 1910.

22. *Ibid.*

23. *Winston S. Churchill, The Young Statesman, 1901-1914,* p. 285.

24. *Winston S. Churchill, Youth 1874-1900,* p. 357.

25. *Parliamentary Debates,* Fifth Series, XXII, col. 1881, March 13, 1911.

26. W. J. Ashley, "German Steel and Iron," *Quarterly Review,* CCXXVII (April, 1917), 542-43.

27. William Oliver Stevens and Allan Westcott, *A History of Sea-power* (Garden City, 1942), p. 309.

28. Winston S. Churchill, "Sparks from the Anvil," *The Atlantic Monthly*, CLXXXIII (February, 1949), 52.

29. "German Seapower: Its Past and Its Future," *Review of Reviews*, VL (February, 1912), 229-30.

30. E. L. Woodward, *Great Britain and the German Navy* (Hamden, Connecticut, 1935), pp. 404-28.

31. Sir Edward Grey of Fallodon, *Twenty-Five Years* (New York, 1925), II, p. 64.

CHAPTER VI

1. Anatole Mazour, *Russia Tsarist and Communist* (New York, 1962), p. 543.

2. *Ibid.*

3. Bernard Pares, *The Fall of the Russian Monarchy* (New York, 1939), p. 311.

4. Sidney Harcave, *Russia* (Chicago, 1959), p. 448.

5. *Ibid.*

6. David Lloyd George, *War Memoirs* (London, 1933), I, 455.

7. *Ibid.*, p. 409.

8. Alan Moorehead, *Gallipoli* (New York, 1956), p. 364. With permission of Harper and Row, publishers.

9. R. M. F. Cruttwell, *A History of the Great War* (Oxford, 1934), p. 145. By permission of the Clarendon Press and the author.

10. Sir Edward Grey of Fallodon, K. G. *Twenty-Five Years 1892-1916* II (New York, 1925), p. 78.

11. William Oliver Stevens and Allen Wescott, *A History of Sea Power* (Garden City, 1942), p. 341.

12. Stephen Koss, "The Destruction of the Last Liberal Government," *Journal of Modern History*, XL (June, 1968), 262.

13. *Ibid.*, p. 266.

14. *Ibid.*, p. 271.

15. *Ibid.*, p. 275.

16. R. M. F. Cruttwell, *op. cit.*, p. 144. By permission of the author and the Clarendon Press.

17. Howard La Fay, "Be Ye Men of Valour," *National Geographic Magazine*, CXXVIII (August, 1965), 181.

18. *Ibid.*

19. Maurice Grosser, "Art," *Nation*, CLXXXVI (March 22, 1958), 263.

20. Eric Newton, "Churchill, the Artist, an Evaluation," *The New York Times Magazine*, January 2, 1949, p. 20.

21. *Ibid.*

22. *Ibid.*

23. Robert Lewis Taylor, *Winston Churchill, An Informal Study of Greatness,* p. 273.

24. Erich von Ludendorff, *Ludendorff's Own Story* (New York, 1919), II, 8, 340.

25. James Huston, *The Sinews of War: Army Logistics 1775-1953* (Washington, D. C., 1966), pp. 334-35.

CHAPTER VII

1. G. M. Young, *Stanley Baldwin* (London, 1952), p. 88.

2. A. L. Rowse, *The Churchills from the Death of Marlborough to the Present* (New York, 1958), p. 337.

3. Carl Erich Bechhofer Roberts, *Stanley Baldwin: Man or Miracle?* (New York, 1937), p. 160.

4. Victor L. Albjerg, "British Finances: 1914-1939," *Current History,* XXIV (April, 1953), 193-200.

5. Virginia Cowles, *Winston Churchill* (New York, 1953), p. 247.

6. *Parliamentary Debates,* Fifth Series, CVC, 709, May 10, 1926. 1926.

7. Robert Lewis Taylor, *Winston Churchill, An Informal Study in Greatness,* p. 327.

8. *Parliamentary Debates,* Fifth Series, CVC, 116, May 3, 1926.

9. Francis Boyd, *British Politics in Transition* (London, 1964), pp. 13-14.

CHAPTER VIII

1. Charles J. V. Murphy and John Davenport, "The Lives of Winston Churchill," *Life,* XVIII (May 21, 1945), 102.

2. *Parliamentary Debates,* Fifth Series, CCLXXVI, 2790, April 13, 1933.

3. *Ibid.*

4. Winston Churchill, *The Gathering Storm* (London, 1948), pp. 7-9. Hereafter cited as *Gathering Storm.*

5. Werner Richter, *Bismarck* (New York, 1965), p. 101. With permission of G. P. Putnam's Sons and the author, copyright 1964.

6. Franz Neumann, *Behemoth* (New York, 1963), p. 141.

7. Michael Florinsky, *Russia, A Short History* (New York, 1964), p. 456.

8. John Wheeler-Bennett, "From Brest-Litovsk to Brest-Litovsk," *Foreign Affairs,* XVIII (January, 1940), 200. Permission to quote granted by publisher of *Foreign Affairs.*

9. H. R. Trevor-Roper, "Hitler's Gamble," *The Atlantic Monthly* CLXXII (September, 1954), 41.

10. *Gathering Storm*, p. 84.

11. *Parliamentary Debates*, Fifth Series, CCLXXII, 81, November 23, 1932.

12. René Kraus, *Winston Churchill*, p. 316.

13. *Parliamentary Debates*, Fifth Series, CCLXXII, 90, November 23, 1932.

14. *Ibid.*, CCLXXVI, 543, March 23, 1933.

15. *Ibid.*, CCLXXV, 1823, March 14, 1933.

16. *Ibid.*, CCVC, 866-67, November 28, 1934.

17. *Ibid.*

18. *Gathering Storm*, pp. 120-21.

19. *Parliamentary Debates*, Fifth Series, CCVC, 859, November 28, 1934.

20. *Ibid.*, CCCXXI, 1400, March 11, 1937.

21. *Ibid.*, 1404.

22. *Ibid.*, CCCXXXI, 1135-36, November 17, 1938.

23. *Ibid.*

24. *Ibid.*, CCCII, 1492, May 31, 1935.

25. V. L. Albjerg and M. H. Albjerg, *Europe from 1914 to the Present* (New York, 1951), p. 246.

26. Martin Gilbert and Richard Gott, *The Appeasers* (London, 1967), p. 11. Hereafter cited as *The Appeasers*.

27. *Ibid.*, pp. 6-8.

28. *Ibid.*, pp. 21-22.

29. *Parliamentary Debates*, Fifth Series, CCLXXVI, 2791-92, April 13, 1933.

30. *The Appeasers*, p. 31.

31. *Ibid.*

32. Randolph Churchill, *The Rise and Fall of Anthony Eden* (New York, 1959), p. 90.

33. William Rock, *Appeasement on Trial* (Archon Books, 1946), p. 164. Place of publication not given.

34. Archibald Grimke, *William Lloyd Garrison* (New York, 1891), p. 117.

35. *Parliamentary Debates*, Fifth Series, CCCXII, 1447, May 21, 1936.

36. *Ibid.*, 1442.

37. *Ibid.*, 1448.

38. E. M. Robertson, *Hitler's Prewar Policy and Military Plans* (New York, 1967), p. 56.

39. *Gathering Storm*, p. 130.

40. *Ibid.*, p. 132.

41. *The Appeasers*, p. 93.

42. *Parliamentary Debates,* Fifth Series, CCCII, 421, May 22, 1935.

43. Harold Nicolson, *Diaries and Letters, 1930-1939* (New York, 1966), p. 56.

44. *The Appeasers,* p. 41.

45. *Ibid.,* p. 42.

46. William Shirer, *The Rise and Fall of the Third Reich. A History of Nazi Germany,* p. 295.

47. Andreas Dorpalen, "Hitler Twelve Years After," *Review of Politics,* XIX (October, 1957), 502. With the permission of the publisher and the author.

48. *Parliamentary Debates,* Fifth Series, CCCX, 1526, March 26, 1936.

49. *Gathering Storm,* p. 262.

50. *Parliamentary Debates,* Fifth Series, CCCXXXIII, 94-99, March 14, 1938.

51. Max Beloff, *The Foreign Policy of Soviet Russia, 1936-1941* (New York, 1947-1949), II, 50.

52. *Parliamentary Debates,* Fifth Series, CCCXXXIII, 95, March 14, 1938.

53. *Gathering Storm,* pp. 180-81.

54. *Parliamentary Debates,* Fifth Series, CCCXXXVIII, 2959, July 26, 1938.

55. Basil Collier, *Barren Victories, Versailles to Suez, The Failure of the Western Alliance, 1918-1956* (Garden City, 1964), p. 141.

56. *The Appeasers,* p. 130.

57. *Ibid.,* p. 135.

58. *Gathering Storm,* p. 293.

59. *Ibid.,* p. 305.

60. *Ibid.*

61. Keith Feiling, *The Life of Neville Chamberlain* (London, 1946), p. 367.

62. Stuart Hodgson, *The Man Who Made the Peace* (New York, 1938), p. 112.

63. Maurice Crain, *Rulers of the World* (New York, 1940), p. 85.

64. *Parliamentary Debates,* Fifth Series, CCCXXXIX, 364, October 5, 1938.

65. *Ibid.*

66. *Gathering Storm,* p. 362.

67. *Ibid.,* p. 370.

68. *The Life of Neville Chamberlain,* p. 403.

69. *Gathering Storm,* p. 394.

CHAPTER IX

1. *Parliamentary Debates,* Fifth Series, CCCLI, 295, September 3, 1939.

2. James Phinney Baxter, "The Seesaw of Submarine War," *The Atlantic Monthly,* CLXXVIII (August, 1946), 81. By permission of the publisher and the author.

3. *The Appeasers,* p. 346.

4. *Ibid.,* p. 350.

5. The Earl of Birkenhead, *The Life of Lord Halifax* (Boston, 1966), p. 455.

6. *Gathering Storm,* p. 667. With permission of Houghton Mifflin Company.

7. A. W. Baldwin, *My Father: The True Story* (London, 1956), p. 323.

8. *Parliamentary Debates,* Fifth Series, CCCLX, 1502, May 13, 1940.

9. R. B. Mowat, "Fatalism and Direction," *Contemporary Review,* CLIX (March, 1941), 287.

10. *Their Finest Hour,* p. 414.

11. *Ibid.,* p. 115.

12. Fletcher Pratt, "Who Has the Best Submarines," *Harper's Magazine,* CIIC (February, 1949), 66.

13. *Ibid.,* p. 65.

14. James Phinney Baxter, "The Seesaw of Submarine Warfare," *The Atlantic Monthly,* CLXXVIII (August, 1946), 86.

15. Vice Admiral Kurt Assmann, "Why the U-Boat Failed," *Foreign Affairs,* XXVIII (July, 1950), 670.

16. *Ibid.*

17. "The Seesaw of Submarine Warfare," *The Atlantic Monthly,* CLXXVIII (August, 1946), 86.

18. John Wheeler-Bennett, *John Anderson, Viscount Waverley* (New York, 1962), p. 245.

19. "Winston Churchill's Approval of Fascism," *Literary Digest,* CDXXXXII (February 26, 1927), 18.

20. Winston Churchill, "Dictators on Dynamite," *Collier's Weekly,* CII (September 3, 1938), 17-26.

21. *Their Finest Hour,* pp. 121-22.

22. *Triumph and Tragedy,* p. 528.

23. *Their Finest Hour,* p. 20.

24. Arthur Bryant, *Triumph in the West* (Garden City, N. Y., 1950), p. 31.

25. *Ibid.,* p. 115.

26. Arthur Bryant, *The Turn of the Tide, A History of the War Years Based upon the Diaries of the Imperial Field Marshal Lord*

Alanbrooke, Chief of the General Staff (Garden City, N. Y., 1957), p. 418.

27. Arthur Bryant, "Britain's Greatest General Speaks," *Look*, XX-1 (May 28, 1957), p. 97.

28. *The Turn of the Tide*, p. 432.

CHAPTER X

1. Michael Florinsky, *Russia, A Short History*, p. 546.

2. Yves Delbars, *The Real Stalin* (London, 1953), p. 292.

3. *Ibid.*, p. 291.

4. I. Deutscher, *Stalin, A Political Biography* (New York, 1949), p. 464.

5. Winston Churchill, *The Hinge of Fate* (Boston, 1949), p. 758. Hereafter cited as *The Hinge of Fate*.

6. Winston Churchill, *The Grand Alliance*, p. 372.

7. *The Hinge of Fate*, p. 259.

8. Trumbull Higgins, *Winston Churchill and the Second Front* (New York, 1957), p. 61.

9. *The Grand Alliance*, p. 383.

10. William L. Shirer, *The Rise and Fall of the Third Reich*, p. 853.

11. Vice Admiral Kurt Assmann, "The Battle for Moscow, Turning Point of the War," *Foreign Affairs*, XXVIII (January, 1950), 325-26.

12. *Europe from 1914 to the Present*, p. 535.

13. Winston Churchill, "The Lights Are Going Out," *Vital Speeches* (November 1, 1938), p. 50.

14. *Their Finest Hour*, p. 24.

15. *Ibid.*

16. *Europe from 1914 to the Present*, p. 523.

17. Ralph G. Martin, *Jennie, The Life of Lady Randolph Churchill, The Romantic Years, 1854-1895*, p. 340.

18. *Their Finest Hour*, p. 553.

19. *Twenty-first Report to Congress on Lend-Lease Operations for the Period Which Ended September 30, 1945*, pp. 12-14.

20. *The Grand Alliance*, p. 23.

21. Edward R. Stettinius, *Roosevelt and the Russians* (New York, 1949), p. 70.

22. *The Grand Alliance*, p. 607.

23. *Ibid.*, p. 608.

CHAPTER XI

1. Herbert Feis, *Churchill, Roosevelt, and Stalin. The War They Won, and the Peace They Sought* (Princeton, 1967), p. 44.

2. *Ibid.*, p. 45.

3. Richard M. Leighton, "Overlord Revisited: An Interpretation of the American Strategy in the European War, 1942-1944," *The American Historical Review*, LXVI (July 1963), 919-37.

4. Henry L. Stimson and McGeorge Bundy, *On Active Service in Peace and War* (New York, 1947), p. 414.

5. *The Grand Alliance*, pp. 683-84.

6. *Congressional Record*, pt. 9, 77th Congress, 1st Session, November 26, 1941 to January 2, 1942, pp. 1017-18.

7. Lord Charles Moran, *Churchill, Taken from the Diaries of Lord Moran, The Struggle for Survival, 1940-1965* (Boston, 1966), p. 17.

8. *Ibid.*

9. *The Grand Alliance*, p. 706.

10. *Ibid.*, p. 447. Permission to quote from Houghton Mifflin Company.

11. Eleanor Roosevelt, *This I Remember* (New York, 1949), pp. 243-44.

12. Moran, *Diaries*, p. 27.

13. *Ibid.* Permission to quote from Houghton Mifflin Company.

14. Vice Admiral Sir Arthur Hezlet, *The Submarine and Sea Power* (London, 1949), p. 181.

15. H. H. Arnold, *Global Mission* (New York, 1949), p. 303. Permission to quote from Harper and Row, publishers.

16. Trumbull Higgins, *Winston Churchill and the Second Front*, p. 97.

17. *Ibid.*, p. 63.

18. Robert Sherwood, *Roosevelt and Hopkins, An Intimate History* (New York, 1948), pp. 521-28.

19. *Ibid.*, p. 563.

20. *Ibid.*

21. William McNeill, *Survey of International Affairs* (London, 1953), p. 182.

22. Feis, *op. cit.*, p. 83.

23. Maurice Matloff and Edwin Snell, *Strategic Planning for Coalition Warfare 1941-42* (Washington, D. C., 1953), p. 221.

24. Dwight D. Eisenhower, *Crusade in Europe* (Garden City, N. Y., 1948), p. 70.

25. J. A. Spender, *Life, Journalism and Politics* (New York, 1927), II, 70. Winston Churchill, *The Hinge of Fate*, p. 433.

26. Ernest King, *A Naval Record* (New York, 1952), p. 425.

27. *Winston Churchill and the Second Front*, pp. 142-43.

28. *The Hinge of Fate*, p. 383.

29. *Winston Churchill and the Second Front*, p. 147.

30. *Roosevelt and Hopkins*, p. 609.

31. *On Active Duty in Peace and War*, p. 437.

32. Kent Robert Greenfield, *American Strategy in World War II* (Baltimore, 1963), p. 30.

33. *Ibid.*

34. Gordon Harrison, *Cross Channel Attack* (Washington, D. C., 1951), pp. 29-30.

35. *Strategic Planning for Coalition Warfare*, p. 159.

36. *Winston Churchill and the Second Front*, p. 152.

37. *Ibid.*

38. *Ibid.*

39. *Turn of the Tide*, p. 433.

40. Anne Armstrong, *Unconditional Surrender: The Impact of the Casablanca Policy on World War II* (New Brunswick, 1961), pp. 7-13.

41. Harold Macmillan, *The Blast of War, 1939-1945* (New York, 1968), pp. 121-22.

42. *Winston Churchill and the Second Front*, pp. 190-91.

43. Armstrong, *op. cit.*, p. 41.

44. *Closing the Ring*, p. 663.

45. Michael Foot, *Aneurin Bevan, A Biography* (New York, 1963), p. 431.

46. *Ibid.*, p. 432.

47. Forrest Davis, "What Really Happened at Teheran," *Saturday Evening Post*, CCXXII (May 13, 1944), 13, 39.

48. *Crusade in Europe*, p. 207.

49. William McNeill, *Survey of International Affairs*, p. 203.

50. Moran, *Diaries*, p. 173.

51. *Ibid.*, by permission of Houghton Mifflin Company and the author.

52. *Ibid.*, pp. 161-62.

Chapter XII

1. Omar Bradley, *A Soldier's Story* (New York, 1951), p. 316.

2. *Ibid.*, p. 291.

3. G. A. Harrison, *Cross Channel Attack*, p. 447.

4. William Shirer, *The Rise and Fall of the Third Reich, A History of Nazi Germany*, p. 1038.

5. *Triumph and Tragedy*, p. 6.

6. *Ibid.*, p. 13.

7. Cornelius Ryan, *The Longest Day, June 6, 1944* (New York, 1959), p. 303.

8. Basil Collier, *The Battle of the V-Weapons, 1944-1945* (New York, 1945), pp. 141-45.

9. *Closing the Ring*, p. 235.

10. Nigel Tangye, "Flying Bombs and Rockets," *Foreign Affairs,* XXIV (October, 1945), 41.

11. Joseph Warren Angell, "Guided Missiles Could Have Won the War," *Atlantic Monthly,* CLXXXVIII (December, 1951), 29.

12. Nigel Tangye, *op. cit.,* pp. 47-48.

13. Forrest C. Pogue, *The Supreme Command* (Washington, D. C., 1954), p. 252. With permission of the Department of the Army and the Office of the Chief of Military History.

14. *Ibid.,* p. 248.

15. *Ibid.,* p. 246.

16. Larry Collins and Dominique Lapierre, *Is Paris Burning?* (New York, 1965), p. 335.

17. Bernard Montgomery, *The Memoirs of Field-Marshal the Viscount Montgomery of Alamein, K. G.* (New York, 1958), p. 235. With permission of World Publishing Company.

18. *Ibid.,* pp. 234-35.

19. *Crusade in Europe,* p. 306.

20. Pogue, *op. cit.,* pp. 312-13.

21. *Ibid.,* pp. 314-15.

22. *Ibid.,* p. 298. With permission of the Department of the Army and the Office of the Chief of Military History.

CHAPTER XIII

1. *Foreign Relations of the United States, Diplomatic Papers, Malta and Yalta* (Washington, D. C., 1955), p. 726.

2. *Ibid.,* p. 728.

3. James F. Byrnes, *Speaking Frankly* (New York, 1947), p. 23. Hereafter cited as *Speaking Frankly.*

4. William Henry Chamberlin, *America's Second Crusade* (Chicago, 1950), p. 208.

5. *Triumph and Tragedy,* p. 347.

6. *Ibid.,* pp. 347-48.

7. *Ibid.*

8. *Foreign Relations of the United States,* p. 678.

9. *Ibid.*

10. *The New York Times,* March 1, 1972.

11. *Speaking Frankly,* p. 27.

12. *Foreign Relations of the United States,* p. 878.

13. *Speaking Frankly,* p. 27.

14. *Ibid.,* p. 28.

15. Jesse Clarkson, *A History of Russia* (New York, 1961), pp. 654-55.

16. *Speaking Frankly,* p. 78.

17. William Leahy, *I Was There* (New York, 1950), pp. 318-19.

18. *The United States News and World Report* (April 15, 1955), 60.

19. William Leahy, *I Was There,* p. 318.

20. Raymond Sontag, "Reflections on the Yalta Papers," *Foreign Affairs,* XXXIII (July, 1955), p. 622.

21. *Triumph and Tragedy,* p. 402.

Chapter XIV

1. Trumbull Higgins, *Hitler and Russia* (New York, 1966), p. 268.

2. Stephen Ambrose, *Eisenhower and Berlin* (New York, 1967), p. 94.

3. Montgomery of Alamein, *Memoirs,* pp. 296-97. With permission of World Publishing Company.

4. Bradley, *A Soldier's Story,* p. 535.

5. *Triumph and Tragedy,* p. 460.

6. *Ibid.,* pp. 460-61.

7. Stephen Ambrose, *Eisenhower and Berlin,* p. 102.

8. *A Soldier's Story,* pp. 508-9.

9. *Crusade in Europe,* p. 402.

10. *A Soldier's Story,* p. 535.

11. *Memoirs,* p. 296.

12. *Ibid.*

13. *Triumph and Tragedy,* pp. 464-66.

14. *Ibid.,* p. 466.

15. *Congressional Digest,* XXV (May, 1946), 135.

16. James Huston, *The Sinews of War: Army Logistics 1775-1953* p. 489.

17. *Congressional Digest, op. cit.,* p. 136.

18. *The Sinews of War,* p. 489.

19. John Wheeler-Bennett, *John Anderson, Viscount Waverley,* p. 327.

Chapter XV

1. Harold Macmillan, *Tides of Fortune* (London, 1969), pp. 27-28.

2. Roy Jenkins, *An Interim Biography, 1945-1955* (London, 1969), p. 247.

3. Macmillan, *op. cit.,* p. 31.

4. Dennis Bardens, *Churchill in Parliament* (South Brunswick and New York, 1969), p. 311.

5. Quintin Hogg, "A Conservative Forecast," *Foreign Affairs,* XXII (October, 1943), p. 310.

6. "The Atlantic Report," *The Atlantic Monthly,* CLXXVI (September, 1945), 5. Lord Woolton, "We're Planning for a Better Britain," *Rotarian,* XVI (April, 1945), 16-18.

7. Lester Velie, "Churchill's New Battle for Britain," *Collier's Weekly*, CXXIII (March 26, 1945), 83.

8. Moran, *Diaries*, p. 310.

9. *Triumph and Tragedy*, pp. 675-76.

10. Kay Halle, *The Irrepressible Churchill* (New York, 1969), p. 276.

11. D. N. Pritt, *The Labour Government 1945-1951* (London, 1963), p. 64.

12. Moran, *Diaries*, p. 338.

13. *Ibid.*, p. 173.

14. *Ibid.*

15. Moran, *Diaries*, p. 338.

16. *U.S. News and World Report*, LXIX (September 28, 1970), 57.

17. *U.S. Economic Assistance Programs Administered by Agency for International Development and Predecessor Agencies*, pp. 66-67.

18. *U.S. News and World Report*, LXIX (December 28, 1970), 20-23.

19. *Parliamentary Debates*, Fifth Series, CCCCLXXXVII, 2161, May 10, 1951.

20. John Fisher, "The Scared Men in the Kremlin," *Harpers Magazine*, CLXXXXIII (August, 1946), 100.

21. *Parliamentary Debates*, Fifth Series, CCCCLXXIII, 198-99, March 28, 1950.

22. *Ibid.*, IIIM, 446, March 5, 1952.

23. *Ibid.*, 433-37.

24. *Ibid.*, CCCCLXXIII, 191, March 28, 1950.

25. *Ibid.*, 194.

26. Clement Attlee, "British Plan for India, *Vital Speeches*, 516, June 3, 1947.

27. *Parliamentary Debates*, Fifth Series, CCCCXXXIV, 677, March 6, 1947.

28. *Tides of Fortune*, p. 271.

29. *Ibid.*

30. *Parliamentary Debates*, Fifth Series, CCCCLVII, 250-51, October 28, 1948.

31. Alfred Lilienthal, *What Price Israel* (Chicago, 1953), pp. 26-27.

32. James Parkes, *A History of Palestine from 115 A.D. to Modern Times* (New York, 1949), p. 292.

33. Richard van Alstyne, "Whither Palestine," *Current History*, XIV (February, 1948), 292.

34. Esco, "Foundations for Palestine, Inc.," *Palestine, A Study in Jewish-Arab and British Policies* (New Haven, 1949), p. 112.

35. *Ibid.*, p. 1024.

36. *Ibid.*, p. 1034.

37. James Parkes, *op. cit.*, p. 356.

38. Edward Browne, *The Persian Revolution* (New York, 1956), p. 328.

39. Edward Ashley Bayne, "Crime and Confidence in Iran," *Foreign Affairs* (July, 1951), XXIX, 579.

40. *Parliamentary Debates*, Fifth Series, IXD, 990, July 30, 1951.

41. Henry Ayteo, "Iran Oil Flows," *Foreign Policy Bulletin*, XXXIV, #7 (December 15, 1954), 49-50.

42. Peter Avery, *Modern Iran* (New York, 1969), pp. 453-54.

43. Francis Hunter Farrell, "Britain and Egypt," *Current History*, XXIV (April 1, 1954), 236.

44. *Parliamentary Debates*, Fifth Series, VIID, 79, November 6, 1951.

45. Francis Hunter Farrell, "Britain and Egypt," 238.

46. *Parliamentary Debates*, Fifth Series, IXD, 981-83, July 30, 1951.

47. *Ibid.*, 981.

48. *Ibid.*, XVD, 2378, March 20, 1951.

49. *Ibid.*, VIID, 79, November 6, 1951.

50. *Ibid.*

51. *Tides of Fortune*, pp. 515-16.

52. Moran, *Diaries*, p. 540.

53. *Ibid.*

54. *Parliamentary Debates*, Fifth Series, DIII, 270, July 1, 1952.

55. Freda Kircheway, "Atlee versus Truman," *The Nation*, CLXXI, December 9, 1950, 519-20.

56. *Parliamentary Debates*, Fifth Series, IVD, 968, February 26, 1952.

57. Harold Laski, "Labor Viewpoint," *The New York Times Magazine* (August 5, 1945), p. 8.

58. Pauline Gregg, *Modern Britain, A Social and Economic History Since 1760* (New York, 1967), p. 573.

59. D. E. Butler, *The British Election of 1951* (London, 1952), p. 237.

60. Moran, *Diaries*, pp. 434-42.

61. *Parliamentary Debates*, DXXXV, 1109, December 9, 1954.

62. F. Lee Benns and Mary Elisabeth Seldon, *Europe 1939 to the Present* (New York, 1971), p. 237.

63. *Tides of Fortune*, pp. 304-5.

64. *United Nations Statistical Yearbook*, 1966, pp. 156, 160, 163.

65. R. K. Webb, "Britain in the Sixties," *Headline Series*, #156, p. 21.

Selected Bibliography

From Conservative Convictions to Liberal Contentions

CHURCHILL, RANDOLPH. *Winston Leonard Spencer Churchill, Youth 1874-1900*. Boston: Houghton Mifflin, 1966. Valuable source, well written, and based upon extensive research. Lacks historical distinctiveness. Offers few interpretations.

—————. *Young Statesman, 1901-1915*. Boston: Houghton Mifflin, 1967. Second volume of the projected 5-volume biography. Reveals Churchill's political independence, administrative capacity and political strength.

CHURCHILL, WINSTON LEONARD SPENCER. *Lord Randolph Churchill*. 2 vols. London: Macmillan, 1906. Remarkably unbiased considering his devotion to his father, and the hostility of many toward Lord Randolph and also toward Winston. Established Winston as a superior author.

—————. *From London to Ladysmith, via Pretoria*. London: Longmans Green, 1900. An interesting account of his experiences in South Africa during the Boer War. Gives his recommendations for British future policy toward the Boer states.

—————. *Great Destiny; Sixty Years of the Honorable Life of the Man of the Century, Recounted by his own Incomparable Words*. Edited by F. W. Heath, New York: Putnam, 1965. Based upon extracts of his books, with the exception of his Second World War volumes. Excellent description of his political colleagues.

—————. *Painting as a Pastime*. New York: Whittlesey House, 1950. Reveals his joy in pursuing his avocation, as well as his proficiency with the brush.

—————. *The River War*. 2 vols. London: Longmans Green, 1908. An account of Britain's campaign against the Sudanese dervishes. Describes the first meeting with Lieutenant Beatty, later Admiral. Critical of Kitchener's treatment of the defeated army and its leader.

—————. *A Roving Commission, My Early Life*. New York: Scribner's, 1930. Brilliantly written. Relates his part in all significant movements. Reveals his serious objectives as well as his jovial moods, his shifts from parties, and the significant roles that he played.

JAMES, ROBERT RHODES. *Lord Randolph Churchill, Winston Churchill's Father*. London: Barnes, 1960. Material contribution to the late Victorian period. Excellent example of superior historical biography.

LESLIE, ANITA. *The Remarkable Mr. Jerome.* New York: Henry Holt, 1954. Highly laudatory. Traces Leonard Jerome's career from northern New York State to his successes in New York City. Describes his diversity of interests, his accomplishments, and his financial misfortunes.

MARTIN, RALPH G. *Jennie, The Life of Lady Randolph Churchill, The Romantic Years, 1854-1895.* Englewood Cliffs, New Jersey: Prentice Hall, 1969. Candid and intimate account of her career from her birth until the death of Lord Randolph Churchill.

Jubilation Smothered in Humiliation

ASQUITH, HERBERT HENRY. *Memories and Reflections, 1852-1927.* 2 vols. Boston: Little Brown, 1928. These two volumes scarcely qualify as memoirs or an autobiography because of their lack of unity and coherence, for they constitute his momentary reaction to issues and incidents as they occurred. They reveal Asquith as a scholar and fine character. He was intimate with a large number of people, among whom was Winston Churchill.

BALFOUR, ARTHUR JAMES, FIRST LORD OF. *Retrospect, an Unfinished Biography.* Boston: Houghton Mifflin, 1930. The author reveals himself as somewhat of a dilettante, and as one of the most interesting of the late Victorians. Balfour's death prevented completion of the project.

BEAKE, ROBERT. *The Unrepentant Tory, The Life and Times of Andrew Bonar Law, 1858-1923.* New York: St. Martin's Press, 1956. The author has exposed the falsity of Asquith's slur against Bonar Law as "the Unknown Prime Minister." He has revealed the human qualities of honesty and friendship, though these were subdued in his relations with Churchill.

BEAVERBROOK, WILLIAM MAXWELL AIKEN. *The Decline and Fall of Lloyd George.* London: Collins, 1963. Reviews the political collapse of the Little Welsh Attorney who served as Prime Minister from 1916 to 1922. Includes gossipy trivialities.

BROMAGE, MARCH C. *Churchill and Ireland.* Notre Dame: University of Notre Dame Press, 1964. Author credits Churchill with persistent effort to establish peace in Ireland.

CHURCHILL, WINSTON LEONARD SPENCER. *Marlborough, His Life and Times.* 6 vols. New York: Scribner's, 1933-1938. An attempted refutation of Macaulay's *Life of Marlborough* in which Churchill smothered splenetic urges and produced one of the great biographies in historical literature. It embodies sound scholarship based upon a survey of the battlefields where Marlborough commanded armies and won battles. He also consulted documents never before utilized.

——. *The Unknown War on the Eastern Front.* New York: Scribner's, 1931. This volume is confined almost exclusively to the Eastern front during World War I. Churchill describes this as a gigantic struggle. This was the best single-volume treatment of the contest for many years after its appearance.

——. *The World Crisis.* 4 vols. New York: Scribner's, 1923-1929. A running, sometimes rambling account of European history in the ten years following World War I, during part of which period (1924-1929) he was Chancellor of the Exchequer. It includes a hostile diatribe against Lenin, another evidence of his profound hostility toward Communist Russia.

CRUTTWELL, ROBERT MOBRAY FRASER. *A History of the Great War, 1914-1918.* Oxford: Clarendon Press, 1934. The author was a former army officer who had turned historian following his career on the battlefield. He produced a volume distinctive for its scholarship, balance, and fairness. One of the very best volumes on the war.

FALLS, CYRIL BENTHAM. *The Great War.* New York: Putnam, 1959. An able treatment of World War I by the official British historian of that conflict. It emphasizes the part played by the British navy.

FISHER, ADMIRAL OF THE FLEET LORD. *Memories.* London: Hodder and Stoughton, 1919. A salty account of his career in the navy to 1919. In Chapter V, "The Dardanelles," he gives his side of the story, not always with sincerity.

FISHMAN, JACK. *My Darling Clementine.* London: D. McKay, 1963. An informal admiring picture of Mrs. Churchill. A journalist's report rather than a biographer's characterization.

GREY, SIR EDWARD, OF FALLODON. *Twenty-five Years, 1892-1916.* 2 vols. New York: Stokes, 1925. The volumes deal primarily with his administration of the Foreign Office from December, 1905, to 1916, during which he was a colleague of Churchill's. The volume reveals his opposition to Germany's efforts in the period to shatter its encirclement. He assumed the initiative in bringing Italy into the war on the side of England and France. Failing eyesight led to his resignation in 1916.

HALDANE, R. B. *An Autobiography.* London: Hodder and Stoughton, 1929. An exceptionally readable and interesting account which reveals his deep interest in philosophy, and his significant contribution to politics and government. He was an elder statesman when Churchill was a promising young parliamentarian and administrator.

HAMILTON, GENERAL SIR IAN. *Gallipoli Diary.* 2 vols. London: Doran,

1920. Tells a tragic story . . . "with the art of a poet and the precision of a soldier." An endorsement of Churchill and Kitchener.

HANKEY, LORD M. P. A. *The Supreme Command, 1914-1918.* 2 vols. London: Allen and Unwin, 1961. As Secretary to the Committee of Imperial Defence for a quarter of a century following 1912, he was in a position to command significant information for the writing of these volumes. One of the most authoritative books on World War I.

HASSAL, CHRISTOPHER. *Edward Marsh, Patron of Arts.* London: Longmans Green, 1959. Reveals Marsh's deep and wide interest in art. It also evinces his relations with Churchill, and the extent to which he influenced his employer.

HIGGINS, TRUMBULL. *Winston Churchill and the Dardanelles—A Dialogue in Ends and Means.* New York: Macmillan, 1963. Based upon exhaustive research. Sympathetic toward Churchill.

HYAM, R. *Elgin and Churchill at the Colonial Office, 1905-1906.* New York: St. Martin's Press, 1969. The author portrays Churchill as the subordinate who formulated policies, and secured their adoption by crediting his senior with originality and ingenuity.

JONES, THOMAS. *Lloyd George.* Cambridge: Harvard University Press, 1951. Sympathetic yet realistic treatment of the Little Welsh Attorney. Author appreciates merits and failings of his subject. The study is drawn from sources that had been unavailable until then.

JUDD, DENNIS. *Balfour and the British Empire: A Study in Imperial Evolution, 1874-1932.* New York: St. Martin's Press, 1968. Reveals Balfour as an excellent leader in imperial affairs, and a failure as chief of the Conservative Party.

KEYES, ADMIRAL SIR ROGER BROWNLOW. *Naval Memoirs, The Narrow Seas to the Dardanelles, 1910-1915.* New York: Dutton, 1934. Covers the period during most of which Churchill was First Lord of the Admiralty. During that interval Keyes was Commodore in charge of submarine service and Chief of Staff of the Eastern Mediterranean Squadron. The Gallipoli Compaign also occurred during that period.

LIDDELL HART, BASIL HENRY. *The Tanks: The History of the Royal Tank Regiment and its Predecessors, Heavy Branch Machine-gun Corps, Tank Corps, 1914-1945.* New York: Praeger, 1959. Vivid account of the development of the tank, and its effectiveness in war.

LLOYD GEORGE, DAVID. *War Memoirs.* 6 vols. London: Nicholson, 1933-1936. A revelation of the author's dynamic mobilization of all England, men, women, and resources for winning World War I. The author takes the reader into his confidence in all of his activities. Restraint in writing is no more one of his virtues than in his denunciation of the opposition in the House of Commons. His volumes lack precise information.

MENDELSSOHN, PETER DE. *The Age of Churchill, Heritage and Adventure, 1874-1911.* New York: Knopf, 1961. Having drawn heavily upon secondary sources, the author has produced an entertaining and illuminating volume that is packed with information.

MORLEY, JOHN VISCOUNT. *Recollections.* 2 vols. New York: Macmillan, 1917. Deals in personalities, principles and incidents during his career. A generous assessment of Churchill.

NICOLSON, HAROLD. *King George the Fifth, his Life and Reign.* London: Constable, 1952. An authorized biography, highly laudatory of George V. Gives the King's attitude on political issues and on personalities, including Winston Churchill.

OWEN, FRANK. *Tempestuous Journey, Lloyd George, his Life and Times.* New York: McGraw-Hill, 1951. Characterizes Lloyd George as a congenital radical, eager to improve the lot of the poor, a man with inexhaustible zest and verve. Journalism rather than history.

PITT, BARRIE. *The Last Act.* New York: Norton, 1963. "As good a treatment of the last year of World War I as Barbara Tuchman's first five months of that conflict."

SPENDER, J. A., AND CYRIL ASQUITH. *Life of Henry Herbert Asquith, Lord Oxford and Asquith.* 2 vols. London: Hutchinson, 1932. Most of the earlier chapters were written by Asquith's son; the latter chapters by a noted journalist who knew intimately what was going on behind the scenes during the premiership. Has the merits and defects of an official project.

SPENDER, JOHN ALFRED. *Fifty Years of Europe: A Study in Pre-War Documents.* 2 vols. London: Stokes, 1933. A collection and analysis of documents dealing with the outbreak of World War I.

TAYLOR, ALAN JOHN PERCIVAL. *The First World War, An Illustrated History.* London: Hamilton, 1963. Insists that Germany was not alone to blame for instituting World War I. An excellent volume.

THOUMAN, RICHARD LODOIS. *The First World War.* London: Secker and Warburg, 1963. Condensation of General Thouman's three-volume *La Grande Guerre.*

TUCHMAN, BARBARA W. *The Guns of August.* New York: Macmillan, 1962. Excellent exposition of World War I from August to

December 31, 1914, especially as it affected Britain. Opening chapter is especially brilliant.

————. *The Proud Tower. A Portrait of the World 1890-1914.* New York: Macmillan, 1966. Brilliantly written résumé of international relations from 1890 to World War I and British diplomatic adjustments to the situation on the Continent.

Interest in Social Welfare

CLAPHAM, JOHN HAROLD. *Economic History of Modern Britain: Machines and National Rivalries.* 3 vols. New York: Macmillan, 1938. A masterly work of enduring excellence. Author presents the growth and development of industry, and reveals its economic, political, and sociological results.

CLARKE, E. W. B. *The Economic Effort of the War.* London: Allen and Unwin, 1940. Comparison of the economic strength of the belligerent groups. Critical of England's economic policy under Neville Chamberlain.

COLE, GEORGE DOUGLAS HOWARD. *British Trade and Industry, Past and Future.* London: Macmillan, 1932. Discusses the causes, both national and international, of the depression of 1929. Since the economic blizzard was worldwide, it could be solved only by international action.

ENSOR, ROBERT CHARLES KIRKWOOD. *England, 1870-1914.* Oxford: Clarendon Press, 1936. An excellent historical background to Churchill's career. Treats the subject matter skillfully and impartially.

FAY, C. R. *Great Britain from Adam Smith to the Present.* London: Longmans Green, 1957. Traces the growth of industrial development; exposes the deplorable conditions of labor, relates this to England's commercial relations with other countries.

JONES, G. P., AND A. G. POOL. *A Hundred Years of Economic Development in Great Gritain.* New York: Macmillan, 1940. An excellent economic history of Britain.

————. *Liberalism and the Social Problem.* London: Doran, 1909. A collection of Churchill's speeches endorsing the enactment of England's new social laws. His literary style forecasts the excellence of his last speeches prior to World War II.

MORRISON, HERBERT STANLEY. *Prospects and Policies.* New York: Knopf, 1944. A defense of the Labour Party's policies during and after World War I. Places emphasis upon economic affairs.

PETRI, CHARLES. *The Chamberlain Tradition.* New York: Frederick Stokes, 1938. Embraces the political and diplomatic careers of Joseph Chamberlain and his two sons, Austin and Neville. Author has failed to provide satisfactory treatment of the three, each of whom held important offices during critical times.

The Wherefore of World War II

CHURCHILL, WINSTON LEONARD SPENCER. *Step by Step, 1936-1939*. New York: 1939. A collection of the author's articles on home and foreign affairs from 1936 to 1939. In this volume he reveals his efforts to awaken the British people to the threatening danger.

————. *While England Slept: A Survey of World Affairs, 1932-1938*. New York: 1938. A compilation of speeches which Churchill delivered mainly in the House of Commons. The test of the quality of these speeches rests upon the accuracy of his foresight.

COLLIER, BASIL. *Barren Victories, Versailles to Suez, The Failure of the Western Alliances, 1918-1956*. Garden City: Doubleday, 1964. A clear analysis by the writer on the factors that influenced European policy after 1918.

DORPALEN, ANDREAS. "Hitler Twelve Years After," *Review of Politics*, XIX (October, 1957). An excellent and informative article which focuses on Hitler's personality.

FEILING, KEITH. *The Life of Neville Chamberlain*. London: Macmillan, 1946. An attempt to explain the policy and conduct of Chamberlain, neither condemning nor approving. Based in part on Chamberlain's diaries and journals.

GILBERT, MARTIN, AND RICHARD GOTT. *The Appeasers*. Boston: Houghton Mifflin, 1963. The authors make no apologies for the appeasers and are staunch supporters of Churchill's policy.

HIGHAM, ROBIN. *The Military Intelligence in Britain, 1918-1939*. New Brunswick, New Jersey: Rutgers University Press, 1966. Provides a useful military guide for the period between the two wars.

NICOLSON, HAROLD. *Diaries and Letters, 1930-1938*. New York: Atheneum, 1966. A frank and lively assessment of the growing tension as seen by a man who appreciated Churchill's warnings.

ROBERTSON, E. M. *Hitler's Pre-war and Military Plans*. New York: Citadel, 1967. A careful study of Hitler's foreign policy from his assumption of the Chancellorship to the outbreak of World War II.

ROWSE, A. L. *Appeasement: A Study in Political Decline, 1933-1939*. New York: Norton, 1961. Analysis of the appeasers' point of view.

SHERWOOD, ROBERT E. *Roosevelt and Hopkins*. New York: Harper, 1948. A vast fund of significant information about the relationship between Churchill and Roosevelt, and the part that Hopkins played in the relationship between the two leaders.

TAYLOR, A. J. P. *Origins of the Second World War*. London: Atheneum, 1961. Author maintains that Hitler hoped to avoid a major war from 1933 to 1939. He insists that the Fuehrer was merely struggling for a revision of the peace treaties following World War I.

Commander-in-Chief

ARMSTRONG, ANNE. *Unconditional Surrender: The Impact of the Casablanca Policy on World War II.* New Brunswick: Rutgers University Press, 1961. Volume deals more with political questions than with military problems.

BALDWIN, HANSON W. *Battles Lost and Won.* New York: Harper and Row, 1966. Author bases his thesis upon eleven major campaigns of World War II in which Hitler committed blunders, and his opponents made mistakes.

BIRKENHEAD, F. W. F. S. *The Professor and the Prime Minister.* Boston: Houghton Mifflin, 1962. Complex portrait of an involved personality. A vindication of the role of Professor Lindemann, Churchill's adviser.

BRADLEY, OMAR. *A Soldier's Story.* New York: Holt, 1951. Gives the best account of how the American-British armies fought the Axis, and tangled with each other on the question of strategy. While the author is charitable, he concedes nothing and promotes nobody.

BRYANT, ARTHUR. *The Turn of the Tide—A History of the War Years Based on the Diaries of Field Marshal Lord Alan Brooke, Chief of the Imperial General Staff.* Garden City, N. Y.: Doubleday, 1957. Packed with significant information relating to the contest between the American and the British Chiefs of Staff. It also divulges the clashes between Churchill and his Chief of the Imperial General Staff, Alan Brooke.

—————. *Triumph in the West, A History of the War Years Based upon the Diaries of Field Marshal Lord Alan Brooke, Chief of the Imperial General Staff.* Garden City, N. Y.: Doubleday, 1959. Reveals the relationship between Churchill and the Imperial General Staff.

BUTCHER, HARRY CECIL. *My Three Years with Eisenhower.* New York: Simon and Schuster, 1946. An informal picture of General Eisenhower, embracing the period from 1942 to the end of the war, written largely in the form of a diary.

BUTLER, JAMES RAMSEY MONTAGU, ed. *Grand Strategy (History of the Second World War: United Kingdom Military Series),* 4 vols. in 5 bindings. London: Her Majesty's Stationery Office, 1953-1956. Detailed and integrated account of British armed services in the war. An excellent set.

CHURCHILL, WINSTON LEONARD SPENCER. *The Second World War*. Boston: Houghton Mifflin, 1948-1953, 6 vols. A comprehensive survey of the background and prosecution of World War II. Much of it is supported by documents and letters. Indispensable for treatment of World War II. The six volumes are: *The Gathering Storm* (1948); *Their Finest Hour* (1949); *The Grand Alliance* (1950); *The Hinge of Fate* (1950); *Closing the Ring* (1951); and *Triumph and Tragedy* (1953).

COLLIER, BASIL. *The Second World War: A Military History*. New York: Morrow, 1967. The author, an Englishman, treats World War II with deference to Churchill's ideas by devoting a disproportionate space to campaigns in the Mediterranean and North Africa.

COLLINS, LARRY, AND DOMINIQUE LAPIERRE. *Is Paris Burning?* New York: Simon and Schuster, 1965. Compression of this volume would improve it very much. Reveals the appointment of General von Choltitz to command the German forces in Paris with orders to burn the city rather than surrender it to the Allies.

EADE, CHARLES, ed. *Churchill by his Contemporaries*. New York: Simon and Schuster, 1954. A compendium of forty essays written by distinguished personalities and authors, assessing Churchill from as many angles. Most of these were British, who after World War II felt kindly toward him and revealed this in their contributions.

EISENHOWER, DWIGHT DAVID. *Crusade in Europe*. Garden City, N. Y.: Doubleday, 1948. A straightforward account of American participation in World War II, told in his own vernacular, without flourishes or any effort to garner glory for himself. Without belligerence or bitterness he reveals his differences with Montgomery and Churchill. Maps are excellent.

EISENHOWER, JOHN S. D. *The Bitter Woods*. New York: Putnam, 1968. Reveals that the United States had outgrown Britain in production and superseded it in manpower, and that the members of the Imperial General Staff found it awkward to play second fiddle. The clash in strategy between Eisenhower and Montgomery is also revealed.

ELLIS, MAJOR L. F. *The War in France and Flanders, 1939-1940*. London: Her Majesty's Stationery Office, 1953. A vivid account of Britain's unpreparedness for the war in 1939, its courageous but feeble effort to halt the German advance, and the resolution to prosecute the war alone.

FULLER, MAJOR GENERAL JOHN FREDERICK CHARLES. *The Conduct of War, 1789-1961*. London: Eyre and Spottiswoode, 1961. This volume is based upon sound scholarship. The author believes

that warfare cannot be properly appreciated without a compre-
hension of the contending countries' culture.

HARRISON, GORDON. *The United States Army in World War II. The
European Theater of Operations, The Cross-Channel Attack*,
edited by K. R. Greenfield. Washington, D. C.: Office of the
Chief of Military History, Department of the Army, 1951. En-
dorses the invasion of northwestern France rather than the
prosecution of a war in the Mediterranean.

HIGGINS, TRUMBULL. *Hitler and Russia, The Third Reich in a Two-
Front War, 1937-1943*. New York: Macmillan, 1966. An account
of the "Fierce Friendship," followed by Hitler's attack on Russia,
and the ferocious fighting until May 3, 1945.

HULL, CORDELL. *The Memoirs of Cordell Hull*. New York: 2 vols.
London: Hodder and Stoughton, 1948. With few exceptions
these memoirs are detached and impartial. They vindicate, in
his mind, his policies as they affected Europe, including his
treatment of De Gaulle.

LEIGHTON, RICHARD M. "Overlord Revisited: An Interpretation of
American Strategy in the European War, 1942-1944," *American
Historical Review*, LXVI (July, 1963), 919-37. Analyzes British
and American strategies for the defeat of Germany. Author
maintains that British policy was "a pragmatic, flexible, even in
some respects 'peripheral' strategy, continuously responsible to
the political realities and the changing military needs."

LEAHY, WILLIAM. *I Was There*. New York: Whittlesey, 1950. The
personal Chief of Staff of President Roosevelt and President
Truman writes about the war without affectation or desire for
personal glory. He was not as influential as Harry Hopkins, and
yet the two Chief Executives valued his judgment highly.

LIDDELL HART, BASIL HENRY. *The German Generals Talk*. New
York: Morrow, 1953. The author maintains that wars are not
won by powerful and ruthless bombing and blasting, but by
indirect appeals and persuasion. The book bristles with challenges to those who decline to accept his doctrine.

LYTTLETON, OLIVER. *The Memoirs of Viscount Chandos. An Unexpected View from the Summit*. New York: The New American
Library, 1963. The volume is divided into three parts: Public
life as a soldier, cabinet minister regulating commerce, and
statesman during World War II. His memoirs are distinctive
for honesty, insight, and entertainment.

MACDONALD, CHARLES B. *The Siegfried Line Campaign*. Washington,
D. C.: Office of the Chief of Military History, Department of
the Army, 1963. Reveals the conflicting strategies of the British
and American staffs.

MACMILLAN, HAROLD. *The Blast of War*. New York: Harper and Row, 1968. Since Macmillan served in North Africa and with the Mediterranean military forces, he gives much information about events in that region.

MATLOFF, MAURICE, AND EDWIN SNELL. *Strategic Planning for Coalition Warfare, 1941-1942*. Washington, D. C.: Office of the Chief of Military History, Department of the Army, 1953. This volume deals with the various plans for conducting the war during the early part of World War II. One phase of this treatise concerns itself with plans for the engagement of the United States forces during 1942, and another with the results of the execution of these plans upon the prosecution of the war.

MCNEIL, WILLIAM HARDY. *Survey of International Affairs, 1939-1946: America, Britain and Russia, Their Cooperation and Conflict, 1941-1946*. New York: Oxford, 1953. Scholarly, balanced, drawn from many sources.

MONTGOMERY, BERNARD LAW. *The Memoirs of Field-Marshall the Viscount Montgomery of Alamein, K. G.* Cleveland: World, 1958. This is a personal account of Montgomery's career from boyhood to the end of his fifty years' service in the army. The volume defends his actions and denounces those whose views differed from his own, especially Eisenhower.

————. *Normandy to the Baltic*. London: Hutchinson, 1958. A controversial volume which contributes little material that is new.

MOOREHEAD, ALAN. *Montgomery, A Biography*. New York: Coward-McCann, 1946. First significant biography of Montgomery. It concentrates on the desert campaign, and on differences with Eisenhower regarding the cross-Channel invasion, and the Battle of Berlin.

MORAN, LORD CHARLES. *Taken from the Diaries of Lord Moran. The Struggle for Survival, 1940-1965*. Boston: Houghton Mifflin, 1966. Packed with intimate information about Churchill's physical condition and the effect of his illness upon his personality and policies.

MORISON, SAMUEL ELIOT. *Strategy and Compromise*. Boston: Little Brown, 1958. Recounts the differences which arose between the British and American Chiefs of Staff during World War II, and the resulting compromises adopted.

NICKERSON, HOFFMAN. *Arms and Policy, 1914-1944*. New York: Putnam, 1945. The author divides his project into three parts: (1) The causes of World War II; (2) review of the six years of war; (3) lessons of the war. Author was a military theorist of the first rank. Opposed area-bombing tactics of the inhabitants, a useless and terroristic imposition upon the victims.

POGUE, FORREST C. *The Supreme Command. The European Theater of Operations.* Washington, D. C.: Office of Military History, 1954. This volume deals with the integrated command of Allied forces on the Western Front in 1944-1945. It reveals the conflicting strategic plans of General Eisenhower and Mr. Churchill. A scholarly volume.

RYAN, CORNELIUS. *The Longest Day: June 6, 1944.* New York: Simon and Schuster, 1959. A vivid and detailed description of the day of invasion from personal interviews and from extensive research, well-written.

STIMSON, HENRY L., AND MCGEORGE BUNDY. *On Active Duty in Peace and War.* New York: Harper, 1948. Vigorous advocacy of cross-Channel invasion. Favored an early execution of project. Actively opposed to the strategy of the British General Staff.

THOMPSON, REGINALD WILLIAMS. *Churchill and the Montgomery Myth.* Philadelphia: Evans, 1968. The author maintains that Churchill needed a victory, and a hero, and Montgomery was selected for the role. The author's motive in writing the volume was to reduce Montgomery to his proper size.

Taps

BRAY, ROBERT ALEXANDER. *Crisis in Britain: Plans and Achievements of the Labour Government.* Berkeley: University of California Press, 1950. An examination of the Government's plans and their execution from 1945 on.

CHURCHILL, RANDOLPH SPENCER. *Rise and Fall of Anthony Eden.* New York: Putnam, 1959. Caustic treatment of his subject.

COLE, GEORGE DOUGLAS HOWARD. *The Postwar Condition of Britain.* London: Rutledge and Paul, 1956. Comparison of the economic conditions of England between 1937 and 1956.

COOMS, DAVID. *Churchill and his Paintings.* Cleveland: World, 1967. Traces Churchill's development in painting which led him to pursue an impressionistic style.

HOWELL, ROY. *Churchill's Last Years.* New York: McKay, 1966. Intimate account of Churchill's physical, mental, and emotional condition from 1958 to 1965.

MOOREHEAD, ALAN. *Winston Churchill in Trial and Triumph.* Boston: Houghton Mifflin, 1955. A brilliant sketch.

TRUMAN. *Year of Decision,* and *Years of Trial and Hope.* New York: Doubleday, 1953. Two biased volumes in favor of Mr. Truman and the Democratic Party.

Index